Preventing Torture and Monitoring Places of Detention

Tom Daems · Olivia Nederlandt ·
Aurore Vanliefde De Keyser
Editors

Preventing Torture and Monitoring Places of Detention

The Role of National Preventive Mechanisms in Europe

palgrave
macmillan

Editors
Tom Daems
Leuven Institute of Criminology
KU Leuven
Leuven, Belgium

Olivia Nederlandt
UCLouvain Saint-Louis—Bruxelles
Brussels, Belgium

Aurore Vanliefde De Keyser
Leuven Institute of Criminology
KU Leuven
Leuven, Belgium

ISBN 978-3-032-28284-2 ISBN 978-3-032-28285-9 (eBook)
https://doi.org/10.1007/978-3-032-28285-9

Cover illustration: Vertigo3d

This Palgrave Macmillan imprint is published by the registered company Springer Nature Switzerland AG
The registered company address is: Gewerbestrasse 11, 6330 Cham, Switzerland

Preface

The chapters included in this volume were first presented and discussed in Leuven, on 30 October 2025, at a workshop on national preventive mechanisms (NPMs) in Europe. This workshop was organised by Research Line n°8 ('Punishment and Control') of the Leuven Institute of Criminology (LINC), KU Leuven and the Groupe de Recherche en matière Pénale et Criminelle (GREPEC), UCLouvain Saint-Louis—Bruxelles. The workshop aimed to mark the twentieth anniversary of the entry into force of the UN Optional Protocol to the Convention Against Torture (OPCAT).

The eight countries selected for this workshop and subsequent edited volume were selected for a number of (practical) reasons as, unfortunately, we were not able to cover all NPMs in Europe in this book. It should therefore not be inferred from our selection that the experiences in other countries are any less relevant or important to the broader understanding of OPCAT implementation than the ones that are included in this volume. Our hope is that this volume can foster curiosity and create paths for researching and better understanding the structure, mandate, challenges and opportunities of NPMs in Europe. We are grateful to our authors, coming from different parts of Europe, who shared their expertise on their countries' processes in ratifying OPCAT as well as the establishment and functioning of the NPMs. We also would like to thank Josie Taylor and her team at Palgrave Macmillan for showing genuine interest in our project and for all their help and support in producing this book.

Leuven, Belgium	Tom Daems
Brussels, Belgium	Olivia Nederlandt
Leuven, Belgium	Aurore Vanliefde De Keyser
March 2026	

Contents

List of Contributors

Alessandro Albano Office of the National Guarantor for the Rights of Persons Deprived of Liberty—Italian NPM, Roma, Italy

Ariane Amado CNRS, CRESPPA, Paris, France

Barbara Bernath Subcommittee On Prevention of Torture (SPT), Geneva, Switzerland

Jean-Sébastien Blanc National Commission for the Prevention of Torture—Swiss NPM, Bern, Switzerland

Kerstin Buchinger Austrian Ombudsman Board—Austrian NPM, Vienna, Austria

Johannes Carniel Austrian Ombudsman Board—Austrian NPM, Vienna, Austria

Tom Daems KU Leuven, Leuven, Belgium

Sam Gluckstein UK NPM, London, UK

Pauline Jacobs Tilburg University, Tilburg, The Netherlands

Adriano Martufi University of Pavia, Pavia, Italy

Olivia Nederlandt UCLouvain Saint-Louis, Bruxelles, Belgium

Sarah Rennie UK NPM, London, UK

Elīna Šteinerte Subcommittee On Prevention of Torture (SPT), Geneva, Switzerland

Julia Schmitz Ecole de Droit, Université de Toulouse Capitole, Toulouse, France

Milan Svoboda Office of the Public Defender of Rights—Czech NPM, Brno, Czech Republic

Miriam Tomášková Department of Constitutional Law, Palacký University Olomouc, Olomouc, Czech Republic

Aurore Vanliefde De Keyser KU Leuven, Leuven, Belgium

List of Tables

Monitoring Places of Detention Under OPCAT: Spotlight on NPMs in Europe

Tom Daems, Olivia Nederlandt, and Aurore Vanliefde De Keyser

In 2006, Marco Mona, a former President of the Association for the Prevention of Torture (APT), commented as follows on the power of saffron:

> If you add three threads of saffron the next time you prepare rice, you will immediately see how the saffron rapidly spreads throughout even the largest pots of rice, imbuing it with rich colour and delicious spicy perfume – a striking effect, considering the small size of those few threads! (cited in APT, 2007, p. 40)

T. Daems (✉) · A. Vanliefde De Keyser
KU Leuven, Leuven, Belgium
e-mail: tom.daems@kuleuven.be

A. Vanliefde De Keyser
e-mail: aurore.vanliefde@kuleuven.be

O. Nederlandt
UCLouvain Saint-Louis, Brussels, Belgium
e-mail: olivia.nederlandt@uclouvain.be

T. Daems et al. (eds.), *Preventing Torture and Monitoring Places of Detention*,
https://doi.org/10.1007/978-3-032-28285-9_1

For Mona, the ingredients contributed by APT and its partners to the wider discussion on torture prevention "(…) have had a similar effect as those three threads of saffron. And we still have more precious threads of saffron to add to the pot, when and just as much as needed, to make utopia become reality" (APT, 2007, p. 40). Undoubtedly, many in the world of torture prevention at the time will have applauded the prospect of having an increasing number of National Preventive Mechanisms (NPMs), as it would potentially amplify the "striking effect" of torture prevention globally, by securing a permanent presence in States Parties and boosting the capacity for organising visits to places of detention which even the best resourced international preventive body would never be able to achieve. Unsurprisingly, then, Malcolm Evans, a former president of the Subcommittee on Prevention of Torture (SPT), referred to the NPMs as "…the most innovative element of the OPCAT, and helping establish and support NPMs is the SPT's most important role" (Evans, 2023, p. 5).

1 Twenty Years of OPCAT

The year 2006 was, indeed, a very important year in the history of torture prevention: on 22 June 2006, the Optional Protocol to the Convention against Torture and other Cruel, Inhuman or Degrading Treatment or Punishment (OPCAT), which was adopted on 18 December 2002 by the fifty-seventh session of the General Assembly of the United Nations, entered into force.[1] The objective of the OPCAT is "…to establish a system of regular visits undertaken by independent international and national bodies to places where people are deprived of their liberty, in order to prevent torture and other cruel, inhuman or degrading treatment or punishment".[2]

The entry into force of the OPCAT in 2006 was the culmination of a long historical process, the origins of which lead us back to the 1970s,

[1] Optional Protocol to the Convention Against Torture and Other Cruel, Inhuman or Degrading Treatment or Punishment, *UN Doc.* A/RES/57/199, 18 December 2002.

[2] Art. 1 OPCAT.

when the "revival of torture" (Buchanan, 2020, p. 183) came to attract the attention of the global community. In December 1975, the General Assembly of the UN adopted the Declaration on the Protection of All Persons from Being Subjected to Torture and Other Cruel, Inhuman or Degrading Treatment or Punishment. Two years later, the Commission on Human Rights was requested to draft a treaty, which eventually, in 1984, led to the UN Convention against Torture (UNCAT) (Rodley, 2009).

Against this background, the Swiss former banker and philanthropist Jean-Jacques Gautier became interested in the issue of torture (De Vargas, 1980; Mischler, 2003). Gautier contributed to a study by the Institut Henry-Dunant on the protection of political prisoners, for which he drafted the conclusions. In this, he incorporated ideas he had previously outlined in embryonic form in a letter of 25 September 1974 to Hélène Engel. Gautier drew particular attention to the UN's inability to ensure respect for human rights and the need to approach the issue of implementation from an entirely different perspective:

> My feeling is that we should try to tackle the problem from the other end, that is to say, persuade three or four European states to sign a convention among themselves providing not only for the abolition of all forms of torture, but also for investigations to be carried out by a neutral body and the publication of their findings. If a few other states then join this convention, we will at least have succeeded in stemming this epidemic of torture, which has spread alarmingly over the last few decades. (Gautier, 1974, p. 43, translated from French)

Some years later, he would again insist on this: "... there is legitimate reason to doubt the utility of a new convention if it does not strengthen the existing procedures for implementation" (Gautier, 1980, p. 32). Inspired by the experiences of the International Committee of the Red Cross, Gautier therefore proposed the establishment of an independent international body that would be granted unrestricted and unhindered access to places of detention in order to verify on the spot that everything was being carried out in accordance with the rules. Two years later, he published his proposals in the journal *La Vie protestante* (Gautier,

1976). In 1977, Gautier founded the Comité suisse contre la torture (which was renamed to the current APT in 1992) with the primary aim of establishing the proposed monitoring body.

The history has been recounted many times—we do not need to rehearse the details here (see e.g. Evans & Haenni-Dale, 2004; Boeglin, 2005; Murray et al., 2011). For our purposes and for the reader of this book, it is, however, important to realise that the first attempts to establish such a preventive mechanism at an international level backfired, as there was insufficient support for such a monitoring system at the level of the UN. This explains why the first international monitoring mechanism, embodying the ideas of Gautier, came to be established at a regional level, in Europe, with the adoption of the European Convention for the Prevention of Torture and Inhuman or Degrading Treatment or Punishment (ECPT) on 26 November 1987, which entered into force on 1 February 1989. The European Committee for the Prevention of Torture and Inhuman or Degrading Treatment or Punishment (CPT) held its first meeting in November 1989 and conducted its first visit in May 1990 to Austria (Bicknell et al., 2018; Evans & Morgan, 1998).

2 OPCAT's Two-Pillar System

The OPCAT system rests on two pillars. On the one hand, the OPCAT establishes the SPT. The SPT is an international committee with access to all places where people are deprived of their liberty. The SPT initially comprised ten members, who were elected in October 2006 and met for the first time in Geneva on 19 February 2007. Following the fiftieth ratification of the OPCAT (by Switzerland on 24 September 2009), the SPT had to be expanded to 25 members.[3] The fifteen additional members were elected on 28 October 2010, and the expanded SPT met for the first time in February 2011. Furthermore, the OPCAT stipulates that each State Party shall designate or establish one or several NPMs. Such NPMs must be able to operate independently, visit persons in detention and make recommendations. The SPT is expected to assist Member States

[3] Art. 5.1 OPCAT.

in establishing or designating the NPMs. Furthermore, the SPT must maintain contact with the NPMs and support them where necessary.[4]

After each visit, the SPT draws up a confidential report which forms the basis of the dialogue with the Member State. Reports may be published in three circumstances: (1) where the State concerned gives its consent; (2) where the State concerned itself publishes part of the report; and (3) in the absence of cooperation, the SPT may request the CAT to make the report public. In the latter case, the SPT may also ask the CAT to issue a public statement. In addition, the SPT must draw up an annual report for the CAT. This is publicly accessible.[5] Furthermore, the SPT may also propose organising a short follow-up visit if it deems this necessary.[6]

Member States undertake to designate or establish a NPM within one year of ratifying the OPCAT.[7] A deferral is possible, but is limited to a maximum of three years. This period may be extended once by two years by the CAT.[8] Apart from a number of general remarks on independence, professionalism, resources and respect for the Paris Principles, the OPCAT does not prescribe exactly what form the NPMs should take.[9] On the contrary, the SPT recognises the importance of having NPM models which are well embedded within a country's political, social, cultural and institutional landscape to carry out its torture prevention mandate (Bernath & Šteinerte, this volume). There is therefore no ideal model prescribed for NPMs (Murray, 2008; Šteinerte & Murray, 2009). The SPT's fourth annual report makes the following observation on this matter:

> The form and structure of the NPM is likely to reflect a variety of factors which are particular to the country concerned, and it is not for the Subcommittee to say in the abstract what may or may not be appropriate.

[4] Art. 11(b) OPCAT.
[5] Art. 16 OPCAT.
[6] Art. 13.4 OPCAT.
[7] Art. 17 OPCAT.
[8] Art. 24 OPCAT.
[9] Art. 18 OPCAT.

> All NPMs must of course be independent. Beyond this, the Subcommittee looks at NPMs from a functional perspective, and recognizes that just because one model works well in one country does not mean it will work well in another.[10]

Nevertheless, the SPT had already drawn up a number of preliminary guidelines in its first annual report[11] and further supplemented and revised these in its fourth annual report.[12]

3 NPMs in Europe

This book focuses on Europe. As we have discussed earlier, before the entry into force of the OPCAT, Europe already had considerable experience with monitoring places of detention by the CPT. There are many similarities between the UN and the Council of Europe systems, but also (at least) two differences: first, the European monitoring model does not foresee a two-pillar structure; and second, the CPT's membership is larger, that is, it consists of "a number of members equal to that of the Parties".[13] The SPT must cooperate with the relevant UN bodies and other international, regional and national institutions.[14] This is particularly relevant within the European context, as most European states have ratified both the ECPT and the OPCAT. In the foreword to its sixteenth annual report, the CPT welcomed the entry into force of the OPCAT and stated that cooperation, complementarity and synergy should characterise the relationship between the CPT and the SPT.[15] Following its first visit to Europe (which was a visit to Sweden in March 2008), the

---

[10] SPT, Fourth annual report of the SPT, *UN Doc.* CAT/C/46/2, 3 February 2011, para 62.

[11] SPT, First annual report of the Subcommittee on Prevention of Torture and other Cruel, Inhuman or Degrading Treatment or Punishment, *UN Doc.* CAT/C/40/2, 14 May 2008, 'Preliminary guidelines for the ongoing development of NPMs.'

[12] SPT, Guidelines on National Preventive Mechanisms, *UN Doc.* CAT/OP/12/5, 9 December 2010; Fourth annual report of the SPT, *UN Doc.* CAT/C/46/2, 3 February 2011.

[13] Art. 4.1 ECPT.

[14] Arts. 11(c) and 31 OPCAT.

[15] CPT, *16th General Report on the CPT's activities covering the period 1 August 2005 to 31 July 2006*, CPT/Inf (2006) 35, 16 October 2006, p. 5.

SPT had consulted with the CPT. This explains why the SPT adopted "a more targeted approach", which resulted in a focused visit of shorter duration.[16]

In the best of worlds, the co-existence of multiple monitoring bodies would lead to cross-fertilisation and complementarity in torture prevention; for Europe in particular, that would imply making the most of the "triangular relationship" between the CPT, the SPT and the NPMs (Bicknell & Evans, 2017). And indeed, it is in that spirit that the NPMs have been received and welcomed in Europe. In its 22nd annual report, the CPT (2012) reflected again, and more at length, on its relationship to the NPMs, which were referred to as "...natural partners for the CPT": "...the effectiveness of efforts to assist States in Europe to prevent torture and other forms of ill-treatment will in future depend to a large extent on the quality of the interaction between the Committee and these mechanisms".[17] In this annual report, the CPT highlighted that, during its own visits, it is attentive to whether the NPMs in Europe meet the key requirements (e.g. functional independence of NPMs and its personnel, adequate resources, requirements with respect to membership, mandate and powers), as laid down in the OPCAT and the SPT's guidelines on NPMs. It also mentioned its own involvement and engagement with NPMs in Europe, in particular through the (then) "European NPM Project" and, since 2016, the "European NPM Forum".[18] Over the years, it has become common practice for CPT visiting delegations to consult with NPMs at the start of a visit or, if a NPM is non-existent or not functioning well, to bring such deficiencies to the attention of state authorities and recommend to take appropriate action, as has happened, for example, for Belgium and Ireland, the two countries in the European Union that so far have failed to ratify OPCAT.[19]

---

[16] SPT, First annual report of the Subcommittee on Prevention of Torture and other Cruel, Inhuman or Degrading Treatment or Punishment, *UN Doc.* CAT/C/40/2, 14 May 2008, p. 8.

[17] CPT, *22nd General Report of the CPT*, CPT/Inf (2012) 25, 6 November 2012, p. 15.

[18] European Union & Council of Europe, *European NPM Forum,* https://www.coe.int/en/web/implementation/european-npm-forum.

[19] CPT, Rapport au Gouvernement de la Belgique relatif à la visite effectuée en Belgique par le CPT du 27 mars au 6 avril 2017, CPT/Inf (2018) 8, 8 March 2018, p. 11; Report to the Irish Government on the visit to Ireland carried out by the CPT from 21 to 31 May 2024, CPT/Inf (2025) 22, 24 July 2025, p. 10.

However, having multiple monitoring bodies, working under different flags yet with similar mandates and objectives, also comes with definite risks: first, the risk of duplication if monitoring bodies, unaware of (or indifferent to) each other's activities, are targeting the same countries and institutions; second, "the risk of diverging approaches and interpretations vis-à-vis given situations",[20] and, third, "monitoring fatigue" (somewhat akin to "compassion fatigue"), that is, the risk that institutions may feel the burden of being exposed too much. In order to avoid these risks, it is in the interest of all actors involved in the "triangular relationship" (Bicknell & Evans, 2017) to cooperate as closely as possible. And in this respect, the NPMs do, indeed, play a key role, both in terms of conducting visits (that is, the NPMs can visit places within national borders at a much higher frequency and pace than the SPT or CPT could ever do) as well as in the post-visit phase (that is, in disseminating findings and monitoring the follow-up of recommendations). One key concern for monitoring bodies across the globe is addressing the question "what happens after the report?" (Daems, 2017), and here NPMs can and should play a decisive role: the baton must pass on to others (*cf.* Morgan & Evans, 2001).

4 Overview of the Chapters

This book is composed of 11 chapters in total, which are written both by academics and authors who have professional experience with the SPT or the NPMs in their home countries. In chapter 2 ("The SPT and NPMs: An Evolving Relation"), Barbara Bernath and Elīna Šteinerte reflect on the development of the relationship between the SPT and the NPMs. The chapter examines the SPT's work in three domains: (1) advising and assisting the States Parties vis-à-vis the NPMs, (2) advising and supporting the NPMs themselves, and (3) advancing the prevention of torture under a tripartite cooperation (that is, the SPT, the State Party and the NPM). The main part of the book is then composed of eight chapters, discussing the development and practice of NPMs in

[20] CPT, *22nd General Report of the CPT*, CPT/Inf (2012) 25, 6 November 2012, p. 17.

eight different countries. These were selected for a number of (practical) reasons as, unfortunately, we were not able to cover all NPMs in Europe in this book: one should therefore not infer from our selection that the experiences in other countries are any less relevant or important to the broader understanding of OPCAT implementation than the ones that are included in this volume.

In chapter 3 ("The French Contrôleur général des lieux de privation de liberté: Towards a Panoptic Control?"), Julia Schmitz and Ariane Amado discuss the creation of the French *Contrôleur général des lieux de privation de liberté* (CGLPL), against the background of the ratification of the OPCAT by France. The French NPM has some peculiar features, as it is, in fact, a single-person body, assisted by a team of inspectors. Chapter 4 ("The Czech Republic and OPCAT: Reflection on Almost 20 Years of the Czech NPM") offers an overview of almost two decades of the NPM's activity in the Czech Republic. Milan Svoboda and Miriam Tomášková highlight how the Czech Republic ratified the OPCAT already in 2006 and explore how the Czech NPM operates with the institution of the Public Defender of Rights and the Defender of Children's Rights (the Czech Ombudsman). In chapter 5 ("Ten Years of NPM in Italy: Some Reflections on the Past and the Possible Ways Ahead"), Alessandro Albano and Adriano Martufi explore the institutional design, the legal prerogatives and the practice of the NPM in Italy (the *Garante nazionale dei diritti delle persone private della libertà personale*, GNPL), which was established in 2014 in the follow-up to Italy's ratification of the OPCAT. Chapter 6 ("The Dutch NPM. A New Horizon for Prevention of Torture Against Torture and Other Cruel, Inhuman or Degrading Treatment or Punishment in the Netherlands?") discusses the developments in the Netherlands. Here, Pauline Jacobs points to the difficulties in the Dutch NPM's history from a complex multi-body NPM, which became dormant, to a centralised NPM within the Dutch Human Rights Institute since 1 January 2024. In chapter 7 ("The United Kingdom's National Preventive Mechanism: Lessons in Coordination and Collaboration"), Sam Gluckstein and Sarah Rennie present the UK NPM, which has a peculiar and unique umbrella structure composed of 21 statutory bodies, which brings a set of challenges and opportunities to implement the NPM mandate.

In chapter 8 ("15 Years of the Swiss National Preventive Mechanism: Reflecting on Impact and the Boundaries of Deprivation of Liberty"), Jean-Sébastien Blanc reflects on fifteen years of the National Commission for the Prevention of Torture (NCPT) in Switzerland, a centralised NPM in an otherwise complex federal state, which has aimed to advance monitoring practices by expanding its mandate to forced deportation flights, federal asylum centres and nursing homes. In chapter 9 ("The Austrian Ombudsman Board as National Preventive Mechanism: A Unique Approach Combining OPCAT and CRPD Mandates"), Kerstin Buchinger and Johannes Carniel offer an overview of the functioning of the Austrian Ombudsman Board (AOB) as NPM in Austria and draw special attention to how it combines OPCAT and CRPD mandates. In chapter 10 ("Belgium's Long Road to OPCAT Ratification: Challenges and Prospects of the Belgian NPM"), Olivia Nederlandt and Aurore Vanliefde De Keyser trace the unaccomplished road to Belgium's OPCAT ratification and development of the Belgian federal NPM, established in 2024, from the conceptual choices underpinning its umbrella design and the selection of its specialised bodies to the opportunities and challenges of the current model.

Chapter 11 ("Conclusion: 20 Years of NPMs in Europe—Highlights of a Varied Preventive Monitoring Landscape") offers a conclusion to the volume, reflecting on the advances of torture prevention monitoring through NPMs, shedding light on places of deprivation of liberty and on the shadows cast by institutional choices in terms of mandate, resources and organisation.

Bibliography

Association for the Prevention of Torture [APT]. (2007). *Letting in the light. 30 years of torture prevention*. APT.

Bicknell, C., & Evans, M. (2017). Monitoring prisons: The increasingly complex relationship between international and domestic frameworks. In T. Daems & L. Robert (Eds.), *Europe in prisons* (pp. 11–35). Palgrave.

Bicknell, C., Evans, M., & Morgan, R. (2018). *Preventing torture in Europe.* Council of Europe Publishing.

Boeglin, N. (2005). History of the optional protocol to the UN convention against torture. In Inter-American Institute for Human Rights & Association for Prevention of Torture (Eds.), Optional protocol to the United Nations convention against torture and other cruel, inhuman or degrading treatment or punishment. A manual for prevention (pp. 33–59). Inter-American Institute for Human Rights & Association for Prevention of Torture.

Buchanan, T. (2020). *Amnesty international and human rights activism in Postwar Britain, 1945–1977*. Cambridge University Press.

Daems, T. (2017). Slaves and statues: Torture prevention in contemporary Europe. *British Journal of Criminology, 57*(3), 627–643.

De Vargas, F. (1980). History of a Campaign. In International Commission of Jurists & Swiss Committee Against Torture (Eds.), Torture: How to make the international convention effective. A draft optional protocol (pp. 41–46). International Commission of Jurists.

Evans, M. D., & Haenni-Dale, C. (2004). Preventing torture? The development of the optional protocol to the UN convention against torture. *Human Rights Law Review, 4*(1), 19–55.

Evans, M. D., & Morgan, R. (1998). *Preventing torture. A study of the European convention for the prevention of torture and inhuman or degrading treatment or punishment*. Clarendon Press.

Evans, M. D. (2023). *Tackling torture: Prevention in practice.* Bristol University Press.

Gautier, J.-J. (1974/2003). Lettre de Jean-Jacques Gautier à Hélène Engel (25 septembre 1974). In N. Mischler (Ed.), *Jean-Jacques Gautier et la prévention de la torture: de l'idée à l'action. Recueil de textes* (pp. 41–44). APT.

Gautier, J.-J. (1976/2003). La proposition de Jean-Jacques Gautier. In N. Mischler (Ed.), *Jean-Jacques Gautier et la prévention de la torture: de l'idée à l'action. Recueil de textes* (pp. 229–232). APT.

Gautier, J.-J. (1980). The case for an effective and realistic procedure. In International Commission of Jurists & Swiss Committee Against Torture (Eds.), *Torture: How to make the international convention effective. A draft optional protocol* (pp. 31–38). International Commission of Jurists.

Mischler, N. (2003). Introduction. In N. Mischler (Ed.), *Jean-Jacques Gautier et la prévention de la torture: de l'idée à l'action. Recueil de textes* (pp. 17–36). APT.

Morgan, R., & Evans, M. (2001). *Combating torture in Europe.* Council of Europe Publishing.

Murray, R. (2008). National preventive mechanisms under the optional protocol to the torture convention: One size does not fit all. *Netherlands Quarterly of Human Rights, 26*(4), 485–516.

Murray, R., Šteinerte, E., Evans, M., & Hallo de Wolf, A. (2011). *The optional protocol to the UN convention against torture.* Oxford University Press.

Rodley, N. (2009). *The treatment of prisoners under international law.* (3rd ed.). Oxford University Press.

Šteinerte, E., & Murray, R. (2009). Same but different? National human rights commissions and ombudsman institutions as national preventive mechanisms under the optional protocol to the UN convention against torture. *Essex Human Rights Review, 6*(1), 54–72.

Šteinerte, E. (2013). The changing nature of relationship between the United Nations subcommittee on prevention of torture and national preventive mechanisms: In search for equilibrium. *Netherlands Quarterly of Human Rights, 31*(2), 129–155.

Šteinerte, E. (2014). The jewel in the crown and its three guardians: Independence of national preventive mechanisms under the optional protocol to the UN torture convention. *Human Rights Law Review, 14*(1), 1–29.

The SPT and NPMs: An Evolving Relation

Barbara Bernath and Elīna Šteinerte

1 Introduction

The Optional Protocol to the UN Convention against Torture and Other Cruel, Inhuman or Degrading Treatment or Punishment (OPCAT)[1] is an innovative human rights treaty. It focuses on the prevention of torture through an operational rather than normative approach by establishing a system of visits to places of deprivation of liberty undertaken by both international and national independent bodies. This two-pillar system is certainly the most innovative feature of the OPCAT. Indeed, in

Disclaimer: Views provided in their personal capacity

[1] Optional Protocol to the Convention Against Torture and Other Cruel, Inhuman or Degrading Treatment or Punishment, *UN Doc*. A/RES/57/199, adopted by the UN General Assembly on 18 December 2002 by 127 votes to 4, with 42 abstentions; came into force on 26 June 2006.

B. Bernath (✉) · E. Šteinerte
Subcommittee On Prevention of Torture (SPT), Geneva, Switzerland
e-mail: bernathbarbara@gmail.com

T. Daems et al. (eds.), *Preventing Torture and Monitoring Places of Detention*,
https://doi.org/10.1007/978-3-032-28285-9_2

addition to accepting visits to places of deprivation of liberty by an international body—the UN Subcommittee on Prevention of Torture and Other Cruel, Inhuman or Degrading Treatment or Punishment (SPT)—, States Parties have the obligation to establish an independent national body, a National Preventive Mechanism (NPM).[2]

For the first time, an international treaty defines key requirements and mandates of a national body, while leaving it to the discretion of the State regarding the type and form of the body, and provides it with the same broad powers of access to places of detention, persons deprived of liberty and documentation as the international body. By doing so, the OPCAT introduces an innovative triangular relation between the SPT, the State Party and the National Preventive Mechanism.

The SPT, in addition to its visiting mandate, is therefore also mandated to advise and assist States in the designation and effective functioning of NPMs, as well as NPMs in their preventive work. According to Article 11 b) of the OPCAT, which defines the role of the SPT in relation to National Preventive Mechanisms, it shall:

(i) Advise and assist States Parties, when necessary, in their establishment;
(ii) Maintain direct, and if necessary confidential, contact with the national preventive mechanisms and offer them training and technical assistance with a view to strengthening their capacities;
(iii) Advise and assist them in the evaluation of the needs and the means necessary to strengthen the protection of persons deprived of their liberty against torture and other cruel, inhuman or degrading treatment or punishment;

[2] The original 1980 draft of the OPCAT submitted by Costa Rica to the UN Human Rights Commission, and its revised 1991 draft, included only an international visiting mechanism. The European Convention for the Prevention of Torture adopted by the Council of Europe on 26 June 1987 also created a single body: the European Committee for the Prevention of Torture. In 2001, during the negotiations, Mexico proposed the addition of national visiting bodies. The two-pillar approach was integrated in a new text proposed by the Chair of the Working Group in 2002, that was presented for adoption by vote at the Human Rights Commission and eventually adopted by vote by the UN General Assembly on 18 December 2002. For the history, see Nowak et al. (2019).

(iv) Make recommendations and observations to the States Parties with a view to strengthening the capacity and the mandate of the national preventive mechanisms for the prevention of torture and other cruel, inhuman or degrading treatment or punishment.

Over two decades of the OPCAT's implementation have meant a development of a unique relationship between the SPT and NPMs, the dissection of which is the aim of the present chapter. Following a brief overview of the SPT's main features, the chapter will proceed to examine in detail the SPT's work in three domains: (1) advising and assisting the States Parties vis-à-vis the NPMs; (2) advising and supporting the NPMs themselves; and (3) advancing the prevention of torture under a tripartite cooperation.

The main argument of the present chapter lies with an acknowledgement that the OPCAT does not envisage a hierarchy between the SPT and the NPMs, nor does it vest the SPT with any decision-making power towards the choice of the States Parties vis-à-vis their NPM. Therefore, it is not for the SPT to "approve", "accredit" or otherwise the NPMs. However, the SPT holds advisory functions that it regularly exercises through its country visits as well as with other advice both to the State Parties and to the NPMs.

2 The Subcommittee on Prevention of Torture: A Brief Overview

The SPT is the largest UN human rights treaty body with 25 members elected for a four-year period, chosen by OPCAT States Parties from "among persons of high moral character, having proven professional experience in the field of the administration of justice, in particular criminal law, prison or police administration, or in the various fields relevant to the treatment of persons deprived of their liberty".[3] All members serve in their individual capacities, bound by the principles of independence and impartiality.

[3] Article 5 (2) OPCAT.

Internally, the SPT is led by a bureau, composed of the Chair and four Vice Chairs, of which one Vice Chair holds the overall responsibility over the SPT's engagement with the NPMs. Moreover, the SPT is organised in four regional teams: Africa, the Americas, Asia Pacific and Europe, and each of the 25 members act as designated country rapporteurs for four to five OPCAT States Parties in the region (see Sect. 3). The main aim has been to ensure there is a clear focal point for each OPCAT State Party and especially for each NPM.

The SPT mandate as the OPCAT treaty body is three-fold: to visit places of deprivation of liberty in the States Parties,[4] to advise and assist NPMs and States on their preventive work,[5] and to cooperate with relevant regional and internal bodies.[6] Regarding cooperation, Article 31 of the OPCAT also encourages the SPT to consult and cooperate with regional bodies instituting a system of visits, "to avoid duplication and promoting effectively the objectives" of the OPCAT. In Europe, the SPT has formalised cooperation with the European Committee for the Prevention of Torture and Inhuman or Degrading Treatment or Punishment (CPT) through a reciprocal exchange of letters[7] and organises regular meetings and exchanges to ensure coordination between the two bodies in terms of visits. In its work, the SPT is guided by the principles of confidentiality, impartiality, non-selectivity, universality and objectivity,[8] and the SPT and the State Parties shall cooperate in the implementation of the OPCAT.

The secretariat support for the SPT's work is ensured by the Office of the High Commissioner for Human Rights (OHCHR), as is the case for all other UN human rights treaty bodies. However, this support appears to follow the core modalities of the mandates of other UN human rights treaty bodies, whereas the unique features of the SPT's mandate, especially in relation to the NPMs, are not duly recognised. The budget for the SPT covers only sessions in Geneva and in-country visits, but there is no dedicated budget line to support the work of the SPT vis-à-vis

[4] Article 11.1 a) OPCAT.

[5] Article 11.1 b) OPCAT.

[6] Article 11.1 c) OPCAT.

[7] SPT, Twelfth annual report, *UN Doc.* CAT/C/66/2, 13 March 2019, para 33.

[8] Article 2.3 OPCAT.

the NPMs. This has had a significant impact on the ability of the SPT to discharge this part of its mandate effectively. Notwithstanding this significant financial constraint, over the two decades, the SPT has been creative and assertive in discharging its mandate vis-à-vis the NPMs.

3 SPT Advice and Assistance to States Parties Regarding NPMs

The SPT is mandated to advise States Parties on the designation and operation of their NPMs, yet has to provide this guidance in a way that would not undermine the independence of the NPMs. Without a doubt, this constitutes a careful balancing act which pushes the States to establish and maintain their NPMs in full accordance with the requirements of the OPCAT without providing a ground for the States to intervene in the NPMs' ability to exercise their preventive mandate with independence and rigour.

There are three distinct phases that can be distinguished when examining the SPT's mandate to advise and assist the States Parties regarding their NPMs: the very initial phase, the establishment of the NPMs (or failure to do so), the ongoing operation of the NPMs, which encompasses the obligation of the States to maintain their NPMs, and the protective mandate, which is triggered when the NPM faces challenges from the State.

Advising and Assisting with the NPM Establishment

The obligation to set up or designate an institution, an NPM in the case of the OPCAT, as a means to implement obligations arising from an international treaty is a very novel approach towards responsibilities stemming from an international human rights treaty.[9] The OPCAT

[9] The other example of the obligation to establish independent monitoring mechanisms is found in Article 33 (2) of the UN Convention on the Rights of Persons with Disabilities (CRPD), *UN Doc.* A/Res/61/106, adopted by the UN General Assembly on 13 December 2006, entry into force in 2008.

however does not prescribe what form or shape these NPMs are to take, although it includes a time limit for their establishment post-ratification. States Parties to the OPCAT are to "maintain, designate or establish" their own NPMs, composed of one or more bodies, whether entirely new or existing mechanisms, within a year of ratifying the OPCAT.[10] Aside from that, the OPCAT only sets out the key institutional features of the NPMs in relation to their independence, including independence of the personnel, functional and financial independence[11] and invites the States Parties to "give due consideration to" the so-called Paris Principles.[12] The OPCAT also provides for the central elements of the NPM operational mandate, including the right to visit all places of deprivation of liberty and their facilities and installations; to have access to information concerning persons deprived of their liberty; to interview, in private, persons deprived of their liberty and others; to issue recommendations to authorities with the view of preventing occurrences of torture and ill-treatment; and the corresponding obligation of the authorities to engage in a dialogue with the NPM about the implementation of these recommendations.[13]

Without a blueprint for an NPM, the OPCAT States Parties are left considerable freedom in their NPM choice. To this end, the SPT has repeatedly emphasised that a "one size fits all" approach is not suitable for the effective implementation of the obligation towards the NPM establishment and there is no model for the NPM.[14] Instead, the SPT has insisted that, when choosing the NPM, it is imperative that the mechanism, whatever form it may take, is structured and carries out its mandate

---

[10] Art. 17 OPCAT.

[11] Art. 18 OPCAT.

[12] UN Principles relating to the Status of National Institutions (The Paris Principles), adopted by the UN Human Rights Commission by Resolution 1992/54, and by the UN General Assembly in its Resolution 48/134 on National institutions for the promotion and protection of human rights *UN Doc.* A/RES/48/134, 20 December 1993. See Art. 18 (4) of the OPCAT.

[13] Arts. 19–20, 22 OPCAT.

[14] SPT, Seventeenth annual report, *op. cit.*, Annex I, para 2; SPT, Ninth annual report, *UN Doc.* CAT/C/57/4, 22 March 2016, Annex, para 17; Report on the visit of the SPT to Cyprus undertaken from 25 to 29 January 2016: observations and recommendations addressed to the State Party, *UN Doc.* CAT/OP/CYP/1, Sept 22, 2017, para 89.

in accordance with the requirements of the OPCAT.[15] The rationale behind this is that NPMs must mould within the existing geo-political, legal, socio-economic and cultural realities of their respective jurisdictions to be able to fulfil the torture prevention mandates. Hence, starting from its very first annual report[16] and the initial visit reports,[17] the SPT has rather consistently advised on the constitutive and operational overall features of the NPMs, always clearly indicating that the responsibility over the NPMs rests with both the State Parties and the NPMs themselves as well. This advice culminated with the adoption of the Guidelines on the NPMs[18] in 2010, which is the most comprehensive advice on the NPMs issued by the SPT to date. These Guidelines follow the earlier approach in distinguishing the responsibilities of the State Party in the initial setting up/designation of the NPM, in maintaining the NPM (see the next section), and in the NPM's responsibilities. While overall comprehensive, these Guidelines do not address the role of civil society in monitoring the process of the designation and functioning of the NPM, a role which is particularly significant as a guarantor of the NPM's (perceived) independence.[19]Although this is not to say that the SPT has not recognised the important role of civil society in effective torture prevention, either as part of the NPM formally[20] or through collaborating with the NPM.[21]

In relation to the choice of the NPMs, Article 18 (4) of the OPCAT stipulates that they should be designated in accordance with the Paris

[15] SPT, Seventeenth annual report, *op. cit.*, Annex I, para 2; See also Murray (2008).

[16] SPT, First annual report, *UN Doc.* CAT/C/40/2, 14 May 2008, paras 28–29.

[17] While the first visit report, on the visit to Mauritius, remains confidential the second visit report, on the visit to the Maldives, contains a dedicated section on the guidelines on NPMs with separate paras for the State and the NPMs. See SPT, Report on the visit of the SPT to the Maldives, *UN Doc.* CAT/OP/MDV/1, 26 February 2009, paras 71–72. Similarly, the third visit report, on the visit to Sweden, contains guidelines on NPMs. See SPT, Report on the visit of the SPT to Sweden, *UN Doc.* CAT/OP/SWE/1, 10 September 2008, para 42.

[18] SPT, Guidelines on National Preventive Mechanisms, *UN Doc.* CAT/OP/12/5, 9 December 2010.

[19] See further: Šteinerte (2014).

[20] SPT, Report to the NPM on the visit of the SPT to Kyrgyzstan, *UN Doc.* CAT/OP/KGZ/2, 15 July 2019, para 26.

[21] SPT, Report to the NPM on the visit of the SPT to the United Kingdom of Great Britain and Northern Ireland, *UN Doc.* CAT/OP/GBR/RONPM/1, 16 December 2020, para 73.

Principles. In light of this, it is noteworthy that a large majority of NPMs worldwide are National Human Rights Institutions (NHRIs) or have NHRIs as a constitutive part. Hence, the SPT has deemed it necessary to address various issues of NHRIs acting also as NPMs on a number of occasions (see Sect. 3 below). Critically, the SPT has clarified that NHRIs are not to be equated with NPMs and the SPT "has no input into this peer-review system and that, consequently, any assessment by the Subcommittee on Accreditation [of the Global Alliance of National Human Rights Institutions] should not be taken to represent the Subcommittee's views as to whether any particular national preventive mechanism complies with the requirements of the Optional Protocol".[22] The SPT has thus somewhat distanced itself from the accreditation system of the NHRIs, making it clear that this is not to be taken as some form of assessment of the NPMs as per the OPCAT requirements.

As of 1 December 2025, roughly two thirds of the 96 OPCAT States Parties have designated their NPM among which the most "popular choice" has been the designation of the NHRIs, be these Human Rights Commissions[23] or Ombudsperson,[24] acting alone[25] or together with other institutions[26] or civil society organisations[27] albeit there are a

[22] SPT, Seventeenth annual report, *op. cit.*, Annex III, para 3.

[23] For example, the Human Rights Commission of the Maldives has been the country's NPM since 2006.

[24] For example, the Commissioner for Human Rights of Azerbaijan has been the designated NPM of Azerbaijan since 2009.

[25] For example, the Ombudsman of the Republic of Bulgaria has been the NPM since 2011 while Burkina Faso's *Commission Nationale des Droits de l'Homme* has been the NPM since 2010.

[26] For example, the NPM of New Zealand is comprised of four institutions: the Human Rights Commission (with the NPM coordinating role), The Ombudsman's Office, The Children's Commissioner, The Police Complaints Authority and The Judge Advocate General while the Swedish NPM is composed of two institutions: the Parliamentary Ombudsman and the Chancellor of Justice.

[27] For example, the NPM of Moldova is comprised of Centre for Human Rights (Ombudsman) in combination with the Consultative Council which is composed of the civil society representatives.

handful of States Parties, which have established entirely new institutions for the purposes of their NPM.[28]

The Failure to Establish an NPM: Article 17 List

The obligation to designate an NPM is to be implemented by a State Party within a year of the OPCAT ratification.[29] While the vast majority of the States Parties have fulfilled this obligation, there is a small number of States Parties which have not, and yet a smaller number whose failure to designate an NPM now stretches to a few years, or even a decade.[30] The SPT has limited recourse in how to address such instances and in a remarkable departure from its general approach towards the principle of cooperation and confidentiality applicable to its work with all States Parties, since 2016 the SPT has published the so-called "Article 17 list": a list of OPCAT States Parties whose compliance with the obligation to designate an NPM is *significantly* overdue (emphasis added).[31] From its inception, this list became akin to public "naming and shaming", appearing in each annual report and a dedicated section on the SPT's website too.

In addition to this list, the SPT has clarified five cumulative criteria it requires to be satisfied in order to ascertain of the fact that the NPM has been established: (1) the fact of such establishment; (2) a copy of the legal instrument establishing the NPM; (3) the name of the head of the NPM; (4) the postal address of the NPM; and (5) the email address

---

[28] For example, France established *Contrôleur Général des lieux de privation de liberté* as its NPM in 2008 while Switzerland established its *Commission nationale de prévention de la torture* in 2009.

[29] Notable exception is provided by Art. 24 of the OPCAT which allows postponing the implementation of the obligation to designate an NPM for a year; a further extension of up to three years may be granted by the Committee against Torture. To date, two countries availed themselves of this possibility: Kazakhstan (1 year) and Australia (1 + 3 years).

[30] For example, Burundi ratified the OPCAT in 2013 but still has not designated its NPM; Liberia ratified the OPCAT in 2004 but is yet to set up its NPM while Democratic Republic Congo and Gabon, both OPCAT State Parties since 2010, remain without their respective NPMs to date.

[31] SPT, Non-compliance with Article 17, https://www.ohchr.org/en/treaty-bodies/spt/non-compliance-article-17 (consulted 5 October 2025).

and phone number of the NPM.[32] These are to be communicated to the SPT via note verbale from each OPCAT State Party[33], which is crucial to indicate the official choice of the State Party regarding its NPM.

As noted above, the so-called "Article 17 list" is a notable exception to the overall SPT approach to confidentiality and cooperation in its relations with the OPCAT States Parties. The speed (or rather the slowness) at which States Parties are removed from this list begs the question of the effectiveness of the tool in accelerating the establishment of NPMs. There are States Parties who have been on this list since its very inception, which clearly indicates the need for a different SPT approach towards the delivery of advice and assistance in the establishment of their NPMs.

Advising and Assisting in Maintaining the NPM

The obligations of the States Parties vis-à-vis their NPMs do not cease with the establishment and designation of the NPM but extend to maintaining it.[34] The SPT has formulated the continuous obligation of States Parties as "the effectiveness of the NPM should be subject to regular appraisal by both the State and the NPM itself, taking into account the views of the SPT, with a view to its being reinforced and strengthened as and when necessary".[35]

Despite the considerable financial constraints imposed on the SPT, it has issued a substantive body of advice over the past two decades. This comprises, *inter alia*, advice on NPM legislation, once again confirming that any such NPM legislation "should take into account the idiosyncrasies of national realities"[36]; a variety of guidance regarding the independence of the NPMs and their funding, especially in the context

---

[32] SPT, Sixteenth annual report, *UN Doc*. CAT/C/76/2, 15 March 2023, para 32.

[33] Ibid.

[34] Arts. 3 and 17 OPCAT.

[35] SPT, Guidelines on National Preventive Mechanisms, *UN Doc*. CAT/OP/12/5, 9 December 2010, para 15.

[36] SPT, Ninth annual report, *op. cit.*, Annex, para 17.

of SPT visits[37]; and advice on NHRIs that have been vested with the NPM mandate.[38]

Another central theme of advice is the interpretation of the terms "places of deprivation of liberty", such as in the first General Comment of the SPT, adopted in 2024 on Article 4 of the OPCAT.[39] This was motivated by several reports which the SPT received stating that "in practice, some national preventive mechanisms have, at different times, faced difficulties or restrictions in conducting visits to some places of deprivation of liberty".[40]

The way the SPT has implemented its advisory function towards the continuous work of the NPMs clearly implies that the SPT places great emphasis on the continuity of the obligations arising for the States Parties vis-à-vis their NPMs. The obligations of the State Party do not end with the establishment of an NPM: they are permanent and ongoing, especially in providing adequate funding, safeguarding independence and implementing the NPM recommendations.

Protecting the NPMs

The Subcommittee recognises the central role of the NPMs to advance the overall torture prevention aims of the OPCAT. The SPT has therefore stepped in to protect the NPMs around the globe in crisis situations. The most recent such example surrounds the decision of the Kyrgyz authorities to abolish their long-standing NPM, the National Centre for the Prevention of Torture, and transfer the NPM mandate to the country's Akyikatchy (the Ombudsperson) through a rushed adoption of a new Constitutional Law. While the details of the discussions with the State Party remain confidential, the SPT issued a press release expressing

---

37 See, for example, SPT, Report to the State Party of the visit of the SPT to Croatia, *UN Doc.* CAT/OP/HRV/ROSP/1, paras 18–19; Report of the visit of the SPT to Bosnia and Herzegovina, *UN Doc* CAT/OP/BIH/ROSP/1, 5 December 2024, paras 19–23.

38 SPT, Seventeenth annual report, *op. cit.*, Annex I, paras 1–7, Annex 3.

39 SPT, General Comment No. 1 (2024) on Article 4 of the Optional Protocol (Places of Deprivation of Liberty), *UN Doc.* CAT/OP/GC/1, 4 July 2024.

40 Ibid., para 5.

its "dismay" over the Kyrgyz decision.[41] By doing so, the SPT made it public that it had travelled to the country for high-level talks over the fate of the NPM and concluded that the transfer of the NPM mandate had taken place through "a completely opaque process, with no public consultation, no engagement with stakeholders, and not even the text of the amendments made publicly available" which "is plainly incompatible with the requirements of the OPCAT".[42]

The SPT's support to the Brazilian NPM in 2019–2022, when funding for the Brazilian NPM was revoked and its members dismissed without formally ceasing the institution, was more successful. In December 2019, the SPT issued for the first time public views, concluding that Brazil should ensure that its "system of prevention of torture functions efficiently and independently, with financial and structural autonomy and adequate resources, in accordance with its international obligations under the Optional Protocol".[43] This was followed by the SPT visit to Brazil for high-level talks at the very start of 2022 (the visit was planned earlier but was delayed by the COVID pandemic), which ultimately led to a positive outcome for restoring the work of the Brazilian NPM.[44]

What these two contrasting examples show is the readiness of the SPT to take bold steps to support and protect the NPMs who are facing situations critical to their very survival. The ultimate outcome of these efforts, however, requires strong national support of the SPT's efforts.

---

[41] OHCHR Press Statement of 30 June 2025, *Kyrgyzstan: Independent torture prevention watchdog should not be replaced, UN experts warn*: https://www.ohchr.org/en/press-releases/2025/06/kyrgyzstan-independent-torture-prevention-watchdog-should-not-be-replaced-un.

[42] Ibid.

[43] SPT, Views of the Subcommittee on Prevention of Torture on the compatibility with the Optional Protocol to the Convention against Torture of presidential decree No. 9.831/2019 relating to the national preventive mechanism of Brazil, *UN Doc*. CAT/OP/8, 16 December 2019, para 35.

[44] United Nations, *UN torture prevention body applauds Brazil Supreme Court's decision safeguarding national preventive mechanism*, 1 April 2022, https://www.ohchr.org/en/press-releases/2022/04/un-torture-prevention-body-applauds-brazil-supreme-courts-decision

4 SPT's Role in Advising NPMs and Strengthening Their Role

According to Evans (2023, p. 103), "it is the 'twin-pillar' approach, based on the interplay between the international and national mechanisms which makes the OPCAT so unique". Indeed, the possibility for the SPT and NPMs to have direct contact is one of the most innovative features of the OPCAT. The OPCAT also foresees an advisory role for the SPT towards NPMs, which the SPT is mainly implementing through general guidelines and during its visits.

Direct Contacts Between the SPT and NPMs

The possibility for an international entity (in this case: the SPT) to have direct contact with a national body (in this case: the NPM) and vice versa is certainly "one of the most powerful powers granted by the OPCAT"[45] to both the SPT and the NPMs. The SPT can maintain "direct, if necessary confidential, contacts" with NPMs.[46] States Parties not only have to grant their NPMs the "right to have contacts with the Subcommittee on Prevention, to send it information and to meet with him"[47] but also undertake to "encourage and facilitate contacts between" them.[48] The fact that these contacts can be "if necessary confidential" both underlines and strengthens their respective independence (Nowak et al., 2019, p. 814).

This essential component of the SPT mandate, as already noted, however, is not covered by any budgetary provisions of the OHCHR, an issue already raised by the SPT in its first annual report some two decades ago, where it noted that it is keen to "continue and intensify its direct contacts with NPMs" however "there is no specific provision within the regular budget for the SPT's mandate to work in direct contacts with

[45] Association for the Prevention of Torture (APT), NPM Toolkit 'Interaction with the SPT', www.apt.ch/knowledge-hub/npm-toolkit (consulted 5 October 2025).

[46] Art. 11 b) ii OPCAT.

[47] Art. 20 f OPCAT.

[48] Art. 12 c) OPCAT.

NPMs".[49] The situation has not changed since then, and the OHCHR only provides a budget for SPT plenary sessions in Geneva and in-country visits. The SPT has therefore developed strategies to maintain direct contacts within these budgetary constraints.

At the institutional level, the position of Vice-Chair on NPMs not only provides a clearly designated point of contact within the SPT on all issues concerning the NPMs but also sends an unmistakable signal of the importance the SPT attaches to the proper functioning of the NPMs in the wider torture prevention architecture of the OPCAT.[50] Further, the internal work within the SPT is organised through regional teams with the SPT members designated as country rapporteurs[51] to undertake and coordinate the NPM-related activities of the Subcommittee within each region. For the past years, SPT's four regional teams have organised annual webinars during SPT sessions with all NPMs in their region,[52] to discuss operational and/or substantive issues. Country rapporteurs engage with their NPMs on a regular basis, outside of sessions, at the initiative of the rapporteur or of the NPM, to discuss developments, activities, challenges and opportunities the NPMs may face. The underlying idea is for NPMs to have one identified focal point within the SPT to turn to and for the SPT to be able to maintain contacts with NPMs despite their growing number and in the absence of dedicated funding from the OHCHR. NPMs also regularly contact the SPT, mainly through the country rapporteur, to request advice on the interpretation of the OPCAT or on methodological or substantive issues. They also share their annual reports that are published on SPT's website and form the basis of an exchange between the NPM and the country rapporteur.

The SPT also maintains direct contacts by inviting NPMs to meet during its sessions, either in plenary or with the regional teams. These bilateral meetings can take place in person for NPMs able to travel

---

[49] SPT, First annual report, *UN Doc.* CAT/C/40/2, 14 May 2008, para 50.

[50] SPT, Fifth annual report, *UN Doc.* CAT/C/48/3, 19 March 2012, para 39.

[51] See SPT webpage for the Regional Teams and Country Rapporteurs: https://www.ohchr.org/en/treaty-bodies/spt/regional-teams (consulted 27 March 2026).

[52] See for example SPT, Eighteenth annual report, *UN Doc.* CAT/C/82/2, 26 March 2025, paras 30-34; Seventeenth annual report, *op. cit.*, paras 26–30.

to Geneva, and—with the development of videoconferencing—have increasingly been held online. The meetings are mentioned in SPT's annual reports under the section "dealing with developments on NPM".

The SPT has been able to provide further training and technical assistance owing to invitations from civil society organisations, regional organisations, academia and others to participate in face-to-face national or regional workshops and conferences. From the beginning of its work in 2009, a "pilot programme for assistance to NPMs enabled the SPT to participate in bilateral and regional workshops with European NPMs.[53] These invitations continue to represent a great opportunity to engage in person with NPMs and exchange bilaterally as well as collectively.[54] Recently, the OHCHR capacity-building programme has facilitated the participation of SPT members in NPM regional activities.[55] Finally, through the OPCAT Special Fund established in accordance with Article 26 of the OPCAT, which funds projects related to NPM education and/or implementation of SPT recommendations following visits, the SPT may also be able to provide assistance, training and advice to NPMs.

Advising NPMs Through General Advice

The SPT's mandate to "advise and assist NPMs" has also been exercised through the publication of general advice and guidelines on NPMs' settings and operations, issued by the SPT on its own initiative or in response to requests for advice from NPMs. They cover a wide range of issues, from core institutional questions, in particular related to NPMs, which are part of NHRIs, to more practical issues related to the methodology of visits.

---

[53] The programme was supported by the Council of Europe and implemented by the APT, i.e. SPT, Second annual report, *UN Doc.* CAT/C/42/2, 7 April 2009, para 37; Third annual report, *UN Doc.* CAT/C/44/2, 25 March 2010, para 45; Fourth annual report, *UN Doc.* CAT/C/46/2, 3 February 2011, para 27.

[54] See for example SPT, Eighteenth annual report, *op. cit.*, paras 38–39; Seventeenth annual report, *op. cit.*, paras 31-34.

[55] For example, in 2023, OHCHR capacity-building programme organised two sub-regional conferences on the OPCAT in Dakar for West Africa and in Yaounde for Central Africa, see SPT, Seventeenth annual report, *op. cit.*, para 37. In 2025, it facilitated the participation of one SPT member in the Second meeting of the Network of African NPMs in Cape Verde.

As already noted above, guidance on the establishment and ongoing operation of the NPMs, addressed both to States Parties and NPMs, was set out in SPT's first annual report,[56] followed by the 2010 Guidelines on NPMs.[57] The Section on Operations contains Points for NPMs where the SPT underlines the OPCAT obligations and adds institutional and methodological elements, such as the establishment of a visit programme, the issuance of visit reports, and the need for the NPM to review its working methods and undertake training. It also notes, for the first time, its position regarding designation of NHRIs as NPMs: "where the body designated as the NPM performs other functions in addition to those in the Optional Protocol, its NPM functions should be located within a separate unit or department, with its own staff and own budget".[58] This paragraph continues to serve as a reference point and has been further elaborated upon over the years by the SPT.[59]

Further, in 2012, the SPT published its analytical self-assessment tool for NPMs, which is addressed directly and solely at NPMs, noting that "the SPT should have a view on the manner in which the NPM addresses core areas of its mandate in order to advise it in its work".[60] This assessment tool emphasises the development of NPM as an ongoing obligation and lists what NPMs "should" do to implement their mandate effectively. This includes the development of a strategy, internal organisation, visits and reports, including annual reports, prevention of reprisals and cross-cutting issues. However, arguably most of the value added by this tool rests with its companion, the self-assessment matrix, which is a practical and hands-on instrument, listing detailed elements of the NPM mandate, thus enabling a relatively straightforward self-assessment by the NPM itself.

---

56 SPT, First annual report, *UN Doc.* CAT/C/40/2, 14 May 2008, para 28.

57 SPT, Third annual report, *UN Doc.* CAT/OP/12/5, 9 December 2010; Guidelines on National Preventive Mechanisms, *op. cit.*

58 Ibid., para 32.

59 SPT, Eighteenth annual report, *op. cit.*, Annex III; Seventeenth annual report, *op. cit.*, Annex I, A. and Annex III.

60 SPT, Analytical self-assessment tool for National Prevention Mechanisms (NPM), *UN Doc.* CAT/OP/1, 6 February 2012, para 3.

The SPT has also utilised its annual reports as vehicles to publish a generic response to an NPM-specific request, with the premise that "such advice is of general interest".[61] After all, when an NPM from one country approaches the SPT with a request for advice on an emerging issue, it is likely that similar challenges have arisen or may arise in the work of another NPM. The SPT has therefore started to compile its responses in the form of general advice, usually not publicly naming the NPM who approached it for advice, to amplify their potential impact among NPMs. NPM requests to the SPT cover a broad range of issues, which can be grouped into three categories. First, there are requests on the scope of the OPCAT mandate, with interpretation of Article 4,[62] monitoring of compulsory quarantine,[63] or cross-border monitoring.[64] A second type of requests deals with the issue of NPMs that are part of an NHRI. The SPT's responses can be clustered in organisational issues, i.e. financial autonomy, hierarchical relations or NHRI functions versus preventive functions and the independence of the mechanism.[65] Thirdly, certain requests and corresponding advice deal with the implementation of the mandate, such as access to information to be provided to NPM under Article 20, application of the principle of confidentiality, or body searches and pat-downs of the NPM members.[66] The publication of the SPT's responses to specific requests in the form of advice is a creative way of exercising its advisory role by building on individual and specific requests to engage with the NPM community as a whole.

Advice to Operational NPMs in the Context of Visits

Within its budgetary limitations, one of the most effective ways for the SPT to engage in direct contacts with NPMs is during its country

---

61 SPT, Ninth annual report, *op. cit.*, para 26.

62 SPT, Ninth annual report, *op. cit.*

63 SPT, Advice provided by the Subcommittee to the National Preventive Mechanism of the United Kingdom of Great Britain and Northern Ireland regarding compulsory quarantine for coronavirus (COVID-19 virus), *UN Doc.* CAT/OP/9, 31 March 2020.

64 SPT, Ninth annual report, *op. cit.*, Annex, V.

65 SPT, Ninth annual report, *op. cit.*, Annex, III and I, A.

66 SPT, Ninth annual report, *op. cit.*, Annex I, B, II and IV.

visits. In countries where there is a designated NPM, and so from the first round of visits in 2007,[67] the SPT dedicates part of the visit to engage with the NPM. These, however, only provide a limited opportunity for thorough engagement with the NPMs, leading the SPT to introduce a new type of NPM advisory visits in 2012. These visits were aimed at closer joint work with an operational NPM, based on a new methodology, shorter, with joint visits to places of detention, following a programme agreed jointly in advance. These visits were to allow a better understanding of the challenges the NPM faced.[68] These visits were followed by two confidential reports, one to the State Party on issues related to the set-up of the NPM and one to the NPM, which could be made public by recipients.[69] While initially heralded by the SPT as a "great success",[70] these visits were abandoned as it was later felt that categorising visits into different types "hindered the full and robust exercise of its [the SPT's] mandate".[71] Consequently, the SPT reverted to one type of "full" visits from 2016. Notwithstanding this, the engagement concerning the establishment of the NPMs still forms a significant part of the visit when there is no NPM designated yet. Equally, in countries with an operational NPM, the SPT visits always include meetings with the NPM, joint visits to places of deprivation of liberty to enable peer-to-peer learning and exchanges on visiting methodology. At the end of the visit, the SPT continues to produce two distinct reports, one to the State Party and one to the NPM, which follows a shorter format since 2021, and several NPMs have authorised publication of the reports.

In its report to NPMs, the SPT makes recommendations regarding institutional issues, such as the NPM's legal framework, where it

---

[67] SPT, Report on the visit of the SPT to the Maldives, *op. cit.*; Report on the visit of the SPT to Sweden, *op. cit.*

[68] The SPT conduct advisory visits in 2012 to Honduras, the Republic of Moldova and Senegal and in 2013, to Armenia, Costa Rica, Bulgaria and Germany. On the website, in the table listing the visits, the visits are mentioned as 'focus on the NPM.'

[69] The following NPMs have made the reports of the NPM advisory visit public: Armenia (CAT/OP/ARM/2, 8 January 2017) Germany (CAT/OP/DEU/2, 29 October 2013), Honduras (CAT/OP/HND/3, 30 October 2012), the Republic of Moldova (CAT/OP/MDA/2, 23 May 2013) and Senegal (CAT/OP/SEN/2, 14 June 2013).

[70] SPT, Seventh annual report, *UN Doc.* CAT/C/52/2, 20 March 2014, para 44.

[71] SPT, Ninth annual report, *op. cit.*, para 40.

recommends that the NPM take proactive steps to review the legal framework.[72] In the UK, where 21 existing institutions have been designated as NPM, the SPT recommended the NPM to "continue proactively raising with the authorities of the United Kingdom the need for robust legislation as an essential safeguard for the mechanism's independence, effectiveness and credibility, both nationally and internationally".[73] While the adequate NPM funding is the responsibility of the State Parties, and the SPT cannot realistically provide specific guidelines on what would be adequate in a given context, it recommends that the NPMs evaluate their financial needs and submit proposals to the authorities based on these needs,[74] thus ensuring and supporting a more context-based request to ensure regular visits as per the OPCAT. The issue of the functional independence, which "supposes that an NPM cannot be subject to any orders or instructions by any State authorities"[75] is central to the SPT and is regularly noted in NPM reports.[76] When the NHRI is designated as NPM, the SPT recommends the NPM to take steps "to clearly separate the activities and functions"[77] of the NPM from the NHRI or "steps, which may include advocacy for legislative change, to ensure that it is independent within the ombudsperson's office".[78]

---

[72] SPT, Report on the NPM Advisory visit to Armenia, *UN Doc.* CAT/OP/ARM/2, 8 January 2017, para 26; Report to the NPM following the 2018 visit to Portugal, *UN Doc.* CAT/OP/POR/2, 22 August 2019, para 19; Report to the NPM following the 2018 visit to Poland, *UN Doc.* CAT/OP/POL/RONPM/1, 6 February 2020, para 20.

[73] SPT, Report to the NPM following the 2018 visit to UK, *UN Doc.* CAT/OP/GBR/RONPM/1, 8 December 2020, para 50; Report to the NPM following the 2017 visit to Hungary, *UN Doc.* CAT/OP/HUN/2, 4 June 2018, para 19; Report on the NPM Advisory visit to Germany, *UN Doc.* CAT/OP/DEU/2, 29 October 2013, para 34.

[74] SPT, Report to the NPM following the 2018 visit to Poland, *op. cit.*, para 26; Report to the NPM following the 2018 visit to Kyrgyzstan, *UN Doc.* CAT/OP/KGZ/RONPM/2, 11 July 2019, para 37; Report to the NPM following the 2019 visit to Switzerland, *UN Doc.* CAT/OP/CHE/RONPM/1, 5 March 2021, para 32; Report on the NPM Advisory visit to Germany, *op. cit.*, para 37; Report to the NPM following the 2017 visit to Hungary, *op. cit.*, para 45; Report to the NPM following the 2017 visit to North Macedonia, *UN Doc.* CAT/OP/MKD/2, 20 March 2018, para 18.

[75] SPT, Report to the NPM following the 2018 visit to UK, *op. cit.*, para 55.

[76] SPT, Report to the NPM following the 2018 visit to Hungary, *UN Doc.* CAT/OP/HUN/2, 4 June 2018; Report to the NPM following the 2018 visit to UK, *op. cit.*, paras 54–55.

[77] SPT, Report on the NPM Advisory visit to Armenia, *op. cit.*, para 26.

[78] SPT, Report to the NPM following the 2018 visit to Portugal, *op. cit.*, para 18; Report to the NPM following the 2017 visit of the SPT to North Macedonia, *op. cit.*, para 16.

The SPT also recommends that the NPM conduct awareness-raising campaigns to clearly distinguish the two mandates.[79]

The SPT reports to NPMs based on joint visits, also focus on the methodology applied by NPMs, and sometimes include practical recommendations on the teamwork,[80] on the need to wear visible identification,[81] as well as the need to devote attention to safeguards beyond material conditions.[82] The SPT also regularly makes practical recommendations regarding the conduct of private interviews with persons deprived of liberty, including the way the NPM introduces themselves and the mandate, the choice of a safe location and ensuring confidentiality.[83] The SPT further systematically underlines the risks of reprisals against persons deprived of liberty following the visit, and the need to develop strategies and enter into dialogue with the authorities to prevent risks of reprisals.[84]

Overall, the SPT country visits serve two key objectives: its own visits to places of deprivation of liberty with the view of setting out recommendations to the State Party concerned and supporting the work of the NPM or advising on its establishment/designation. This is a very clear

---

[79] SPT, Report to the NPM following the 2018 visit to Portugal, *op. cit.,* para 43; Report to the NPM following the 2018 visit to Poland, *op. cit.,* para 34; Report to the NPM following the 2019 visit to Costa Rica, *UN Doc*. CAT/OP/CRI/RONPM/1, December 9, 2019, para 25; Report to the NPM following the 2017 visit of the SPT to Spain, *op. cit.,* para 17.

[80] SPT, Report to the NPM following the 2018 visit to Poland, *op. cit.,* para 39; Report of the NPM Advisory visit to Germany, *op. cit.*, para 52.

[81] See SPT, Report on the NPM Advisory visit to Germany, *op. cit.*, para 62; Report to the NPM following the 2017 visit to Spain, *op. cit.*, para 17; Report on the NPM Advisory visit to Armenia, *op. cit.*, para 46.

[82] SPT, Report on 2012 NPM Advisory visit to Germany, *op. cit.*, para 39 and recommendations 44; Report to the NPM following the 2017 visit of the SPT to North Macedonia, *op. cit.,* para 33.

[83] SPT, Report to the NPM following the 2018 visit to Spain, *op. cit.,* para 21; Report to the NPM following the 2018 visit of the SPT to Costa Rica, *op. cit.,* para 30; Report to the NPM following the 2018 visit of the SPT to Switzerland, *op. cit.,* para 52–53; Report to the NPM following the 2018 visit of the SPT to Kyrgyzstan, *op. cit.,* para 63–66; Report to the NPM following the 2018 visit to North Macedonia, *op. cit.,* paras 27 and 37.

[84] SPT, Report to the NPM following the 2018 visit to Portugal, *op. cit.*, para 43; SPT Report to the NPM following the 2018 visit to Kyrgyzstan, *op. cit.,* para 78–79; SPT Report to the NPM following the 2019 visit to Costa Rica, *op. cit.,* para 35; SPT Report to the NPM following the 2019 visit to Switzerland, *op. cit.,* para 61; SPT Report to the NPM following the 2019 visit to UK, *op. cit.*, para 106; SPT Report to the NPM following the 2017 visit to Spain, *op. cit.*, para 21.

signal from the SPT that these two elements of its mandate go hand in hand, and the operational effectiveness of the NPM is key to the full implementation of the torture prevention architecture of the OPCAT.

5 Tripartite Cooperation: Substantive Advances in Torture Prevention

The aim of the OPCAT system of visits is to reduce the risks of torture occurring by identifying, understanding and addressing its root causes—instead of asking what has happened, torture prevention asks *why* it has happened.[85] The objective is to ensure that the visits and the subsequent reports and recommendations "offer practical advice and suggestions as to how to reduce the likelihood or risks of torture or ill treatment occurring"[86] and that recommendations are implemented by the authorities. The cooperation between the SPT and NPMs in supporting the States Parties to take measures on torture prevention is slowly increasing and shows significant potential for change.

Broadening the Scope of Torture Prevention, Jointly

In addition to its Approach to torture prevention[87], the SPT has, over the years, published in its annual reports[88] a series of dedicated sections analysing different thematic issues to assist both States Parties and NPMs in their understanding of torture prevention. Topics covered range from the Istanbul protocol,[89] indigenous justice,[90] corruption,[91]

---

[85] APT/APF/OHCHR guide on NHRI.

[86] SPT, The approach of the Subcommittee on the Prevention of torture to the concept of prevention, *UN Doc*. CAT/OP/12/6, 30 December 2010, para 4.

[87] Ibid.

[88] These thematic sections are also available on SPT's website, groups under the heading 'Approaches to prevention,' www.ohchr.org/en/treatybodies/spt/approaches-prevention.

[89] SPT, Second annual report, *op. cit.*, Annex VII; Sixteenth annual report, *op. cit.*, Annex.

[90] SPT, Sixth annual report, *UN Doc*. CAT/C/50/2, 23 April 2013, paras 81–89.

[91] SPT, Seventh annual report, *op. cit.*, paras 72–100.

pre-trial detention[92] to specific groups such as LGBTIQ+ persons[93] and women deprived of liberty.[94] These thematic sections were drafted by SPT members and Secretariat, based on individual expertise as well as on the experience in conducting visits, with limited consultation with NPMs or States Parties.

The COVID-19 pandemic signified a change in practice. Following advice addressed to States Parties and NPMs on the pandemic, the SPT engaged directly with a record number of 44 NPMs[95] and contacted all NPMs and States Parties with requests for information on how they responded to the pandemic. 49 out of 90 States Parties and 64 NPMs responded to that invitation and the information, received, together with ongoing dialogue with NPMs, formed the basis of a follow-up advice[96] as well as the publication of a protocol for NPMs engaged in visits looking at the planning, the conduct and the follow-up of visits.[97] SPT documents were widely used and disseminated, and this experience showed the positive and substantive tripartite cooperation between the States, the NPM and the SPT to mitigate the risks of the pandemic in places of deprivation of liberty. The NPMs demonstrated their commitment and capacity to act, be it to advise authorities or to monitor the implementation of measures and the risk of ill-treatment in places of detention. The SPT acknowledged that "the pandemic underlined the crucial role played by NPMs within the OPCAT, including as the 'front line' in the prevention of torture prevention".[98]

The drafting process leading to the adoption of the SPT's first General Comment on the concept of places of deprivation of liberty in July

92 SPT, Eight annual report, *UN Doc.* CAT/C/54/2, 26 March 2015, paras 73–96.

93 SPT, Ninth annual report, *op. cit.*, paras 48–82.

94 SPT, Prevention of torture and ill-treatment of women deprived of liberty, *UN Doc.* CAT/OP/27/1, 18 January 2016.

95 SPT, Fourteenth annual report, *UN Doc.* CAT/OP/70/2, 8 March 2021, para 17.

96 SPT, Follow-up advice of the Subcommittee to States Parties and national preventive mechanisms relating to the coronavirus disease (COVID-19) pandemic, *UN Doc.* CAT/OP/12, 18 June 2021.

97 SPT, Protocol for national preventive mechanisms undertaking on site visits during the coronavirus disease (COVID-19) pandemic, *UN Doc.* CAT/OP/11, 10 June 2021.

98 SPT, Fifteenth annual report, *UN Doc.* CAT/C/70/2, 10 March 2022, para 44.

2024[99] also positively built on cooperation between the SPT and the NPMs, as well as other stakeholders. In 2020, the SPT established a working group in charge of drafting, and in 2023, a first draft was made public as part of a consultation. 68 submissions were received from different stakeholders, including many NPMs. In June 2023, a day of public discussion took place, with 30 interventions, which was live broadcast, recorded and made available on the UN website.[100] Most of the comments and suggestions were taken aboard and integrated into the revised draft. The SPT General Comment is the result of a consultative and participatory process that offers a new authoritative and broad interpretation of places of deprivation of liberty to be understood as a comprehensive concept, which is grounded in SPT's experience as well as in the "unparalleled insights into domestic realities" offered by the NPMs.[101] It has been disseminated and shared by the SPT with NPMs through regional webinars and is referred to by many NPMs in their annual reports.[102] The SPT's first General Comment constitutes a useful reference tool for both NPMs and States Parties, and this advice will facilitate access by NPMs to any place where people are deprived of their liberty and hence contribute to achieving better torture prevention. The SPT however also has acknowledged in the same General Comment that the concept "evolves with time, allowing for the inclusion of novel situations and circumstances of deprivation of liberty that may arise in new contexts" and therefore underscored the importance of the autonomous decision-making of the NPMs to determine what constitutes a "place of deprivation of liberty".[103]

---

[99] SPT, General Comment No. 1 (2024), *op. cit.*

[100] SPT, Eighteenth annual report, *op. cit.*, para 47.

[101] Ibid., para 48.

[102] See for example: Uruguay, 2024 annual report, para (with link to the contribution of the NPM); 2024 annual report of the NPM of Chile, Prevention of torture and situation of persons deprived of liberty, p. 10 (and other references in the text) www.mnpt.cl; Monitoring places of detention, UK NPM 15th annual report 2023/204, p. 67 (to complement the General comment, the UK NPM also created a Task Force to agree on a succinct definition) see www.nationalpreventivemechanism.uk; The report of the Human Rights Ombudsman of the Republic Slovenia on Implementing the tasks of the National Preventive Mechanism for 2024, p. 42. www.varuh-rs.sl

[103] SPT, General Comment No. 1 (2024), *op. cit.*, para 59.

Using the Potential of Tripartite Cooperation to Advance Implementation of Recommendations

Visits to places of deprivation of liberty are only a means to collect first-hand information about the functioning of these places and produce evidence-based reports and recommendations. The ultimate aim of the visits is to produce changes in policies and practices which contribute to reducing the risks of torture and ill-treatment. This is where the OPCAT architecture can make a difference, in the long term, through the blending of the weight of an international human rights treaty body with the presence and experience of national monitoring bodies. This is an area where more cooperation could develop over time to facilitate the implementation of both the SPT's and the NPMs' recommendations by the States Parties.

During its country visits, the SPT could systematically implement its good practice of insisting with States Parties for NPMs to be invited to the final meeting with the authorities,[104] to ensure follow-up and implementation. Additionally, considering that the OPCAT foresees confidential direct contacts between the NPM and the SPT, the SPT could share information with the NPM about the places it has visited and the main issues it has found, confidentially. Such more substantive discussions between the SPT and the NPMs about the risks of torture and ill-treatment in places of deprivation of liberty would enable stronger coherence in the recommendations of the two bodies. It would also enable the NPM to follow up and conduct visits to the places visited by the SPT, thereby also reducing the risks of reprisals against persons deprived of liberty who had engaged with the SPT. After its visit, the SPT could also consider sharing its report to the State Party with the NPM. Indeed, Article 16 provides that "the SPT shares its report confidentially with the State and, *if relevant, with the NPM*" (emphasis added), leaving the decision to the SPT depending on the overall context and the level of cooperation with the NPM. Thus far,

[104] See recent examples: SPT, Report on the 2023 visit of the SPT to Georgia, *UN Doc.* CAT/OP/GEO/ROSP/1, 9 January 2025, para 6; Report on the 2022 visit of the SPT to Argentina, *UN Doc.* CAT/OP/ARG/ROSP/1, 19 December 2023, para 5; Report on the 2021 visit of the SPT to Bulgaria, *UN Doc.* CAT/OP/BGR/ROSP/1, 28 October 2022, para 6.

the SPT only shares with the NPM the part of its report to the State Party which concerns the NPM. Sharing State Party reports in full would further enable tripartite follow-up discussions between the NPM, the SPT and the authorities on the implementation of SPT recommendations. There are already some interesting and good practices in this regard, such as the Polish NPM thematic report on the implementation of recommendations from international bodies (CPT and SPT).[105]

Tripartite discussions could also cover the implementation of NPM recommendations, based on issues identified in specific visit reports or in the NPM annual reports. The involvement of the SPT, as a UN body, in the dialogue between the NPM and the authorities would give additional weight to the NPM's recommendations and incentivise the States Parties to implement them. It would also capitalise on the unique OPCAT architecture and on the fact that "the OPCAT system has changed the dynamic of prevention by locating the primary engine of oversight at the domestic level, powerfully supported by international machinery" (Evans, 2020, p. 275).

6 Conclusion

The triangular relationship between the SPT, the State Party and the NPM put in place by the OPCAT remains a distinctive feature of the OPCAT. The SPT stands out within the family of the UN treaty bodies as one that finds no parallel in the mandates of all other nine UN treaty bodies.[106] Yet, the way the SPT is supported by the OHCHR through its Secretariat very much mirrors the way the work of the other nine

---

105 Polish Commissioner for Human Rights, Human rights in places of detention. How Poland is implementing into practice the recommendations of the international bodies for the prevention of torture (CPT and SPT), Thematic report by the Polish NPM published in 2021, https://bip.brpo.gov.pl; See also the Compendium of SPT recommendations published by the NPM of Morocco, 2023 annual report, p. 26.

106 Although Art. 33 of the UN CRPD require the States Parties to designate "one or more focal points within governments" and to "maintain, strengthen, designate or establish within the State Party, a framework, including one or more independent mechanisms" to promote, protect, and monitor the implementation of the Convention, the construct is rather different from that instilled by the OPCAT.

UN treaty bodies is organised which is highly problematic as it fails to acknowledge this distinctive nature of the SPT mandate. The SPT is both an operational body conducting visits to places of detention and an advisory body engaging with (currently) 81 NPMs worldwide, as well as 96 States Parties. This requires early and regular engagement with States Parties, direct and regular contacts with NPMs, both responsive and proactive, to support them in achieving the effectiveness and independence needed for impactful torture prevention work. The lack of dedicated funding from the OHCHR to support SPT's advisory role and the overall SPT's scarce—and further diminishing—human and financial resources, put the blended system of cooperation between international and national preventive bodies at risk.

For its part, the SPT has tried, with varied success, to support the NPMs by advising and assisting on both their establishment as well as on their continued work through a wide variety of advisory documents, both general and country-specific, delivered as part of annual reports, dedicated documents and reports arising from the visits.

The SPT's approach towards the NPMs is testament to its own increasing acknowledgement of the inevitable limitations of its own visiting mandate: the SPT cannot be in all 96 States Parties with the frequency that effective torture prevention requires. NPMs with their regular presence in the country and therefore also in the places of deprivation of liberty nationally, undoubtedly, hold much greater potential to further the aims of the OPCAT (Šteinerte, 2013). However, if they are to succeed in that advancement, they are to be the bodies as the OPCAT envisaged them to be: independent, with mandates covering all places of deprivation of liberty, with the requisite financial and human resources. The two decades of practice of many NPMs around the globe show that this is not always the case, and here, the SPT can play an important role by supporting the NPMs, advising and holding Governments to account, thus enabling the NPMs to reach their full OPCAT potential in protecting persons deprived of liberty.

Bibliography

Evans, M. D. (2020). The prevention of torture. In M. D. Evans & J. Modvig (Eds.), *Research handbook on torture. Legal and medical perspectives on prohibition and prevention* (pp. 258–287). Edward Elgar Publishing.

Evans, M. D. (2023). *Tackling torture. Prevention in practice*. Bristol University Press.

Nowak, M., Birk, M., & Monina, G. (2019). *The United Nations convention against torture and its optional protocol: A commentary* (2nd ed.). Oxford University Press.

Murray, R. (2008). National preventive mechanisms under the optional protocol to the torture convention: One size does not fit all. *Netherlands Quarterly of Human Rights, 26*(4), 485–516.

Šteinerte, E. (2013). The changing nature of relationship between the United Nations subcommittee on prevention of torture and national preventive mechanisms: In search for equilibrium. *Netherlands Quarterly of Human Rights, 31*(2), 129–155.

Šteinerte, E. (2014). The jewel in the crown and its three guardians: Independence of national preventive mechanisms under the optional protocol to the UN torture convention. *Human Rights Law Review, 14*(1), 1–29.

The French Contrôleur général des lieux de privation de liberté: Towards a Panoptic Control?

Julia Schmitz and Ariane Amado

1 Introduction: History, Mandate and Structure of the French NPM

The French National Preventive Mechanism (NPM), the *Contrôleur général des lieux de privation de liberté* (CGLPL), was established in 2007[1] in anticipation of the French ratification of the Optional Protocol

[1] Act of Parliament n° 2007-1545 of 30 October 2007, establishing the Contrôleur général des lieux de privation de liberté, *JORF* n°253, 31 October 2007. Hereafter: Act n° 2007-1545 of 30 October 2007 establishing the CGLPL.

J. Schmitz (✉)
Ecole de Droit, Université de Toulouse Capitole, Toulouse, France
e-mail: juliaschmitz31@gmail.com

A. Amado
CNRS, CRESPPA, Paris, France
e-mail: ariane.amado@univ-lille.fr

T. Daems et al. (eds.), *Preventing Torture and Monitoring Places of Detention*,
https://doi.org/10.1007/978-3-032-28285-9_3

to the United Nations Convention against Torture (OPCAT)[2] with a broad mission that consists of "inspecting the conditions of detention of people in custody in order to ensure the effective exercise of their fundamental rights".[3]

The capacity of the various bodies that were previously able to monitor the prison, such as the Justice Department's inspectorate or visits by magistrates, was strongly criticised in a parliamentary report transmitted in 1999 (Canivet, 2000). This report drew a "clearly unacceptable" conclusion and highlighted the "often formal and superficial nature of the monitoring applied to the reality of prisons". Also, a parliamentary commission of inquiry reported that internal and administrative monitoring were "poorly executed" and "formal" or carried out "to a minimum", and that magistrates were "indifferent" in their view of prisons (Hyest & Cabanel, 2000, p. 180).

The new body, which was created in 2007, carries out professionalised monitoring, with the aim of responding to criticism of the insufficient and fragmented approach previously taken to prisons. The CGLPL is a centralised body, composed of an Inspector, a General Secretariat and a team of auditors, whose office is located in Paris and which carries out its mission throughout France, including overseas territories.

2 Composition, Nomination, Structure and Functioning of the CGLPL

Considering the semi-presidential semi-parliamentary regime in France, the CGLPL is appointed "on the basis of their professional skills and knowledge" for a non-renewable six-year term by decree of the President of the Republic,[4] after public consultation with the relevant standing

[2] Act of Parliament n° 2008-739 of 28 July 2008, autorisant l'approbation du protocole facultatif se rapportant à la convention contre la torture et autres peines ou traitements inhumains ou dégradants, *JORF* n°0176, 30 July 2008. The OPCAT was signed by France in 2005.

[3] Art. 1 of the Act n° 2007-1545 of 30 October 2007 establishing the CGLPL.

[4] Art. 2 of the Act n° 2007-1545 of 30 October 2007 establishing the CGLPL.

committee of each parliamentary assembly, which may veto this appointment by a reinforced majority.[5] Even though the CGLPL is appointed by the President of the Republic, the guarantees of independence from political power and its functioning confer the CGLPL with the status of an independent administrative authority.[6] It is specified that they shall not receive instructions from any authority and may not be dismissed or prosecuted for opinions or acts issued in the exercise of their functions, and that they may not engage in other professional activities or hold elective office.[7]

The members of the team are recruited by the CGLPL. Article 4 of the 2007 Act establishing the CGLPL does not specify the number and requirements for inspectors who may be recruited by the CGLPL.[8]

Concerning the 26 full-time inspectors (*contrôleurs)*, the law never gives any balancing indications when it comes to the gender, professional origins or required training. They must only have "competence in areas related to their mission".[9] The decree of the 12th of March 2008 specifies that "the positions of inspectors shall be filled by magistrates, civil servants, hospital practitioners or military personnel seconded under the conditions provided for by their respective statutes, or by non-tenured public law agents. They may also be filled by retired magistrates, civil servants, hospital practitioners, military personnel or non-tenured public law agents".[10] The CGLPL can also recruit external participants, belonging or not to the administration. They keep on working for their main job and earn flat-rate compensation.[11] As a result, many members of the CGLPL have worked in the administration subject to monitoring

---

[5] Art. 13 of the French Constitution.

[6] Act of Parliament n° 2017-55 of 20 January 2017 on independent administrative authorities and independent public authorities, portant statut général des autorités administratives indépendantes et des autorités publiques indépendantes, *JORF* n°0018 of 21 January 2017.

[7] Art. 2 of the Act n° 2007-1545 of 30 October 2007 establishing the CGLPL.

[8] There are currently 26 full-time controllers and 29 external participants.

[9] Art. 2 of the Act n° 2007-1545 of 30 October 2007 establishing the CGLPL.

[10] Art. 2 of the Decree n° 2008-246 of 12 March 2008 relatif au Contrôleur général des lieux de privation de liberté, *JORF* n°0062, 13 March 2008.

[11] Art. 3 of the Decree n° 2008-246 of 12 March 2008 relatif au Contrôleur général des lieux de privation de liberté.

(the judiciary, prison administration, hospitals, police, etc.) or have had experience in the inspection services of these same institutions.

To avoid any conflict of interest and guarantee their independence, incompatibilities with the mandate are set out in the CGLPL's internal regulations: inspectors may not engage in any activity related to the premises being inspected or any activity that generates material or moral interests that could affect the inspector's freedom of judgement. Similarly, inspectors may not participate in visits to sites where they have worked during the previous ten years.[12]

With regard to their budget, the CGLPL appropriations are voted on by Parliament and included in the budget programme 308, "Protection of rights and freedoms, attached to the Government Action Directorate". For the year 2025, they had a total annual budget of 6 million euros.

3 The Mandate and the Powers of the CGLPL

The mandate of the CGLPL is legally defined to "inspect the conditions of detention of people in custody in order to ensure the effective exercise of their fundamental rights".[13]

Due to the preventive nature of their scope of action, the CGLPL's powers remain limited despite their gradual consolidation in legislation.[14] The CGLPL has no power to issue injunctions or sanctions and no decision-making power since they can only make recommendations; they do have extensive access rights and broad investigative powers. As such, they have the right to visit any place under their authority at any time on their own initiative, the right to access all premises and documents, the right to confidentially interview anybody, and to obtain all necessary information, with the possibility of issuing a formal notice in the event of opposition.

[12] Art. 9 of the internal regulations of the CGLPL, *JORF*, 23 December 2018.

[13] Art. 1 of the Act n° 2007-1545 of 30 October 2007 establishing the CGLPL and its subsequent additions in the Act of Parliament n° 2014-528 of 26 May 2014 modifying it.

[14] Act n° 2007-1545 of 30 October 2007 establishing the CGLPL.

As an independent administrative authority receiving no instructions from any public authority, the CGLPL has the prerogative to emit recommendations. The implementation of their power does not depend on queries from people deprived of their liberty, nor is the CGLPL obliged to respond to them.[15] Moreover, it does not depend on any queries from the authorities or places of detention or custody that they can inspect on their own initiative and without prior notice.[16] This discretionary ability to investigate cases allows them to choose the premises they visit and define their scope of action.

The CGLPL's scope of action

The scope of the CGLPL's competence questions the very definition of places of detention and places of custody, which lacks clarity.

The scope of deprivation of liberty is defined in French positive law in a manner that is both restrictive and controversial. In order to limit the scope of Article 66 of the Constitution, which confers the judicial authorities' jurisdiction over matters relating to the protection of individual liberty, the Constitutional Court has restricted this jurisdiction to situations in which the infringement of freedom of movement constitutes a total deprivation and not a mere restriction of liberty.[17] This special judicial protection therefore covers situations of detention in penitentiary centres and closed educational centres for minors, police custody, migration detention and involuntary hospitalisation.[18]

---

[15] Art. 8-1 of the Act n° 2007-1545 of 30 October 2007 establishing the CGLPL simply states that "Any natural person, as well as any legal entity whose purpose is to uphold fundamental rights, may bring to [their] attention any facts or situations that may fall within their competence."

[16] Although the law specifies that the CGLPL may be referred to by the Prime Minister, members of the Government, members of Parliament, and representatives to the European Parliament elected in France, such referrals, who are not mandatory, those cases are rare or even non-existent. It is also specified that "it may also take up matters on their own initiative." Art. 6 of the Act n° 2007-1545 of 30 October 2007 establishing the CGLPL.

[17] French Constitutional Court, Decision n° 2011-214 QPC, 27 January 2012, *Société COVED SA*.

[18] It should be noted that the ECtHR has developed a jurisprudential concept of deprivation of liberty based on a "difference in degree or intensity, not in nature or essence" depending on the specific situation in which people find themselves, taking into account a set of criteria

However, this definition does not stand up to the proliferation of places of confinement such as electronic tagging, socio-medical security centres, residential care homes, centres for people with disabilities, etc., and the trend towards tighter controls in open environments such as judicial supervision, socio-judicial supervision, treatment programmes, technopolice measures, etc. (Darley & Lancelevée, 2013; Margaine, 2016; Medard Inghilterra, 2024; Ollivon, 2023). More specifically, new criminal surveillance measures in open environments include a residential component with time restrictions which, if not respected, result in a violation of the measure and the possibility of imprisonment (this is the case, for example, with judicial supervision with probation for perpetrators of domestic violence who are under surveillance in special security centres or external placement facilities that function like open prisons without being recognised as such).

Measures that result in the restriction of freedom of movement of individuals for a shorter or longer period of time (compulsory fingerprinting, searches, vehicle checks and identity checks) may also be mentioned. These various measures contribute to making the scope of deprivation of liberty vaguer and broader.

While the parliamentary committee that examined existing controls on prisons recommended the creation of a General Prison Monitoring (Canivet, 2000), specialised in prison control, the explanatory memorandum to the Act of Parliament of July 2007 that created the CGLPL emphasised the desire to monitor "all places of detention, regardless of the structure concerned: prisons, specialised hospitals, court detention centres and administrative detention centres, for example". From the outset of the parliamentary debates, an amendment was introduced to extend the scope of the mandate to all psychiatric institutions, including those under private status, provided that they admit people who have been hospitalised involuntarily or at the request of a third party. The CGLPL thus fulfils the mission entrusted to NPMs by Article 4 of

---

such as "gender, the duration, the sentencing process, the effects of which must be examined cumulatively and in combination." E.g. ECtHR, 6 November 1980, *Guzzardi v. Italy*, App. n° 7367/76 §92; ECtHR, G.C. 15 March 2012, *Austin and others v. UK*, App. n° 39692/09 et 2 others, §57 and 59; ECtHR, G.C., 23 February 2017, *De Tommaso v. Italy*, App. n° 43395/09, §80–81.

the OPCAT, which refers to "the placement of someone in a public or private institution for supervision from which he or she is not authorised to leave at will, ordered by a judicial or administrative authority or any other public authority".[19] It also bears resemblance to the mandate of the European Committee for the Prevention of Torture and Inhuman or Degrading Treatment or Punishment (CPT), which is responsible for visiting "any place" where public authorities deprive people of their liberty.

The CGLPL can inspect all kinds of places of custody and detention, i.e. more than 5,000 locations throughout France: prisons, but also psychiatric hospitals or secure wards within hospitals, police custody or customs detention facilities, immigration detention centres and waiting areas, court detention centres or cells, closed educational centres and any vehicle used to transport people deprived of their liberty. Their monitoring was extended not to a new location but to a procedure. Now, their control goes up to the removal of the foreign nationals process until they are handed over to the authorities of the destination country.[20]

Through their panoptic mandate covering the entire field of deprivation of liberty, the CGLPL distances itself from the disciplinary and institutional approaches that typically characterise the legal regime governing deprivation of liberty in various places of confinement. It can therefore monitor establishments in which people are detained due to a penal decision, such as prisons, but also due to a decision taken by an administrative authority, such as the representative of the State at the territorial level of the department. These establishments may be under the authority of the Ministry of Justice, the Ministry of the Interior or the Ministry of Health (e.g. administrative detention centres, police custody facilities or certain mental health establishments).

Moreover, the CGLPL interprets the law of the 30th of October 2007 constructively, which gives it an indeterminate area of competence by referring in general terms to "the conditions of care and transfer of people

---

[19] Council of Europe, Explanatory report to the European Convention for the Prevention of Torture and Inhuman or Degrading Treatment or Punishment, 26 November 1987, p. 32.

[20] Act of Parliament n° 2014-528 of 26 May 2014.

deprived of their liberty" without further clarification.[21] It is explained on their website that the list of places subject to control is not exhaustive, and that certain places are beyond their control (e.g. places where people are placed in "open environments" but not detained).[22] If we examine the CGLPL discourse as a whole—through all its opinions, recommendations and visit reports published on its website—, it proposed identifying situations of deprivation of liberty outside of any continuous care in a place of confinement.

The CGLPL thus failed to extend its jurisdiction to the supervision of the care of elderly people in residential care homes on the grounds that they may "not be allowed to leave their accommodation" (CGLPL, 2013a, p. 291; CGLPL, 2022a, p. 96). They also consider that the use of care programmes provided for in Article L. 3211-2-1 of the Public Health Code "may mask situations as restrictive as compulsory hospitalisation" (CGLPL, 2018a, pp. 13–14). They therefore recommend that the jurisdiction of the liberty and custody judge be extended to care programme measures and that these be "systematically submitted to him at sufficient frequency and at least once a year" (CGLPL, 2024a, p. 122).

The Visits Methodology

The monitoring methodology they have gradually developed and their composition enable them to take an internal and constructive look at professional practices. The institution is able to take an external or internal multidisciplinary view thanks to the recruitment of its members (Fischer, 2016, 2020). Furthermore, the duration (more or less one or two weeks on-site) and protocol of the visits enable them to examine

[21] The CGLPL internal regulations, published in the Official Journal of the French Republic on 23 December 2018, refer more specifically to "any place of deprivation of liberty or any means of transport used for transfer, even temporary or irregular, regardless of its location or purpose within mainland France, the overseas departments and overseas local authorities", https://www.cglpl.fr/app/uploads/2019/01/20181223_R%C3%A8glement-int%C3%A9rieur-du-CGLPL.pdf.

[22] CGLPL website, *Role*, https://www.cglpl.fr/son-role#content-nav-target-2 (consulted 18 December 2025).

the overall functioning of an institution in order to assess the "conditions of care for people deprived of their liberty". The CGLPL can thus develop an in-depth analysis of each situation, taking into account the material conditions of deprivation of liberty as well as the reality of professional practices and their difficulties. Those include something that was neither planned nor intended by the legislator: the "working conditions of staff and various participants insofar as they necessarily impact the functioning of the institution and the nature of relations with people deprived of their liberty".[23]

After every visit and before writing their report, the CGLPL also engages in dialogue with the said authorities by establishing a rigorous adversarial investigation procedure. Opinions on specific topics and urgent recommendations that may be decided upon following complex missions are systematically sent to the ministers before being published in the Official Journal of the French Republic. The responses provided are attached to these publications where applicable. Visit reports are subject to two adversarial procedures: one with the establishment and local authorities concerned at the provisional report stage and one with the minister(s) at the final report stage. This procedure, which arose from practice but was consolidated by the 2014 Act that reformed the institution, enables the CGLPL to strengthen the objectivity of its findings. It also granted the CGLPL the trust and confidence of local authorities by involving them in the development of recommendations, taking into account their difficulties and expectations.

In the same vein, the CGLPL also seeks to identify good practices that are likely to "improve respect for fundamental rights" and that can serve as models (CGLPL, 2019a, p. 92). Since 2021, they also stated that they intended to compile a "collection of best practices" to "assist ministers in implementing these recommendations" (CGLPL, 2021, p. 61).

This joint development of the CGLPL recommendations is thus beginning to show results within the concerned administrations, particularly within the French Prison Service. Three examples can be given.

---

[23] GLPL website, *Mission*, https://www.cglpl.fr/son-role#content-nav-target-2 (consulted 18 December 2025).

As stated in the 2023 annual activity report, in September 2020, the Minister of Justice collected good practices implemented within the various departments of the Ministry. More specifically, within the Prison Service, the reporting of good practices "is a collaborative process involving the central administration, the regional directions of the Prison Service and the research and innovation laboratory which coordinates the process" (CGLPL, 2024a). The Prison Service research and development department (now development department) recruited staff in mid-October 2023 whose mission is to identify good practices in the CGLPL's reports that could be proposed for replication by prisons.

Furthermore, while the CGLPL regrets the lack of follow-up of their recommendations by the monitored administrations, it should be noted that an internal audit unit was set up by the prison administration in January 2017. This unit comes as a result of the recommendations from the reports of the General Inspectorate of Justice's and the CGLPL.

At the local level, a note from the Prison Service issued on the 10th of February 2023 established a Legal Affairs and Expertise Unit (*Mission du droit et de l'expertise juridique*) within each of the ten interregional prison directions that cover many different territories.[24] This creation aims at strengthening the Law within the prison administration in the face of rising litigations. It definitely gives greater importance to the criticisms and recommendations of the CGLPL. These missions are responsible for providing cross-disciplinary legal expertise, investigating administrative and litigation appeals and promoting the law among partners of the prison administration and judicial authorities. As the CGLPL itself points out, they are intended to be "privileged interlocutors for the various stakeholders in the follow-up of injunctions issued by the administrative judge" (CGLPL, 2024b, p. 45).

[24] Auvergne-Rhône-Alpes (Lyon); Grand-Centre (Dijon); Grand-Est (Strasbourg); Grand-Nord (Lille); Grand-Ouest (Rennes); Outre-mer; Sud-Est (Marseille); Sud-Ouest (Bordeaux); Sud (Toulouse) and Île-de-France (Paris).

Producing Reports, Opinions and Recommendations

The CGLPL has diversified its communication tools: in addition to visit reports on specific establishments and opinions on cross-cutting themes summarising their observations following their visits, they have been publishing thematic reports at a rate of one to two reports per year since 2016. Those publications constitute cross-cutting and in-depth analyses of issues relating to one or more categories of places of deprivation of liberty. Additionally, the CGLPL communicates to the broad public through informal publications such as opinion pieces and letters to ministers that are made public.

The COVID-19 crisis has enabled the CGLPL to raise awareness on prison overcrowding and the need to find quick and effective ways to solve it, deploying a range of communication tools such as reports (CGLPL, 2020b), press releases,[25] letters to ministers[26] and joint opinion pieces with other independent authorities.[27]

Its 257 "Minimum Recommendations for Respecting the Dignity and Fundamental Rights of People Deprived of Liberty" published in June 2020, are the result of twelve years of observations and recommendations to public authorities (CGLPL, 2020c). They are presented as a "coherent and logical body of work, in the manner of a code, so that administrations, people deprived of their liberty and their advisers, non-governmental organisations and even judges can easily refer to it" (Hazan, 2020, p. 1396).

---

[25] CGLPL, "COVID-19 en prison: des mesures gouvernementales insuffisantes", press release of 1 April 2020, https://www.cglpl.fr/publications/covid-19-en-prison-des-mesures-gouvernementales-insuffisantes.

[26] CGLPL, "Poursuivre l'effort de déflation carcérale pour mettre fin à la surpopulation en prison", reference of matter to the Minister of Justice, 5 May 2020, https://www.cglpl.fr/publications/poursuivre-leffort-de-deflation-carcerale-pour-mettre-fin-a-la-surpopulation-en-prison; "Situation sanitaire des lieux de privation de liberté: le CGLPL alerte les ministres de la justice, de la santé et de l'intérieur", 17 November 2020, https://www.cglpl.fr/app/uploads/2020/11/20201117_communiqu%C3%A9-lettres-ministres-Covid_final.pdf.

[27] See the joint opinion piece by the CNCDH, the DDD and the CGLPL, "Sauvegardons les droits fondamentaux", *Le Monde*, 20 March 2020, https://www.lemonde.fr/idees/article/2020/03/20/coronavirus-sauvegardons-les-droits-fondamentaux-pendant-la-crise-sanitaire_6033892_3232.html.

As well as all the independent administrative authorities, the CGLPL submits an annual report to the Government and Parliament to account for the exercise of its missions and resources.

4 The CGLPL Reports and Recommendations: Findings

The CGLPL can take up any issues it wishes by cross-referencing their analyses and identifying common issues in different places of deprivation of liberty, such as the protection of the right to an intimate life or the right of defence of people in detention and custody (CGLPL, 2020a; 2022b). The CGLPL's Minimum Recommendations are the doctrinal formulation of this perspective (CGLPL, 2020c).

Their cross-cutting and comparative analysis of different places of confinement finally enabled them to identify what the CGLPL Minimum Recommendations refer to as "additional constraints", namely situations of additional deprivation of liberty within the confines of detention facilities (CGLPL, 2018b). The Minimum Recommendations reflect an adaptation of the recommendations to each place of deprivation of liberty according to its specific purpose. This is the case for healthcare facilities, which have a therapeutic purpose, distinct from the security purpose prevailing in administrative detention centres, or the educational purpose of juvenile centres. The monitoring body also highlighted the problem of overcrowding in prisons and the use of physical restraint in psychiatric hospitals (CGLPL, 2016; 2023b).

Through their monitoring visits in mental health institutions, they have highlighted the reality of practices of restraint and isolation of people placed in forced psychiatric care that were not necessarily provided for in the texts (CGLPL, 2016, pp. VII–VIII). The doctrinal redefinition of these practices as acts of deprivation of liberty has also been recognised by the Constitutional Court. It has been ruled that isolation and restraint measures taken against people hospitalised without their consent constitute measures that deprive them of their liberty, regardless of their duration, due to the degree of physical restraint that is then exercised on them.[28]

The same reasoning was applied by the CGLPL with regard to the possibility of placing foreign nationals held in administrative detention centres in "isolation rooms" where they are sometimes handcuffed (CGLPL, 2019b).

The reports of the CGLPL also focussed on situations involving double deprivation of liberty. While in principle the care provided to detainees should not add to the constraints of imprisonment, many detainees suffering from mental disorders are ultimately treated without their consent in local hospitals due to a lack of space in psychiatric units (*Unités hospitalières spécialement aménagées*[29]). While no legislation specifies the method of psychiatric care for detainees, the CGLPL has observed the practice of compulsory admission, sometimes at the request of the head of the administrative detention centre concerned (CGLPL, 2019c). The CGLPL findings even refer to situations of triple confinement in relation to the psychiatric care of detainees. Numerous visit reports have long noted practices of systematic isolation and restraint of detainees placed in involuntary care in local hospitals (CGLPL, 2019c). Prisoners suffering from mental disorders admitted to psychiatric hospitals under compulsory treatment are often placed in solitary confinement or even subjected to systematic restraint. The CGLPL has therefore observed three levels of deprivation of liberty: imprisonment, compulsory psychiatric confinement, and psychiatric isolation or restraint.

---

[28] Constitutional Court, Decision n° 2020-844 QPC, 19 June 2020, *M. Éric G.* [Monitoring of isolation measures used in psychiatric care without consent].

[29] These are hospitals specialising in the care of prisoners with mental health issues. They are run by hospital staff, but the outer perimeter is monitored by the prison service.

5 The CGLPL Reports and Recommendations: Impact

The CGLPL has no binding power to impose sanctions or injunctions on the institutions they monitor. However, they exercise what might be called a "magistracy of influence" through indirect normative pressure. As such, they mobilise various external levers such as publicity and litigation.

The CGLPL's influence is primarily exerted on public opinion through their power to alert ("sunshine regulation"). The opinions, recommendations and proposals of the CGLPL are systematically published in the Official Journal of the French Republic and on their website. And their annual report's normative power is also amplified when they present their main conclusions to the parliamentary assemblies. Although they have no decision-making or sanctioning powers, the CGLPL nevertheless wields the authority of media coverage by deploying a multimodal communication strategy. For instance, it frequently posts photos of its visits on Instagram and now has a new podcast for constrained people.[30] The CGLPL's ability to access the main means of communication and information is part of this dynamic.

Although the CGLPL cannot sanction nor advise the authorities responsible for managing places of custody or detention, nor compel public authorities to act in a particular way, the discursive force of their findings and recommendations ultimately influences professional practices through a soft law strategy. As the European Prison Rules, the Minimum Recommendations of the CGLPL are intended to encourage public authorities to amend positive law. As former CGLPL Adeline Hazan stated, they correspond to "the definition of soft law, as formulated by the Council of State", with the aim of "guiding and directing the behaviour of the authorities in charge of places of detention towards a greater respect for the dignity and fundamental rights of people in their care" (Hazan, 2020, p. 1396).

Since 2016, they have also incorporated a new communication tool into their annual activity report, enabling them to highlight the actions

[30] CGLPL, Podcast "Les Enfermé·es", https://www.cglpl.fr/publications/les-enferme-es-podcast.

and reactions of public authorities, serving as a "new monitoring tool". (Gallardo & Giacopelli, 2020, p. 13). Following up on their recommendations, they are able to publish the responses, and lack of response, given by public authorities, thereby forcing the competent authorities to be more responsive or to publicly justify their refusal to comply.

Their recommendations can have an impact on professional practices implemented in places of deprivation of liberty. For example, they had an impact on restraint practices in psychiatric hospitals. The CGLPL recommended that the decision to place prisoners in solitary confinement or under restraint be subject to judicial review, which was then enacted in an Act of Parliament on the 22nd of January 2022.[31]

This power to alert is particularly strong when they implement the possibility of immediately publishing 'urgent recommendations' in the Official Journal of the French Republic without waiting for the issuing of the investigation report and even more the authorities' response.[32] This mechanism is used when a serious violation of fundamental rights has been observed during a visit. It has only been used exceptionally (26 urgent recommendations out of more than 1,900 visit reports), which reinforces the exceptional nature of this publication and its normative force.

The conditions of custody in certain prisons have thus been effectively denounced through this communication tool, as evidenced by the urgent recommendations of the 12th of November 2012 relating to the Baumettes prison in Marseille, which were used to support the injunctions issued by the administrative judge in summary proceedings (CGLPL, 2012),[33] or recently, the emergency recommendations of the 4th of July 2025 concerning the Toulouse-Seysses prison, which also formed the basis for the judge's injunctions.[34]

In the case concerning the Baumettes prison in Marseille, the facility was extremely unsanitary. The administrative judge ordered the prison

---

[31] Act of Parliament n° 2022-46 of 22 January 2022 renforçant les outils de gestion de la crise sanitaire et modifiant le code de la santé publique, *JORF* n°0019, 23 January 2022.

[32] Art. 9 of the Act n° 2007-1545 of 30 October 2007 establishing the CGLPL.

[33] French Council of State, ordinance 22 December 2012, n° 364584.

[34] Administrative Tribunal of Toulouse, 25 July 2025, n° 2505053.

administration to carry out pest control measures at the facility within a very short period of time.

In the case concerning the Toulouse-Seysses facility, the establishment was overcrowded and dirty. The administrative judge ordered the prison administration to take measures to clean up the facility, organise activities within the prison and provide access to medical care. They also conducted a census of prisoners who were vulnerable due to their age, disability, medical condition or pregnancy in order to take all the necessary measures to ensure that these prisoners would not have to sleep on mattresses placed directly on the floor.

This strategy sometimes led to the closure of specific establishments or to mobilise the authorities' internal monitoring resources, such as General Inspectorates. For example, the mother and baby unit at the Réau prison was only able to admit mothers and children several years after the opening of the prison because the CGLPL had pointed out the lack of partnership with the child protection services to ensure that the fundamental rights of the children in care were respected (CGLPL, 2013b, p. 55, 257).[35] Similarly, the CGLPL recently ordered the emergency closure of the La Valentine juvenile centre in Marseille. Part of the facility will be closed for renovation and the Minister has announced that they have commissioned an inspection of the facility by the General Inspectorate of Justice (CGLPL, 2025).

In general, litigation concerning undignified conditions of custody is now being pursued by numerous associations defending prisoners' rights, which are taking cases to court to compel the State to take action. In addition to cases brought before the administrative judge, in particular the administrative judge hearing applications in emergency, there is a new application process before the judicial judge (the *juge des libertés et de la détention or the juge de l'application des peines*) for the imprisonment conditions to be challenged.[36]

In these litigations, associations defending prisoners' rights and bar associations acted upon the judge based on the CGLPL findings. The

---

[35] The mother and baby unit only opened in 2017 whereas the entire prison was inaugurated in 2013.

[36] Act of the Parliament n° 2021-403 of 8 April 2021 aimed at guaranteeing the right to respect human dignity in custody or detention, *JORF* n°0084, 9 April 2021.

CGLPL is now even directly involved in certain cases brought before the European Court of Human Rights,[37] through third-party intervention or by monitoring the implementation of the Court's judgements before the Council of Ministers (Robert, 2020, p. 72).

In their annual activity report for 2021, the CGLPL thus expanded its mission in terms of training and expertise for judges and lawyers.

For example, since 2022, in addition to the usual reports on visits to prisons, they have been producing a new format of reports specifically devoted to custody conditions (CGLPL, 2022a, p. 8). These "reports on the dignity of custody conditions" focus on the situation in a particular detention or custody unit in order to assess detention conditions using objective indicators (such as the minimum space in cells, time in cells, cleanliness, heating and lighting...) adopted by the European Court of Human Rights, the Council of State and the Court of Cassation. Those reports can thus be easily used to support individual applications.

Moreover, bar association presidents have the right, since 2022, to visit places of deprivation of liberty.[38] They have made a habit of sending their visit reports to the CGLPL, in line with the latter's supervisory role (CNB, 2023, p. 5). The CGLPL findings are useful to bar association presidents, who may also initiate legal proceedings. The CGLPL has also "made their experience available to bar association presidents who wish to use it to help them exercise their right of access" (CGLPL, 2023a, p. 19).

6 Complementarity with the Defender of Rights and the NHRI

Other independent administrative authorities hold a mandate to monitor places of detention and custody, such as the Defender of Rights (*Défenseur des droits*, DDD), which is responsible for ensuring "respect for rights and freedoms by State administrations, local authorities, public

[37] ECtHR, 30 January 2020, *J.M.B. v. France*, App. n° 9671/15.

[38] Art. 18 of the Act of the Parliament n°2021-1729 on confidence in the judicial institution of 22 December 2022, *JORF* n°0298, 23 December 2021.

institutions, and any body entrusted with a public service mission, or in respect of which the organic law confers powers upon it".[39] This authority carries out the tasks previously entrusted to the National Security Ethics Committee, which was responsible for ensuring compliance with ethical standards by people carrying out security activities on the territory of the Republic.[40] Their remit also covers other situations involving the prison service and concerning the infringement of individuals' rights by the operation of that service, situations of discrimination or the infringement of the best interests and rights of a detained minor or the child of a detained person. The Organic Act on strengthening the role of the Defender of Rights of 21 March 2022 also enables them to protect the whistleblowers' rights.[41] Situations that may be referred to the Defender of Rights may thus be subject to shared control with the CGLPL. The two authorities formalised this sharing of powers in an agreement on the 8th of November 2011, which provides for the Defender to refer cases to the CGLPL when it receives a complaint relating to matters involving the State, the organisation or functioning of a detention facility, the transfer of people deprived of their liberty or a fundamental right of that person. Conversely, the CGLPL shall refer matters to the Defender when someone considers that they have been harmed by administrative malfunction, a violation of the rights or best interests of the child, discrimination or a breach of professional ethics and security.

Although the establishment of the CGLPL was called into question during the parliamentary debates on the creation of the DDD—with a proposal to integrate it into this constitutional authority—the specific nature of their role ultimately protected it from being absorbed. Their roles are in fact complementary, as they do not perform the same function nor do they have the same monitoring powers.

The monitoring of the CGLPL differs from the mediation role entrusted to the Defender of Rights, which is based on the handling

[39] Art. 71 of the Constitution (Constitutional Act of Parliament n° 2008-724 of 23 July 2008, de modernisation des institutions de la Ve République, *JORF* n° 0171, 24 July 2008).

[40] Act of Parliament n° 000-494, 6 June 2000.

[41] Organic Act of Parliament n° 2022-400 of 21 March 2022 on strengthening the role of the Defender of Rights, *JORF* n°0068, 22 March 2022.

of individual complaints. Such as the OPCAT,[42] this preventive monitoring is not intended to respond to a specific complaint or violation of an individual right, but to raise structural issues relating not to "individual matters" but to "the state of affairs and the way in which the service is organised" (CGLPL, 2011, p. 250).

The law states that the CGLPL shall cooperate with the relevant international bodies in monitoring the implementation of the OPCAT.[43]

In their concluding observations on France's seventh periodic report, the Committee against Torture (CAT) highlighted the strengthening of the CGLPL powers through the legislative reform of the 26th May 2014.[44] They particularly welcomed the recommendations regarding the use of restraint in psychiatric institutions.[45]

In their concluding observations on France's eighth periodic report, the CAT once again welcomed the work carried out by the CGLPL but recommended that the French State ensure better implementation of the recommendations made by this institution. They also recommended revising the law of the 30th of October 2007 establishing the CGLPL to extend their scope to medical-social establishments, medical-educational institutes and residential establishments for dependent elderly people.[46]

The CGLPL and the National Human Rights Commission—which act as the NHRI in France[47]—have signed an agreement to clarify their coordination in order to carry out joint work and share information. In particular, as part of France's universal periodic review, the two institutions are required to consult each other on the issues they wish to raise before United Nations bodies. Within the framework of the Council of Europe, the two institutions must consult each other when they are asked for an opinion by the Legal Affairs Directorate of the Ministry of

[42] Art. 1 of the OPCAT.

[43] Art. 12 of the Act n° 2007-1545 of 30 October 2007 establishing the CGLPL.

[44] CAT, Consideration of Seventh periodic reports of States parties due in 2014, France, *UN Doc.* CAT/C/FRA/7, 29 July 2015, paras 17–27.

[45] CAT, Observations finales concernant le septième rapport périodique de la France, *UN Doc.* CAT/C/FRA/CO/7, 10 June 2016.

[46] CAT, Observations finales concernant le huitième rapport périodique de la France, *UN Doc.* CAT/C/FRA/8, 8 May 2025.

[47] Act of the Parliament n° 2007-292 of 5 March 2007 relative à la Commission nationale consultative des droits de l'homme, *JORF* n°55, 6 March 2007.

Foreign Affairs on the measures necessary to enforce a judgement of the European Court of Human Rights (ECtHR) relating to deprivation of liberty. The CNCDH, which monitors cases brought before the European Court, regularly informs the CGLPL of disputes relating to its field of action. The Convention also provides for the possibility of joint third-party interventions in support of certain applications brought before the ECtHR or joint observations transmitted to the Committee of Ministers with a view to the execution of certain judgements delivered by the European Court.

7 Conclusion

The French CGLPL has several specific features. Firstly, it is a concentrated, single-person body, assisted by a small team of inspectors. Secondly, the distinctive feature of this institution lies within its preventive, rather than corrective nature, which is based on the model used by the CPT. The third distinctive feature of this type of monitoring remains its very broad scope of intervention, which extends beyond prisons alone. It should be noted that the specificity of the CGLPL inspections is none other than their cross-cutting nature. This broad and wide monitoring of all places of confinement enables them to develop an informed and critical view of deprivation of liberty as a whole.

Bibliography

Canivet, G. (2000), *Rapport sur l'amélioration du contrôle extérieur des établissements pénitentiaires*. La Documentation française. https://www.vie-publique.fr/rapport/24366-amelioration-du-controle-exterieur-des-etablissements-penitentiaires-r

CGLPL. (2011). *Rapport d'activité pour 2010*. Dalloz.

CGLPL. (2012, December 6). *Recommandations en urgence relatives au centre pénitentiaire des Baumettes à Marseille*, *JORF* n° 0284.

CGLPL. (2013a). *Rapport d'activité 2012*. Dalloz.

CGLPL. (2013b). *Rapport de visite du Centre Pénitentiaire Sud Francilien de Réau (Seine-et-Marne)*.

CGLPL. (2016). *Isolement et contention dans les établissements de santé mentale*. Dalloz.

CGLPL. (2018a). *Rapport annuel d'activité 2017*. Dalloz.

CGLPL. (2018b). *Les droits fondamentaux à l'épreuve de la surpopulation carcérale*. Dalloz.

CGLPL. (2019a). *Rapport d'activité 2018*. Dalloz.

CGLPL. (2019b). *Avis relatif à la prise en charge sanitaire des personnes étrangères au sein des centres de rétention administrative*, *JORF* n° 44, 21 February 2019.

CGLPL. (2019c). *Avis relatif à la prise en charge des personnes détenues atteintes de troubles mentaux*, *JORF*, n° 271, 22 November 2019.

CGLPL. (2020a, June 25). *Avis du 23 avr. 2020 relatif à la défense dans les lieux de privation de liberté*, *JORF* n° 0156.

CGLPL. (2020b). *Les droits fondamentaux des personnes privées de liberté à l'épreuve de la crise sanitaire*. Dalloz.

CGLPL. (2020c, June 4). *Recommandations minimales pour le respect de la dignité et des droits fondamentaux des personnes privées de liberté*, *JORF*.

CGLPL. (2021). *Rapport d'activité 2020*. Dalloz.

CGLPL. (2022a). *Rapport annuel d'activité 2021*. Dalloz.

CGLPL. (2022b). *L'intimité au risque de la privation de liberté*. Dalloz.

CGLPL. (2023a). *Rapport d'activité 2022*. Dalloz.

CGLPL. (2023b, September 14). *Avis relatif à la surpopulation et à la régulation carcérales*, *JORF*.

CGLPL. (2024a). *Rapport annuel d'activité 2023*. Dalloz.

CGLPL. (2024b). *L'effectivité des voies de recours contre les conditions indignes de détention*. Dalloz.

CGLPL. (2025, August 29). Recommandations en urgence relatives à l'établissement pénitentiaire pour mineurs de Marseille - La Valentine (Bouches-du-Rhône). *JORF* n°0200.

Conseil national du barreau (CNB). (2023). *Guide du droit de visite du bâtonnier et ses délégués des lieux de privation de liberté* (2nd ed.). CNB.

Darley, M., & Lancelevée, C. (2013). Où sont les murs ? Penser l'enfermement en sciences sociales. *Cultures & Conflits, 90* [online]. https://doi.org/10.4000/conflits.18703

Fischer, N. (2016). Entre droit et savoirs professionnels. L'action des membres du contrôleur général des lieux de privation de liberté français. *Déviance et Société*, *40*(4), 411–43.

Fischer, N. (2020). La production d'un regard « indépendant » par les membres du Contrôleur général des lieux de privation de liberté. In B. François & A. Vauchez (Eds.), *Politique de l'indépendance. Formes et usages contemporains d'une technologie de gouvernement*. Presses universitaires du Septentrion. https://doi.org/10.4000/books.septentrion.77991

Gallardo, E., & Giacopelli, M. (2020). *L'élaboration d'un droit de la privation de liberté. Étude autour des recommandations minimales du Contrôleur général des lieux de privation de liberté*. Lexis Nexis.

Hazan, A. (2020). Les Recommandations minimales du Contrôleur général des lieux de privation de liberté. *AJDA*.

Hyest, J.-J., & Cabanel, G.-P. (2000). *Prison: une humiliation pour la République. Rapport de commission d'enquête n°449*. French Senate, 1. https://www.senat.fr/notice-rapport/1999/l99-449-notice.html

Margaine, C. (2016). *Étude des obligations applicables en milieu ouvert. Une analyse de la dimension coercitive de la probation. Rapport de recherche CIRAP*. Presses de l'ENAP. https://hal.science/hal-05056090v1/document

Medard Inghilterra, R. (2024). L'instauration d'une "technopolice" administrative en milieu urbain: cadre et enjeux juridiques. *La Revue des droits de l'homme, 25* [online]. https://journals.openedition.org/revdh/19033

Ollivon, F. (2023). Enfermées à l'air libre. Approche géographique de l'expérience des personnes placées sous surveillance électronique. *Criminologie, 56*(2), 121–142. https://doi.org/10.7202/1107600ar

Robert, A.-G. (2020). La circulation de la norme produite par le CGLPL dans la jurisprudence de la CEDH. In E. Gallardo & M. Giacopelli (Eds.), *L'élaboration d'un droit de la privation de liberté. Étude autour des recommandations minimales du Contrôleur général des lieux de privation de liberté*. LexisNexis.

The Czech Republic and OPCAT: Reflection on Almost 20 Years of the Czech NPM

Milan Svoboda and Miriam Tomášková

1 The Journey of the Czech NPM from Ratification of the OPCAT to Its First Visits

Almost 20 years of National Preventive Mechanism (NPM) mandate operation in the Czech Republic shows how the challenges faced by monitoring mechanisms of this type are changing. Interestingly, the fundamental changes often concern the very definition of the scope of these institutions. However, in the Czech Republic, the legislator implemented the mandate arising from the Optional Protocol to the

M. Svoboda (✉)
Office of the Public Defender of Rights—Czech NPM, Brno, Czech Republic
e-mail: milan.svoboda@ochrance.cz

M. Tomášková
Department of Constitutional Law, Palacký University Olomouc, Olomouc, Czech Republic
e-mail: miriam.tomaskova01@upol.cz

T. Daems et al. (eds.), *Preventing Torture and Monitoring Places of Detention*,
https://doi.org/10.1007/978-3-032-28285-9_4

Convention against Torture (OPCAT)[1] in a relatively broad manner. As we will introduce below, this has made it easier for the NPM to adapt its portfolio of interests to current social and legal challenges. The following section describes how the legal framework for the exercise of the NPM mandate was created and what the initial experiences with its implementation have been.

Implementation of the OPCAT at the National Level (establishment of NPM)

At the end of the 1980s, the UN Convention against Torture (UNCAT)[2] was ratified, which strengthened and clarified the protection of certain rights guaranteed by the International Covenant on Civil and Political Rights—the right to life, the right not to be tortured, and the right to human dignity.[3] In 2002, the OPCAT was adopted in New York. The Czech Republic signed this Optional Protocol on 13 September 2004.[4] Following formal ratification, the OPCAT entered into force for the Czech Republic on 9 August 2006.[5] The Czech Republic thereby undertook to establish the NPM to carry out preventive visits to places where human freedom is restricted in order to prevent, to the greatest extent possible, ill-treatment of persons placed there (Šabatová, 2008, pp. 104–105).[6]

In the Czech Republic, the Public Defender of Rights (Ombudsman) was given the NPM mandate to operate. This was the first extension

---

[1] Optional Protocol to the Convention against Torture and Other Cruel, Inhuman or Degrading Treatment or Punishment (OPCAT), opened for signature February 4, 2003, Communication of the Ministry of Foreign Affairs No. 78/2006 Coll. m. s. (entered into force June 22, 2006).

[2] Ministry of Foreign Affairs, *Decree No. 143/1988 Coll. on the Convention against Torture and Other Cruel, Inhuman or Degrading Treatment or Punishment, 1988.*

[3] Ministry of Foreign Affairs, *Decree No. 120/1976 Coll. on the International Covenant on Civil and Political Rights and the International Covenant on Economic, Social and Cultural Rights,* 1976.

[4] Ministry of Foreign Affairs, *Communication No. 78/2006 Coll. on the ratification of the Optional Protocol to the Convention against Torture, 2006.*

[5] The instrument of ratification of the Czech Republic was deposited with the Secretary-General of the United Nations, the depositary of the Optional Protocol, on 10 July 2006.

[6] Translated from Czech by the authors.

of the mandate of the Czech Ombudsman institution, which has been operating since 2000. By a government decision, a working group was established in 2002 to prepare an amendment to the Public Defender of Rights Act. This came into force on 1 January 2006[7] and required the Ombudsman to carry out preventive visits to places where people are deprived of liberty.[8] The amendment also extended the Ombudsman's personal jurisdiction to all facilities where persons may be deprived of liberty in any way, whether by public authority or for care purposes[9] or whether this takes place in state or private facilities. The Ombudsman or his authorised employees may enter them at any time, even without prior notice, to speak with the persons placed there, and the staff of these facilities are obliged to cooperate with them (Šabatová, 2008).

It should not be forgotten that the first Czech Public Defender of Rights (Ombudsman), Otakar Motejl, a widely respected figure and prominent representative of the Czech judiciary, undoubtedly had a significant influence on the formation of the entire institution (Toman & Šebesta, 2019). As a respected lawyer with extensive experience, he contributed to establishing the NPM as an independent and effective tool. Thanks to his reputation, the NPM was taken seriously and viewed as credible by both the public and state institutions from the very beginning. Another significant and interesting aspect of the NPM's mandate is that the list of Czech ombudsmen includes Anna Šabatová, a former dissident who has personal experience of imprisonment (for political

[7] Act No. 381/2005 Coll., *Amending Certain Laws in Connection with the Adoption of Measures Against Torture and Other Forms of Ill-Treatment.*

[8] Section 1(3) was inserted into Act No. 349/1999 Coll., on the Public Defender of Rights: "The Ombudsman shall conduct visits to places where persons are or may be deprived of their liberty by public authorities or as a result of their dependence on care provided, with the aim of strengthening the protection of such persons against torture, cruel, inhuman, or degrading treatment or punishment, and other ill-treatment."

[9] Section 1(4) was added to Act No. 349/1999 Coll., on the Public Defender of Rights: "The Ombudsman's powers under paragraph 3 shall apply to a) facilities where detention, imprisonment, protective or institutional education, or protective treatment is carried out, b) other places where persons restricted in their liberty by public authority are or may be held, in particular police cells, facilities for the detention of foreigners, and asylum facilities, c) places where persons are or may be deprived of their liberty as a result of their dependence on the care provided, in particular social care institutions and other facilities providing similar care, health care facilities, and facilities for the social and legal protection of children (hereinafter referred to as "facilities")."

reasons).[10] As a former political prisoner, she had a deep understanding of the dignity and rights of persons deprived of their liberty. Her experience enabled her to sensitively identify the risks of abuse, bullying, or mistreatment in various types of institutions (such as prisons, detention centres, and psychiatric hospitals).

Complexities Emerging from the Establishment of the NPM Mandate within the Ombudsman with Its Other Competences

Since its establishment in 2000, the Ombudsman's task has been to protect individuals from actions by authorities and other institutions if such actions are contrary to the law and do not comply with the principles of a democratic state governed by the rule of law and good administration. The list of authorities, institutions, and places that were already covered by the Ombudsman's original jurisdiction includes facilities where remand detention, imprisonment, institutional care for children and juveniles, and protective treatment are carried out. Within this jurisdiction, the Ombudsman has dealt and continues to deal primarily with individual complaints from prisoners, children in institutional care, and patients in psychiatric hospitals.[11] If necessary, it is possible to conduct an on-the-spot inquiry (not preventive, but in reaction to a specific complaint). The outcome of the investigations is a recommendation to public authorities on an individual case of the complainant.

The NPM mandate, as a second mandate of the Ombudsman in relation to places of detention,[12] is linked to the adoption of the OPCAT. In this context, the Czech Republic was obliged to establish an independent body to carry out visits to places where persons are deprived

[10] Anna Šabatová served as Ombudswoman from 2014 to 2020. She was imprisoned in the 1970s for organising a leaflet campaign for parliamentary elections during the communist regime in Czechoslovakia.

[11] For example, the Ombudsman receives around 400 individual complaints a year from prisoners and their relatives. The most common areas of complaint from prisoners are transfers to other prisons, healthcare, and disciplinary proceedings.

[12] Before the OPCAT was implemented in the Czech Republic, no independent body existed to carry out preventive monitoring of detention facilities.

of their liberty. At first glance, these two areas of competence have different purposes. The investigation of individual complaints aims to protect persons from actions by authorities and other institutions that are contrary to the law, do not comply with the principles of a democratic state governed by the rule of law and good administration, as well as from their inaction, thereby contributing to the protection of fundamental rights and freedoms. Visits to places of detention under the NPM mandate aim to strengthen protection against torture, cruel, inhuman, degrading treatment or punishment, and other ill-treatment. Some European NPMs, which are also part of Ombudsman institutions, have chosen to formally separate the complaints agenda from the preventive visits agenda. The Czech NPM unit still combines both mandates.[13]

However, there are also opposing views among domestic experts on the appropriateness of formally separating the two mandates into separate teams or even institutions. This is precisely because of their different goals and concepts. Doubek (2023) describes the differences between so-called reactive and preventive action to protect the rights of persons deprived of their liberty: "the Ombudsman usually focuses on solving individual problems (solving problems based on specific complaints) while the NPM typically acts preventively (for the future) and strives for long-term 'constructive dialogue' with the facilities and state authorities it visits".

Broad Mandate and Understanding of Places of Deprivation of Liberty

Because of the broad definition of powers, the NPM had the opportunity to visit not only so-called hard detention facilities (e.g. prisons, police cells, psychiatric hospitals), where people are held by court order, but also social care facilities, where people are often placed on a contractual basis. However, given their health condition and vulnerability, they are

[13] The Department of Supervision over Places of Detention, which incorporates the National Preventive Mechanism (NPM), has 12 members of staff, the majority of whom also deal with individual complaints.

often de facto entirely dependent on the assistance of third parties, which constitutes a de facto restriction of personal freedom.

This broad interpretation of the NPM mandate was also supported by the UN Subcommittee on Prevention of Torture and Other Cruel, Inhuman or Degrading Treatment or Punishment (SPT) in its General comment No. 1 (2024): "the deciding factor for the qualification of any place, facility, or setting as a place of deprivation of liberty is not the name or title given to it or its categorization in national legislation, but whether individuals are free to leave it at will".[14]

In the Czech Republic, we have not yet encountered any in-depth discussions on the exercise of the NPM mandate in foreign military bases on Czech territory (e.g. military prisons) or on the leasing of detention facilities to other states, which are topics also addressed in the aforementioned General Comment. This is simply because we do not yet have this type of detention facility on our territory.

However, private facilities providing social services for clients with various types of disabilities or other health problems associated with old age represent a phenomenon and a particular challenge for the NPM in the Czech Republic. These are de facto social services, but these private facilities do not meet the registration requirements[15] for operating such facilities:

> The clients of these unregistered residential social service facilities are often people who are in a very vulnerable position due to their dependence on the care of another person. They often do not have families who are willing or able to care for them, and therefore cling to the operator with boundless gratitude. They are willing to pay all their income for their stay, tolerate undignified sanitary conditions, and endure poor treatment. Only in rare cases, clients complained about the conditions

[14] SPT, General Comment No. 1 (2024) on Article 4 of the Optional Protocol (Places of Deprivation of Liberty), *UN Doc*. CAT/OP/GC/1, 4 July 2024.

[15] Requirements for the registration of a social service are laid down in the Social Services Act (Act No. 108/2006 Coll., on Social Services). These include, for example, material and technical requirements, professional qualifications and a clean criminal record of personnel, etc.

in the facility, even though it was clear that the quality of the services provided fell far short of social service quality standards.[16]

The Number and Types of Facilities Visited to Date

In 2006, the first year of the Czech NPM's operation, 44 visits were made to the following types of facilities: police cells, social care institutions for adults with physical disabilities, long-term care facilities, detention facilities for foreigners, prisons with high and maximum security, and facilities for children and juveniles. Since then, the Ombudsman and his team have visited over 600 detention facilities (some on a repeated basis) and inspected the conditions of detention for nearly 33,000 people. An overview of the number of visits and the types of facilities monitored by the NPM is presented in Table 1.

The table shows that the number of visits has declined slightly over the years. This is mainly due to the focus and breadth of topics covered in the NPM′s reports. While the reports from the first visits were written as simple letters of a few pages, more recent reports are published in a structured format, numbering dozens of pages and containing numerous recommendations for improving practice, which places higher demands on the processing of reports.

Expansion of the Ombudsman's Mandates and the NPM

The establishment of the NPM within the Czech Ombudsman's institution was the first expansion of its powers. This was followed by a whole range of other powers, which make the Public Defender of Rights a unique multi-mandate institution (Table 2).

This solution by the legislator, i.e. entrusting a range of diverse powers to a single institution, places increased demands on the Ombudsman in terms of efficiency, work organisation, and information transfer within

[16] Office of the Public Defender of Rights, 2015, Report from visits by the Public Defender of Rights: Facilities providing care without authorisation.

Table 1 Number and types of facilities visited by the Czech NPM

Year	Social services facilities	Facilities for children	Prison facilities	Facilities for foreigners	Police cells	Asylum facilities	Health care facilities	Total
2006	11	4	7	4	19	0	5	50
2007	29	1	3	2	4	2	2	43
2008	21	0	0	0	0	0	8	29
2009	31	0	4	0	0	0	7	42
2010	7	2	7	2	34	2	1	55
2011	1	24	1	1	4	0	13	44
2012	5	18	1	0	5	0	3	32
2013	16	3	0	0	4	0	6	29
2014	7	2	5	1	2	0	2	19
2015	0	0	3	3	8	0	8	22
2016	1	10	2	2	6	0	1	22
2017	6	3	2	0	4	1	6	22
2018	14	1	2	0	6	0	4	27
2019	1	9	3	1	3	0	4	21
2020	5	7	3	2	0	0	3	20
2021	6	7	3	1	5	0	8	30
2022	11	7	3	2	6	0	7	36
2023	10	7	1	0	6	0	7	31
2024	4	10	2	1	6	0	5	28
Total	186	115	52	22	122	5	100	602

the institution. The effective functioning of the NPM in a multi-mandate institution is a challenge that continues to grow with the addition of new mandates, given the need to maintain independence and other specific aspects of its activities.

2 The Current Form of NPM Visits

Over nearly twenty years of the NPM's operation in the Czech Republic, the form, conduct, and outcomes of visits to places of deprivation of liberty have gradually evolved. As the OPCAT and the Public Defender of Rights Act[17] define visits only in broad terms, numerous procedures

[17] Provision of Section 1a(1)(c) of Act No. 349/1999 Coll., on the Public Defender of Rights and the Defender of Children's Rights, 1999.

Table 2 Diagram showing the expansion of the Ombudsman institution's powers in the Czech Republic

Year	Expansion of powers
2000	Establishment of the Office of the Ombudsman by Act No. 349/ 1999 Coll., on the Public Defender of Rights
2001	Protection of individuals against unlawful or otherwise improper conduct or inaction by administrative authorities and other institutions
2006	Agenda of monitoring over restrictions on personal freedom—the Ombudsman becomes an NPM and protects people restricted in their freedom from ill-treatment
2009	Role of national authority for equal treatment and protection against discrimination (equality body)
2011	Monitoring the detention of foreigners and the enforcement of administrative expulsions as part of the prevention of ill-treatment
2018	Function of monitoring body for the implementation of rights enshrined in the Convention on the Rights of Persons with Disabilities
	Assistance to foreign nationals who are citizens of the European Union living or working in the Czech Republic
2025	Establishment of the Office of the Children's Ombudsman
	Establishment of a National Human Rights Institution (NHRI) whose main activity is the protection and independent promotion of human rights

have been developed through practice. Some have been incorporated into the Public Defender of Rights' methodological guidelines on visits and expulsion monitoring,[18] while others remain established internal practices. Certain aspects continue to evolve and raise new questions.[19] Throughout its existence, however, the NPM has consistently pursued the preventive aim enshrined in the OPCAT, complementing ex post traditional approaches that respond to violations of the law ex post,[20] and has adhered to the principles set out in the CAT and OPCAT, including

[18] Public Defender of Rights (2013). *Methodological guideline No. 5/2013 for conducting visits and monitoring expulsions.*

[19] For example, the NPM repeatedly addresses the specific conditions under which the obligation to forward findings from visits to criminal proceedings is fulfilled and the extent to which confidentiality should be breached in such cases.

[20] Association for the Prevention of Torture (APT), The Optional Protocol Implementation Manual, 2010, revised edition, p. 42, https://www.apt.ch/knowledge-hub/publications/optional-protocol-implementation-manual-2010.

independence, effectiveness, "do not harm", protection against retaliation and confidentiality.[21]

Planning and Preparation of Visits

The NPM prepares an annual visit plan specifying the types of facilities to be visited and the approximate number of visits, based on the facilities listed in the Public Defender of Rights Act,[22] without identifying specific facilities. Typically, several types of facilities are selected each year, with visits primarily conducted in thematic series, although individual visits outside a series are also possible.[23] Series-based visits facilitate better preparation of the team and external experts, reflecting ongoing developments in facilities, legislation, and practice. The plan may be amended ad hoc in response to information suggesting possible ill-treatment[24] and also includes follow-up visits to assess compliance with previously issued recommendations and measures.[25]

The selection of a specific facility depends on multiple factors.[26] In the case of series-based visits, facilities are chosen across the entire territory[27]

[21] Art. 13 CAT, Arts. 1, 17, 18/1, 18/2,3, 21, 35 OPCAT.

[22] Provisions of Section 1b(2) of Act No. 349/1999 Coll. Facilities (except for unregistered social services that are outside the legal regime) are established by various laws that determine their purpose and operating regimes. For example, social services are governed by Act No. 108/ 2006 Coll., on social services, police cells by Act No. 273/2008 Coll., on the Police of the Czech Republic, etc.

[23] For example, in 2025, this involves a series of visits to unregistered social service facilities, children's homes, and women's prison wards.

[24] The Ombudsman may obtain information about possible ill-treatment in the course of performing his other duties, such as protecting individuals from the actions of public authorities, monitoring the rights of persons with disabilities, protecting against discrimination, and others. See the provisions of Section 1a(1) of the Act on the Ombudsman and the Children's Ombudsman.

[25] Public Defender of Rights. (2013). *Methodological guideline No. 5/2013 for conducting visits and monitoring expulsions.*

[26] The selection criteria should be clear and transparent and take into account all the rules of operation of the NPM. See Office of the United Nations High Commissioner for Human Rights (OHCHR), Preventing Torture: The Role of National Preventive Mechanisms—A Practical Guide, *UN Doc.* HR/P/PT/21, 2018, p. 42, https://www.ohchr.org/sites/default/files/Documents/Publications/NPM_Guide_EN.pdf.

[27] The Ombudsman, and thus the NPM, has territorial jurisdiction throughout the Czech Republic.

to ensure representation of different sizes, public and private operators (where legally permitted), and both long-established and newly established facilities. Publicly available information, such as facility websites or reports from other inspection bodies, is also taken into account, as well as information provided to the NPM by law[28] or obtained in the performance of its other functions.[29]

Once a facility is selected, preparations for the visit begin. Visits are always conducted unannounced in order to assess the actual situation in the facility[30]; therefore, preparation relies exclusively on publicly available information about the facility,[31] supplemented by data from external sources. The focus is on the target group, organisational structure, and staffing. The team also decides whether the visit will be comprehensive or thematically focused.[32]

Depending on the type of facility and the scope of the investigation, a team of two to four NPM lawyers is assembled, often complemented by external experts (e.g. doctors, nurses, special educators, or social workers)[33] with relevant professional experience.

After defining the team and visit topics, practical arrangements are made. As visits typically last one to three days, accommodation, transport, and meals must be arranged. In addition, all required entry documentation must be prepared, including the authorisation to enter the facility, which includes a brief explanation of the NPM's mandate, the authorisations of team members, and an outline of the visit procedure.

---

28 Pursuant to Section 21c(2), the NPM is required to provide information to, for example, the police regarding the planned expulsion of foreigners.

29 The Ombudsman may obtain information about possible ill-treatment in the course of performing its other duties, such as protecting individuals from the actions of public authorities, monitoring the rights of persons with disabilities, protecting against discrimination, and others. See Section 1a(1) of the Act on the Ombudsman and the Children's Ombudsman.

30 OHCHR, Preventing Torture: The Role of National Preventive Mechanisms—A Practical Guide, *UN Doc.* HR/P/PT/21, 2018, p. 21.

31 It can be based, for example, on public reports from other supervisory bodies (CPT reports included), on information that the facility itself publishes, on publicly available reviews from people who have been through the facility, etc.

32 For example, a series of visits focused on child patients in psychiatric hospitals. See Office of the Public Defender of Rights (2022). *Children in psychiatric hospitals: Summary findings from visits of the Public Defender of Rights.*

33 For more information on the role of experts during NPM visits, see Association for the Prevention of Torture (n.d.). *What is the role of external experts during NPM visits?*

The Course of an NPM Visit

Upon entering the facility, the team first meets the facility manager or a representative for an introductory interview. The preventive nature of the visit, the way in which it is conducted, and the NPM's powers are explained, and a list of required documentation is provided. The manager is also informed of the possibility of night or early morning inspections to assess conditions outside the daytime regime. The NPM's powers include the right to enter all areas without prior notice, to inspect and copy documentation (including medical records), to photograph premises and equipment, to question staff even privately if justified, and to speak with residents alone.[34] If the facility manager refuses to cooperate, the Ombudsman may terminate the visit and inform the superior authority or, if necessary, the public.[35]

Following the interview, the manager gives the team a tour of the facility. The unannounced nature of the visit allows the team to observe daily operations and gain initial insights. The team then divides tasks: studying documentation, interviewing staff and residents, photographing premises,[36] and observing operations in the facility. Work is guided by a pre-prepared checklist that outlines the documents to obtain and the questions to ask. Interviews are ideally conducted by two team members to ensure evidence reliability and prevent accusations of misconduct, with emphasis on confidentiality, anonymity, and cross-verification of data.[37]

The NPM generally collects information without making on-site assessments, except in cases of immediate threats to a person's life or health, where an on-site findings report is drafted with the management

[34] The powers are derived from the provisions of Section 15 of the Act on the Ombudsman and the Children's Ombudsman.

[35] According to the provisions of Section 20 of the Act on the Ombudsman and the Children's Ombudsman.

[36] The protection of the personal data of clients and employees is a matter of course.

[37] OHCHR, Preventing Torture: The Role of National Preventive Mechanisms—A Practical Guide, *UN Doc.* HR/P/PT/21, 2018, p. 33.

to prompt urgent action. The team also conducts "triangulation" meetings during the visit to exchange findings, identify potential issues, and determine information needing verification.[38]

After all information is collected, the visit concludes, ideally with a final interview with the manager. The team expresses appreciation, outlines post-visit procedures, announces forthcoming outputs (e.g. visit report, summary report, roundtable, recommendations), and invites comments on the visit and team conduct. Good practices may be acknowledged, and, if needed, follow-up online interviews may be conducted to ensure comprehensive findings.

Visit Report and Further Procedures After the Visit

Immediately after the visit (usually within one week), each member of the NPM team who carried out the visit creates their official record.[39] This should contain all their findings from the visit, and the form of this record should comply with the Double Smart rules[40] standard structure:

- standard (what should be)
- findings (information from observations, interviews, documentation)
- evaluation (compliance/non-compliance of findings with the standard)
- recommendations (what the facility should do to improve the prevention of ill-treatment)

If the official records contain severe findings about conditions in the facility that were not addressed in the on-site report, a letter may be sent to the facility before the report is issued, calling on it to respond and take measures to remedy the situation (similar to when an on-site

---

[38] Association for the Prevention of Torture (2025). *What should be the structure of a visit report?*

[39] Public Defender of Rights (2013). *Methodological guideline No. 5/2013 for conducting visits and monitoring expulsions.*

[40] Specific, Measurable, Achievable, Results-oriented, Time-bound and Solution-suggestive, Mindful of prioritization, sequencing and risks, Argued, Root cause responsive, Targeted. See Association for the Prevention of Torture. *What makes a good recommendation?*

report is drawn up). The staff member who was responsible for organising the visit then transforms the findings from the official records into a visit report. The report is primarily intended for the management of the visited facility, as well as for its founders,[41] the relevant authorities, and the public. The nature of the report respects the OPCAT rule that it should not condemn the situation in a given facility, but rather help to initiate a dialogue on improving the conditions of persons deprived of their liberty.[42] It may also contain recommendations for corrective measures.[43] Corrective measures differ in urgency, complexity, and implementation timeframe, and are classified as immediate, longer term, or ongoing. Immediate measures address urgent or easily remedied issues and should be implemented within seven days of receipt of the report or as soon as possible. Longer term measures must be completed within a specified deadline (e.g. one or three months), while ongoing measures aim to establish or prevent specific procedures or practices.

The report should be issued no later than two months after the visit; however, this period may be extended due to the volume of information, the need for thorough verification of findings and recommendations, and the requirement for consistency, clarity, and persuasiveness. Extensions are common in facilities requiring extensive data collection, such as social service or children's institutions.[44] Factual accuracy is paramount, as the Supreme Court has classified these reports as public documents whose content is deemed proven.[45]

At the same time as the report is sent, the facility is invited to comment on the report, recommendations, or corrective measures within

[41] In the Czech system of social services, the provider of the service and the founder (establishing authority) of the facility can be two different entities. The provider is the organisation that actually delivers the service (for example, an NGO, a church organisation, or a private company). The founder, on the other hand, is the authority that established the facility—often a municipality, region, or the state. As a result, a social service facility may be founded by one entity but operated by another.

[42] APT, The Optional Protocol Implementation Manual, 2010, revised edition.

[43] Provision of Section 21c(3) of Act No. 349/1999 Coll., on the Public Defender of Rights and the Defender of Children's Rights (1999).

[44] The time limit for issuing a report in such facilities usually ranges from 2 to 5 months.

[45] Supreme Court of the Czech Republic. (2022, November 16). *Judgment No. 30 Cdo 3214/2021.* https://rozhodnuti.nsoud.cz/Judikatura/judikatura_ns.nsf/WebSearch/E9E9DA7EC63E5044C12589480029C42C?openDocument&Highlight=0,null.

a specified period. The Ombudsman may also invite the founder of the facility or the relevant authorities to comment.[46] If the Ombudsman or his representative considers the response of the facility, its founder, or the relevant authorities to be sufficient, the visit is concluded.

After a visit, the report and related communication are published in anonymised form in the Ombudsman's ESO database.[47] If a facility does not cooperate, fails to comment on the report, or implement measures to prevent ill-treatment, the Ombudsman may inform superior authorities or the media,[48] or conduct a follow-up visit to verify compliance. This power has recently been used mainly with unregistered social service facilities.[49]

Following a series of visits, the NPM issues summary reports that aggregate findings and corrective measures for each facility type, propose systemic recommendations and, where appropriate, establish standards of good treatment. These reports guide facilities that have not yet been visited. Publication of summary reports is often accompanied by a roundtable discussion with representatives of the facilities and the professional public, focussing on findings, systemic problems, and potential solutions.

The current method of conducting visits reflects nearly twenty years of development. Each visit generates new insights and experiences, which are incorporated into the methodology. For example, three years ago, the NPM began profiling topics in children's facilities to prioritise areas with a higher risk of ill-treatment. The visit methodology is thus constantly evolving, aiming to maximise the effective protection of persons deprived of liberty.

---

[46] Provisions of Section 21c(3) and (4) of Act No. 349/1999 Coll., on the Public Defender of Rights and the Defender of Children's Rights 1999.

[47] Ombudsman's ESO database (2025).

[48] According to the provisions of Section 20 of the Act on the Ombudsman and the Children's Ombudsman.

[49] For example, the Ombudsman informed the government about another unregistered nursing home | Ombudsman.

3 Other Key Activities of the NPM in the Area of Preventing Ill-Treatment

Visits to places of deprivation of liberty are the core activity of every NPM, including the Czech one. However, the mandate also encompasses a range of additional activities aimed at strengthening the prevention of ill-treatment.[50] These additional activities significantly complement preventive visits to facilities, as these activities are more systematic in nature, which allows the NPM to focus on the causes of problems that pose a risk of ill-treatment or which are repeated across different institutions, and to work towards their solution.

Submission of Proposals and Statements

One key tool (envisaged, inter alia, by the OPCAT[51] and Czech law[52]) is the submission of proposals and opinions on existing or proposed legislation.[53] Where, based on its findings from visits and other activities of the Ombudsman, it finds that the systemic setup does not provide sufficient protection for persons deprived of their liberty against ill-treatment, it issues recommendations for legislative changes or adjustments to practice. Changes do not always happen immediately, so the NPM may sometimes repeat its recommendations. For example, it has long sought to create an effective complaints mechanism for social services.[54] It is also involved in various stages of the preparation of legislation and strategic documents that are important in terms of preventing ill-treatment. Recent examples of its involvement include participation in the preparation of a proposal to improve the status of patients hospitalised without consent developed by the Committee against Torture

[50] OHCHR, Preventing Torture: The Role of National Preventive Mechanisms—A Practical Guide, *UN Doc.* HR/P/PT/21, 2018, p. 27 et seq.

[51] Art. 19(c) OPCAT.

[52] Provisions of Section 22(1) of Act No. 349/1999 Coll., on the Public Defender of Rights and the Defender of Children's Rights 1999.

[53] Art. 19 OPCAT.

[54] For example, Ombudsman—Office of the Public Defender of Rights and Ombudsman for Children (2021). *Annual report 2021, p. 17.*

and Other Inhuman, Cruel, Degrading Treatment and Punishment of the Government Council for Human Rights, comments on the Methodological Guidelines for Hospitalization without Patient Consent, efforts to amend the Social Services Act and introduce a new offense for interference with the dignity, privacy, and integrity of clients, and efforts to introduce uniform rules for the handling of money belonging to prisoners serving prison sentences.[55] It has already achieved several successes in the field of preventing ill-treatment, such as the introduction of an independent complaints mechanism in social services, the enforcement of CPT standards for the floor space of prison cells, changes in the valorisation of prisoners' wages, and improvements in hygiene standards in prisons.

Publications

The NPM also transforms the findings from its visits, the systemic problems identified in the area of prevention of ill-treatment, and other insights from its activities into publications. An important means by which the NPM disseminates its conclusions, proposals, and recommendations is thematic reports summarising good practices and, at the same time, the weaknesses of individual places of deprivation of personal liberty. The reports comprise the Ombudsman's findings on the functioning of these facilities, including specific measures for central government authorities to enhance their functioning, with an emphasis on the prevention of ill-treatment. Since the NPM began operating, it has published thematic reports on virtually every type of facility in the Czech Republic where people are deprived of their personal liberty.[56]

In addition to individual reports and summary reports from visits, the NPM also publishes anthologies focused on various topics and research reports or articles in professional journals. NPM members also regularly participate in the recording of the podcast "Na kávu s ombudsmanem"

[55] Ombudsman—Office of the Public Defender of Rights and Ombudsman for Children, *Annual report 2023; Annual report 2024.*

[56] Office of the Public Defender of Rights and Ombudsman for Children (2025). *Facility visit reports.*

(Coffee with the Ombudsman). All outputs of the NPM are published on the website of the Ombudsman[57] and also on social networks.[58]

Awareness-Raising and Educational Activities

Another equally important area of activity for the NPM is awareness-raising and education. Through awareness-raising, the NPM increases awareness of human rights and possible ill-treatment, thereby also acting preventively against its occurrence.[59] It therefore organises (or actively participates in) seminars, training courses, and conferences intended for staff at visited facilities, as well as for professionals and the wider public. It publishes or contributes to various methodological materials and documents that serve as practical guides on how to prevent ill-treatment and how to ensure dignified conditions for persons deprived of their liberty. Recent activities include the publication of comprehensible instructions for defendants upon admission to custody and instructions for convicts, the implementation of seminars for prosecutors and health professionals working in prisons, and training for staff from long-term and psychiatric care facilities and regional authorities on the prevention of ill-treatment.[60]

Cooperation with Other Entities

In addition to cooperating with external experts on preventive visits, the NPM collaborates with several other entities, both public and private, in the field of preventing ill-treatment. By involving other entities with different focuses, the NPM is able to gain a more comprehensive view

---

[57] Office of the Public Defender of Rights and Ombudsman for Children (2025). *Outputs from activities.*

[58] Office of the Public Defender of Rights and Ombudsman for Children. Ombudsman [Facebook Page]. Facebook. from https://www.facebook.com/verejny.ochrance.prav, Office of the Public Defender of Rights and Ombudsman for Children. [@verejny.ochrance.prav] *Posts* [Instagram Profile]. Instagram. from https://www.instagram.com/verejny.ochrance.prav/?hl=cs.

[59] APT, The Optional Protocol Implementation Manual, 2010, revised edition.

[60] Ombudsman—Office of the Public Defender of Rights and Ombudsman for Children (2023). *Annual report 2023; Annual report 2024.*

and formulate recommendations for changes that are not only legally correct but also practically feasible. Cooperation with non-profit organisations, academia, and professional associations also increases the legitimacy of the findings and ensures that practical experience is reflected in the prevention of ill-treatment.

International cooperation is also a major component of the Czech NPM's activities. It enables the sharing of experience, the improvement of professional standards, and the harmonisation of standards for the prevention of ill-treatment and the protection of human rights in general. For example, the Czech NPM collaborates with foreign ombudsmen, most frequently those from the Visegrad Four countries,[61] the Office of the United Nations High Commissioner for Refugees, and the European Network of National Human Rights Institutions. It participates in international training courses, for example, in cooperation with the Frontex agency (European Union, 2025). Last year, NPM members welcomed colleagues from Ukraine for a study visit and, in turn, gained experience from partners in Norway.

The above list of NPM activities is by no means exhaustive. However, it gives an idea of the systematic work of the NPM and the directions it is taking in the field of preventing ill-treatment in the Czech Republic. From the perspective of preventing ill-treatment, it is crucial that, over nearly twenty years of seeking ways to develop conditions in facilities where people are restricted in their personal freedom, the NPM has managed to build a system of activities that synergistically help to raise the standard of protection against ill-treatment. Although it is clear that its work is far from over, the Czech NPM now has stable procedures and a wealth of experience on which to build in the future.

[61] In addition to the Czech Republic, these countries include Slovakia, Hungary, and Poland.

4 Current Challenges

Efforts to Effectively Combine Mandates

The Ombudsman protects the rights of people in institutions through several areas of competence. The original competence involves reviewing individual complaints, and it also acts as an NPM, focusing preventively on issues involving the risk of ill-treatment, as mentioned above. The Ombudsman's responsibilities also include monitoring how the Czech Republic respects the rights of persons with disabilities under the UN Convention on the Rights of Persons with Disabilities (CRPD). The Office of the Public Defender of Rights has also established the institution of the Children's Rights Defender, known as the Children's Ombudsman. The task of the Children's Ombudsman is to defend and promote children's rights in individual cases and at the systemic level.

In summary, the Ombudsman ensures that the rights of people in various institutions are not violated. However, the purpose of each function is different—to act preventively, to respond, to monitor the respect of rights, or to promote rights.

Problems Associated with Facility Inspections

The various powers of the Ombudsman lead to fragmentation of protection, which causes a number of problems in practice. The institution does not clearly define which aspects of the visit to a facility should be of interest to employees when conducting visits and why. There are repeated discussions across departments about how broadly ill-treatment should be defined and when a situation can actually be declared as ill-treatment.[62] The discussions are about whether to draw inspiration from the case law of the European Court of Human Rights (ECtHR) on Article 3 of the European Convention on Human Rights (ECHR) or the explanatory memorandum to the Public Defender of Rights Act (the

[62] Two teams of the Ombudsman's institution exercising distinct mandates (for example, NPM and CRPD) may visit and monitor the same facility and provide separate sets of recommendations.

concept of the NPM mandate referred to therein is broader than just ill-treatment from the perspective of Article 3 of the ECHR) or even the CRPD.

The Ombudsman institution also lacks common standards for groups of people with the same needs, regardless of the facility in which they are located.[63] For this reason, different views on standards are only discussed at the stage of preparing the report on the visit to the facility, which requires additional work by employees from different departments and significantly prolongs the deadline for preparing the final version of the visit reports and formulating individual recommendations.

The Issue of Harmonisation and the Effective Combination of Different Competences Is Therefore Currently the Biggest Challenge

Furthermore, the NPM conducts comprehensive, in-depth visits, which are time-consuming and labour-intensive (both during the visit and in the subsequent processing of the report). This method of work means that, given the available human resources, they are only able to conduct a limited number of visits. Given the depth of the visits and the volume of findings, it is not realistic to prepare a report in a relatively short time, even in cases where serious violations of rights are found. It is also questionable whether comprehensive reports consisting of dozens of pages of text are of practical benefit to the facilities visited.

The Concept of "Ill-Treatment"

Ill-treatment under the Public Defender of Rights Act[64] encompasses ill-treatment as defined by the ECtHR in its interpretation of Article

---

63 Our objectives for clients in psychiatric hospitals, viewed through the lens of prevention of ill-treatment and through the lens of the CRPD.

64 Act No. 349/1999 Coll., on the Public Defender of Rights and the Defender of Children's Rights 1999.

3 of the ECHR, CRPD[65] or the Convention on the Rights of the Child[66] (CRC) or other human rights documents. The ECtHR assesses the minimum level of severity on a case-by-case basis, and the assessment depends on all the circumstances of the case, including the duration of the treatment, its physical or psychological effects, and, in some cases, the gender, age, and health of the victim. In determining whether the threshold of severity has been reached, the court may also take into account other factors.[67]

The institution is currently compiling an overview of all possible areas that it may address during visits, including an indication of whether a particular area poses a risk of possible ill-treatment. Work has already begun on standards for the treatment of persons deprived of their liberty. Each standard should be accompanied by a clear explanation, including, for example, case law, examples of good practice, and examples of ill-treatment. The published standards could replace the thematic reports that have been issued to date, which may, in the future, take the form of only a short summary (focusing on systemic problems and new phenomena).[68]

Expected Development of the Ombudsman Institution

In 2026, the Ombudsman institution will undergo further development. It expects new powers in the form of monitoring, screening, and asylum procedures with foreigners at the borders of the territory, based on the implementation of current European legislation.[69]

---

[65] Articles 15–16 Convention on the Rights of Persons with Disabilities (CRPD), opened for signature 30 March 2007, entered into force 3 May 2008.

[66] Article 19 CRPD.

[67] European Convention of Human Rights Knowledge Sharing Platform (2025). *The minimum level of severity test in light of Bouyid v. Belgium.*

[68] Office of the Public Defender of Rights, *Project People in Institutions*, Brno, 2024.

[69] Regulation (EU) 2024/1356 of the European Parliament and of the Council introducing the screening of third-country nationals at the external borders and amending related regulations (OJ L 2024/1356). 14 May 2024. https://eur-lex.europa.eu/legal-content/CS/TXT/HTML/?uri=OJ:L_202401356.

5 Conclusion

Currently, the NPM is a crucial tool for safeguarding the human rights of individuals deprived of their liberty in the Czech Republic. However, since its inception, the Czech NPM has undergone dynamic development, whether in terms of its functioning within the framework of the Public Defender of Rights, the establishment of the NPM's activities as such, or the manner in which visits are carried out. In the twenty years of existence, it has gradually established itself as a respected actor ensuring the systematic protection of persons deprived of their liberty in the Czech Republic.

However, this does not mean that the work of the Czech NPM is over. When conducting visits to places where people are deprived of their liberty and in other activities related to preventing ill-treatment, the NPM still encounters several challenges that need to be addressed and problems that require resolution. These relate to the functioning of the NPM (e.g. the integration of the NPM's activities under the Ombudsman's activities with an increasing number of mandates and the harmonisation of these mandates). Similarly, they also relate to the actual conduct of visits (e.g. clarification of the concept of ill-treatment in the Czech context or the creation of standards for the prevention of ill-treatment for detention facilities).

The coming years will therefore test the Czech NPM's ability to adapt to new challenges. It will have to demonstrate that it can respond to social and legislative changes, utilise resources effectively, and maintain a high level of expertise and independence. Maintaining public trust will also be key—without it, the NPM's recommendations and interventions could become less effective. At the same time, it is necessary to strengthen dialogue with the visited facilities and the public so that the results of the NPM's work are not perceived as a formality, but as a tool that genuinely improves the conditions of people deprived of their liberty. Its primary mission remains to defend the human dignity and rights of every person in situations where that person is in the most vulnerable position, that is, in conditions of restriction of personal freedom.

Bibliography

Association for the Prevention of Torture. (2010). *Implementation manual: Optional Protocol to the Convention Against Torture (OPCAT). 2010 Revised edition.* https://www.apt.ch/sites/default/files/publications/opcat-manual-english-revised2010.pdf

Association for the Prevention of Torture. (2025). *What should be the structure of a visit report?* https://www.apt.ch/what-should-be-structure-visit-report

Association for the Prevention of Torture. (n.d.). *What is the role of external experts during NPM visits?* https://www.apt.ch/what-role-external-experts

Association for the Prevention of Torture. (n.d.). *What makes a good recommendation?* https://www.apt.ch/what-makes-good-recommendation

Doubek, P. (2023). Ombudsman jako národní lidskoprávní instituce...: Jak sladit rozličné lidskoprávní působnosti a naplnit požadavek plurality? [The Ombudsman as a National Human Rights Institution: How to harmonize different human rights competences and fulfill the requirement of plurality?]. *Časopis pro Právní Vědu a Praxi, XXXI*(2), 353–379.

European Union. (2025). *European border and coast guard agency.* https://european-union.europa.eu/institutions-law-budget/institutions-and-bodies/search-all-eu-institutions-and-bodies/frontex_cs

European Convention of Human Rights Knowledge Sharing [ECHR-KS]. (2025). Article 3—The minimum level of severity test in light of Bouyid v. Belgium. https://ks.echr.coe.int/documents/d/echr-ks/the-minimum-level-of-severity-test-in-light-of-bouyid-v-belgium

Office of the Public Defender of Rights. (2015). *Report from visits by the Public Defender of Rights: Facilities providing care without authorisation.* Office of the Public Defender of Rights. https://www.ochrance.cz/uploads-import/ESO/28-2014-NZ_Souhrnna_zprava_-_neregistrovana_zarizeni__CJ_.pdf

Office of the United Nations High Commissioner for Human Rights [OHCHR]. (2018). *Preventing torture: The role of national preventive mechanisms—A practical guide.* https://www.ohchr.org/sites/default/files/Documents/Publications/NPM_Guide_EN.pdf

Ombudsman—Office of the Public Defender of Rights. (2021). *Annual report 2021,* p. 17. vyrocni-zprava-2021.pdf

Ombudsman—Office of the Public Defender of Rights. (2023). *Annual report 2023.* https://www.ochrance.cz/dokument/zpravy_pro_poslaneckou_snemovnu_2023/vyrocni-zprava-2023.pdf

Ombudsman—Office of the Public Defender of Rights. (2024). *Annual report 2024*. https://www.ochrance.cz/dokument/zpravy_pro_poslaneckou_snemovnu_2024/vyrocni-zprava-2024.pdf

Ombudsman—Office of the Public Defender of Rights and Ombudsman for Children. (2025a). *Facility visit reports*. https://www.ochrance.cz/eso/zpravy/

Ombudsman—Office of the Public Defender of Rights and Ombudsman for Children. (2025b). *Outputs from activities*. https://www.ochrance.cz/vystupy/

Public Defender of Rights. (2013). *Methodological guideline No. 5/2013 for conducting visits and monitoring expulsions*. Office of the Public Defender of Rights.

Public Defender of Rights. (2025). *ESO database*. www.eso.ochrance.cz

Šabatová, A. (2008). *Ombudsman a lidská práva* [Ombudsman and Human Rights]. Aleš Čeněk.

Subcommittee on Prevention of Torture and Other Cruel, Inhuman or Degrading Treatment or Punishment [SPT]. (2024). *General comment No. 1 on article 4 of the Optional Protocol (places of deprivation of liberty)*. https://docs.un.org/en/CAT/OP/GC/1

Toman, P., & Šebesta, O. (2019). *JUDr. Otakar Motejl*. Advokáti proti totalitě. https://www.advokatiprotitotalite.cz/otakar-motejl/zivotopis

Ten Years of NPM in Italy: Some Reflections on the Past and the Possible Ways Ahead

Alessandro Albano and Adriano Martufi

1 Introduction

This chapter provides an account of the recent history of the National Guarantor for the rights of persons deprived of liberty (GNPL) in Italy.[1] This somewhat long name is the label that designates the Italian

The chapter is the result of a joint endeavour of both authors; Alessandro Albano is the author of Sects. 2, 3, 4, Adriano Martufi is the author of Introduction, Conclusion and Sects. 5 and 6. Alessandro Albano contributed to this chapter in his personal capacity. The opinions expressed in this chapter do not bind the administration he belongs to.

[1] "*Garante nazionale dei diritti delle persone private della libertà personale*" in Italian.

A. Albano (✉)
Office of the National Guarantor for the Rights of Persons Deprived of Liberty—Italian NPM, Roma, Italy
e-mail: alessandro.albano@garantenpl.it

A. Martufi
University of Pavia, Pavia, Italy
e-mail: adriano.martufi@unipv.it

T. Daems et al. (eds.), *Preventing Torture and Monitoring Places of Detention*,
https://doi.org/10.1007/978-3-032-28285-9_5

National Preventive Mechanism (NPM) under the United Nations (UN) Optional Protocol to the Convention against Torture and other Cruel, Inhuman or Degrading Treatment or Punishment (OPCAT).[2] As will be explained, the Italian NPM is a centralised one, upon the accreditation of the GNPL as Preventive Mechanism as per Article 7 of the law establishing the National Guarantor of 2013.[3] However, the present contribution will try to highlight the existence of local non-centralised bodies, whose role constitutes one key peculiarity of the Italian system of torture prevention considered in a broad sense.

The main features of the body accredited as NPM will be discussed in detail as well as its organisation. In a nutshell, the GNPL performs its functions of visiting and reporting about the places of deprivation of liberty (understood broadly under the terms of Article 4 of the OPCAT). Its members are formally appointed by the President of the Republic but are, in fact, chosen by the executive, although this choice must take place upon consultation of the relevant parliamentary committees (of both the Senate and the Chamber of Deputies).

As it will be explained, the NPM's independence hinges critically on the way in which its powers are interpreted in practice. This goes some way to show that the legal framework and the subsequent organisation of the GNPL have considerable room for improvement. Some of these shortcomings were already pointed out in a report based on a visit conducted in 2015 by the Subcommittee on the Prevention of Torture and Other Cruel, Inhuman, or Degrading Treatment or Punishment (SPT), after the formal establishment of the Guarantor (in late 2013) but before it became fully operational in 2016.[4]

This chapter will go on to explain the additional competences of the Italian NPM, and its relationship with the legislature and the judiciary. Though the GNPL is endowed with far-reaching competences, some

---

[2] The OPCAT was adopted on 18 December 2002 at the fifty-seventh session of the General Assembly of the United Nations by resolution A/RES/57/199. The protocol was made available for signature, ratification, and accession as from 4 February 2003 (i.e. the date upon which the original of the Protocol was established) at United Nations Headquarters in New York.

[3] Article 7, Law Decree No. 146 of 23 December 2013, converted into Law No. 10 of 21 February 2014. This provision has been amended several times over the years. Of particular relevance, as will be seen, are the amendments made in 2020.

[4] The SPT's visit was carried out from 16 to 22 September 2015.

concerns were raised regarding the NPM's possibilities to be involved in the law-making process as mandated by Article 19 of the OPCAT, as raised by the 2016 SPT report.[5]

Similarly, we will seek to better understand how the complex relationship between the National Guarantor and the territorial guarantors has developed, both *de jure* and *de facto*. The law explicitly provided only that the GNPL should promote and foster collaborative relationships with the territorial guarantors. Diplomatic correspondence, in designating the Italian NPM, acknowledged that a network structure necessarily implied coordination by the body with national competence. This structure has demonstrated various shortcomings, which the legislator took note of, also on the recommendation of the GNPL. The current structure of the collaborative relationship between the GNPL and the territorial guarantors, including at the NPM level, has developed into a mechanism that leaves the decision to involve the territorial guarantors to the discretion of the GNPL through a formal delegation procedure, which is only possible for certain areas of deprivation of liberty and not for others (see below). The current system implies that the degree of collaboration between the national and local levels depends on the quality of mutual relations and is in any case left to the discretion of the delegating authority. This configuration has led, in fact, to an overall downsizing and progressive fragmentation of the collaborative relationships between the national and territorial levels, which must be monitored carefully in order to understand and even guide future developments (which remain however hard to foresee).

[5] SPT, Report on the visit made by SPT to Italy, *UN Doc.* CAT/OP/ITA/1, 23 September 2016.

2 The Establishment of the Italian NPM: Between Local Experiences and External Constraints

The tasks and the concrete workings of the GNPL can only be understood against the background of pilot experiences and institutions that paved the way, both legally and socially, for its current activity. When one looks back at the chain of events that led to the establishment of the Italian NPM, it is hard to overstate the role played by civil society in the formation of the first prison monitoring bodies at the local level (Albano, 2026).

From a cultural standpoint, the creation of the GNPL marks the end of a decade-long process that drew inspiration from grassroots movements of criminal justice reform (Mellano & Scomparin, 2020). The idea of a nation-wide monitoring body was brought to the fore for the first time during a conference organised in Padua in mid-November 1997, during which a proposal was put forward to establish a national ombudsman for detainees. This idea did not translate into reality right from the start and a bill presented to Parliament the same year was not approved (Anastasia, 2023).

Yet the lively cultural and political debate which followed (as well as the intensive activism of NGOs such as Antigone and A Buon Diritto) sparked a process that led to the creation of local ombudspersons: the first one was appointed in Rome in 2003 (GNPL, 2023c).

The appointment of this prison monitoring body by the city council in Rome was followed by the establishment of other territorial guarantors across various regions and cities in many parts of Italy (Bexelius, 1965) or, as they are often labelled in Italian, "civic defenders" (Della Casa, 2003).

The National Guarantor was only established in late 2013. Though its creation owes much to the prior grassroots experiences at local level, the launch of a national body would not have been possible without a set of peculiar circumstances. To put it roughly, the Italian government was caught up in a series of international constraints, which contributed heavily to overcome some remaining political resistances and paved the way to the creation of a national monitoring organ.

While drawing on the said tradition of prison monitoring bodies at the local level, the establishment of what would soon become the NPM reflects the feeling of urgency (perceived by many policymakers between 2013 and 2016) in the face of the international outcry prompted by the state of detention conditions in Italy (GNPL, 2017).

In 2013 the European Court of Human Rights (ECtHR) was called to take a stance on the issue of systemic overcrowding of the Italian prison system, issuing a ruling in the context of a pilot-judgement procedure (*Torreggiani v. Italy*)[6]: not only did the ECtHR find a violation of Article 3 ECHR owing to poor detention conditions (as shown from a growing number of applications brought to the Court), it also urged national authorities to adopt a set of measures with the purpose of redressing what appeared to be a structural problem.

The process of enforcement of such ruling by Italy would be monitored by the Committee of Ministers of the Council of Europe (CoE) in accordance with Article 46 ECHR. Under the supervision of the most authoritative political body of the Council of Europe, Italian authorities made the decision of establishing the National Guarantor for the rights of persons deprived of liberty.[7] The Decree of its establishment can be understood as an urgent measure adopted by the executive to address the concerns raised by the Strasbourg Court in the *Torreggiani* judgement.

The new institution was designed as "an independent internal mechanism of supervision of detention facilities which will allow the competent authorities promptly to take the necessary corrective measures" to prevent and redress the violation of any prisoner's rights as highlighted by the Council of Europe while taking stock of the measures put up by Italy to execute the ECtHR's ruling.[8]

---

[6] ECtHR, *Torreggiani and Others v. Italy*, 8 January 2013 (Applications no. 43517/09, 46882/09, 55400/09, 57875/09, 61535/09, 35315/10 and 37818/10).

[7] Art. 7 Law Decree no. 146 of 2013.

[8] Committee of Ministers of the Council of Europe, Resolution CM/ResDH(2016)28, Execution of the judgments of the European Court of Human Rights in Two cases against Italy, 8 March 2016.

At the same time, other forms of pressure coming from supranational bodies proved influential in determining the course of events leading to the establishment of the Italian National Guarantor. Most significantly, the obligation to designate a national body as the country's preventive mechanism in accordance with Article 3 of the OPCAT. In April 2014, via a verbal note, the Guarantor was thus designated as a NPM under the OPCAT,[9] adding a further institutional layer—perhaps the most distinctive—to this organ (which would then find its legal basis both in the 2013 Law Decree establishing the GNPL and in the law ratifying the OPCAT).

In fact, Italy had signed the OPCAT on 20 August 2003 and ratified it approximately ten years later with Law No. 195 of 9 November 2012, depositing the instrument of ratification on 3 April 2013. Italy then had one year (counting from 3 May 2013 onwards), pursuant to Article 17 OPCAT, to designate its NPM.[10] The note verbale of 25 April 2014 therefore arrived at the eleventh hour.

A further piece of the puzzle was represented by Italy's obligations as a member of the European Union (EU). In fact, in 2014 the European Commission launched an infringement procedure against Italy for its lack of compliance with the obligation to establish an effective monitoring system of forced repatriations of third-country nationals as defined in the Return Directive (Palma, 2022).[11]

It is fair to say that, at first, Italian authorities crafted this institution mostly as a prison monitoring body, one that would coordinate with local ombudsmen and mainly operate along the lines set by the practice of these organs.[12] However, from the outset, the scope of its

---

[9] The GNPL was initially designated as a NPM through a *note verbale* of 25 April 2014, www.ohchr.org.

[10] The entry into force of the Protocol, pursuant Article 28, has effect on the thirtieth day after the date of deposit of its own instrument of ratification or accession.

[11] Article 8(6) of Directive 2008/115/EC.

[12] The right to visit prisons and meet with inmates for local guarantors had already been provided for by a modification of the so-called law on the "penitentiary order"–namely the Penitentiary Law–(law no. 354 of 1975) adopted in 2009. As of 2013, such norms were extended to cover also the prerogatives of the National Guarantor. It is worth noting that overall the powers attributed to the National Guarantor as an NPM are different and more incisive than those assigned by law to local guarantors.

monitoring mandate was defined in much broader terms as it was meant to cover a wider range of places where deprivation of liberty may take place (including, inter alia, detention centres for irregular migrants for the purpose of their expulsion).

This infringement procedure was only closed after the GNPL had been identified as monitoring body and after it had been verified that this designation meets in practice the requirements of Article 8(6) of the Return Directive (Albano, 2024).[13]

This intricate connection of circumstances which—somewhat independently from one another—contributed to the introduction of the NPM has a major commonality: they are the result of an increasing and combined pressure being brought to bear on Italy by the Council of Europe, the European Union and UN organs as to the treatment of persons deprived of liberty (Caputo & Ciuffoletti, 2018). This turn of events speaks to a broader tendency of the Italian penal system to develop under the pressure of external and, more specifically, supranational constraints (what has been referred to as "inverted panopticon" of human rights bodies in correctional matters, see Cliquennois & Snacken, 2018).

This is even more significant if one considers that Italy has not yet established or identified a National Human Rights Institution (NHRI) meeting the Paris Principles (European Commission, 2025).[14] The mandate of NHRIs is by definition a generalist one. The creation of these authorities should normally predate the establishment of a "specialised" body protecting persons deprived of their liberty. Yet, the process in Italy went the other way around, thereby shaping a wholly unique institutional setting in which the NHRI is still lacking.

[13] The infringement procedure 2014/2235 was closed by the European Commission on 13 July 2017.

[14] This issue persists despite repeated commitments from the Italian government to establish a bespoke body, with few draft laws still pending in late 2025, yet "no concrete actions have been taken to establish a National Human Rights Institution", see 2025 EU Rule of Law Report, Country Chapter on the rule of law situation in Italy. The reference to the Paris Principles is, of course, to the UN General Assembly resolution 48/134 adopted on 19 December 1993 (Principles relating to the Status of National Institutions).

3 The Organisation and Legal Framework of the Italian NPM

The National Guarantor is a public authority with a broad mandate. As said, its origins lie in the set of measures adopted to reduce overcrowding in the prison system. For this reason, it appears that in the eyes of the original drafters of decree law 23 December 2013 the GNPL would work, mostly, as a preventive tool to avoid violations of Article 3 ECHR and address the complaints of prisoners. After all, one of the most pressing criticisms raised by the ECtHR in the *Torreggiani* judgement was the lack of effective remedies available to persons detained in prison.

Although the legislature adopted a set of provisions regulating different avenues to obtain a binding judicial decision to prevent as well as to redress or compensate the violations of fundamental rights in prison,[15] the strengthening of the non-binding role of guarantors of the rights of person deprived of liberty was felt to be necessary and in some ways complementary (Scomparin, 2014).

Albeit the monitoring of the prison system (understood broadly) was the springboard of the GNPL's activity, the decree-law foresaw from the outset other areas of intervention. These included the monitoring of immigration detention centres. As a result, it appeared logical to invest the GNPL with the task of monitoring the process of forced repatriation regulated by the Return Directive.[16]

---

[15] The ECtHR itself noted that the failure to improve the quality of detention was worsened by the fact that rulings by judges in this matter had no binding effect because the generic complaint lodged with them is not of a judicial nature. Therefore, after the *Torreggiani* judgement Italy, by Decree-Law 23 December 2013, No. 146 converted into Law 21 February 2014, No. 10 established a jurisdictional preventive remedy through the introduction of the new Article 35-bis in the Penitentiary Law as well as it established the compensatory judicial remedy introduced by Decree-Law No. 92 of 26 June 2014, converted into Law No. 117 of 11 August 2014, which provided for the new Article 35-ter of the Penitentiary Law. Both of these remedies involve judicial decisions with binding effects. At the same time, Italy, with the same decree-law that had introduced the said preventive judicial remedy, provided for the establishment of the preventive non-jurisdictional remedy represented by the GNPL whose role is complementary to that of the judge and whose recommendations constitute soft law.

[16] As already said, in order to close the infringement procedure 2014/2235 the GNPL was "identified by the Italian State, in a note from the Presidency of the Council of Ministers dated March 12, 2015 (DPE0002621P-4.22.23), as the National Monitoring Body for forced

The organisation of the body now accredited as NPM is crucial to assess its compliance with the OPCAT and, more specifically, to gauge its credentials of independence within the meaning of Article 18 of the Optional Protocol.

The National Guarantor is a Board composed of the president and two members, appointed by decree of the President of the Italian Republic (a third and impartial constitutional organ), upon deliberation by the Council of Ministers and after a consultation with the relevant Parliamentary committees.

The involvement of the Parliament has proved effective to direct the choice of the board members: on one occasion in 2016, after the negative opinion of the Parliament about one specific candidate, a new name was put forward to compose the first National Guarantor Board. This parliamentary scrutiny of the choices made by the Council of Ministers is rightly emphasised because it implies not only formal involvement of the relevant parliamentary committees (Albano, 2021b).

The relationship with the executive is still the most sensitive and problematic one. Hence it is worth looking at it in more detail.

Based on the wording of the relevant legal provisions establishing the GNPL, the current NPM is constituted "at" the Ministry of Justice, not "within" it. This somewhat subtle legal nuance has been taken to mean that the GNPL draws significant resources from that Ministry but is not subject to it nor is part of its functional hierarchy (Albano, 2021b).

This issue was highlighted in a report drafted by the SPT upon a visit to Italy carried out from 16 to 22 September 2015. This report placed emphasis on a number of criticisms as regards the independence of the GNPL as per Article 18 of the OPCAT.

Before addressing the Subcommittee's remarks, two caveats are in order: first, the visit was carried out before the GNPL became operational[17] and, as a result, its findings relate exclusively to the legal/

return operations pursuant to Article 8 paragraph 6 of Directive 2008/115/EC"; see Art. 1(1a), GNPL's Code of Self-Regulation.

[17] As mentioned previously, the authority was established in late 2013. However, the selection process of the three members of the GNPL was finalised in March 2016, when the NPM became operational (GNPL, 2017).

institutional framework designed for it and not to its practical functioning; second, some (although not all) of the criticisms highlighted in the report have been addressed or solved by subsequent legislation and practice.

The SPT, during its visit, acknowledged the GNPL's status of "detached [...] unity [...] within the Ministry of Justice" and that it was endowed with an "autonomous budget". However, it maintained that further steps were needed to adjust the legal framework, particularly in such a way as to secure "the independence of its personnel" (SPT, 2016).[18]

Italy replied to the SPT report after the National Guarantor had already begun operating, explaining inter alia that it "uses the Ministry's resources but it is not included in its hierarchical structure and cannot be considered as one of its branches" (SPT addendum 2016).[19] In a subsequent annual report (GNPL, 2021), the GNPL itself reconfirmed this latter interpretation of how the relationship of instrumentality between the Guarantor and the Ministry of Justice should be understood in concrete terms (Albano, 2021b).

In the years following its establishment, Italy sought to strengthen the independence of the GNPL, starting with the decision of establishing an annual lump-sum allowance for the president and the members of the Board while, originally, their office was meant to be free of charge.[20]

As defined by the law establishing it, the National Guarantor is supported by a technical body assisting it in its activities, the Office of the GNPL, which must be composed of 25 members: we could compare its functions to those of the European Committee for the Prevention of Torture and Inhuman or Degrading Treatment or Punishment's (CPT) Secretariat.[21] Originally, the personnel composing the Office would be

---

[18] SPT, Report on the visit made by the SPT to Italy. Report to the State Party, *UN Doc.* CAT/OP/ITA/1, Distr.: General 23 September 2016, §§ 13–14.

[19] SPT, Visit to Italy undertaken from 16 to 22 September 2015: observations and recommendations addressed to the State party. Report of the Subcommittee. Addendum. Replies of Italy, *UN Doc.* CAT/OP/ITA/1/Add. 1, Distr.: General 2 November 2016, § 104.

[20] This choice was criticised as it would not secure the financial independence of the newly established authority (see Ceresa Gastaldo, 2014).

[21] The GNPL's Office "is the technical body assisting" and supporting "the Guarantor" in its various functions; see Art. 1 (1b), GNPL, Code of Self-Regulation. The CPT's Secretariat is

made, with one exception, of seconded staff of the Ministry of Justice. As of 2019, this organ can rely on the support of at least 20 staff members from the Ministry of Justice, no more than two from the Ministry of the Interior and no more than three from the National Health Service (GNPL, 2019, 2020).

The Office is funded through an operating budget allocation regulated by law, which has varied over the years: initially it was € 200,000 per year, it touched € 400,000 in 2021[22] and currently it stands at € 380,000 per year.[23] This funding does not comprise staff costs, which are mainly borne by the administration of origin of each staff member as well as other relevant costs, such as those relating to the headquarters located outside the Ministry of Justice which are charged to the Ministry of Justice. The institutional consolidation related to the budgetary issues continued with the achievement of accounting autonomy and the enactment of an accounting Regulation starting from 1 July 2021 (as described in GNPL, 2023c).[24]

Despite the progress to reduce the potential dependence on the executive, the configuration of the GNPL remains an odd and critical one. Much of its functional autonomy depends on the way in which the functions are practically performed, especially by the NPM's top officials:

---

composed by CoE's officers supporting the CPT members; see Rules of Procedure, pursuant to Article 6, paragraph 2, of the European Convention for the Prevention of Torture and Inhuman or Degrading Treatment or Punishment. Both–the Office of the GNPL and the Secretariat of the CPT—are composed of administrators and assistants—similar even in number, given that on 3 October 2025 there were 27 members of the Secretariat—who ensure the continuity of their respective institutions.

[22] See Ministry of Justice's "Bilancio di previsione anno finanziario 2021 e per il triennio 2021–2023—Amministrazione trasparente", in the column entitled "Stanziamenti Legge di Bilancio 2021" in www.giustizia.it/giustizia/it/contentview.page?contentId=ART319645.

[23] See Art. 7 (5 bis) Law Decree No. 146 of 2013, Decree of the President of the Council of Ministers (DPCM) No. 89 of 10 April 2019 and "Decreto di ripartizione in capitoli Ministero della Giustizia" in www.rgs.mef.gov.it—in particular see www.rgs.mef.gov.it/_Documenti/VERSIONE-I/attivita_istituzionali/formazione_e_gestione_del_bilancio/bilancio_di_previsione/bilancio_finanziario/2025-2027/LB/LB_2025_LB-04-DRC-050-Giustizia.pdf.

[24] See also the Regulation concerning the Start-up Phase of Accounting Autonomy of National Guarantor for the Rights of Persons Deprived of Liberty—"Regolamento concernente la disciplina per l'avviamento dell'autonomia contabile del Garante nazionale dei diritti delle persone private della libertà personale. Approvato dal Garante con deliberazione del 28/06/2021"—in GNPL, 2022.

in this respect, the personal background of the president and the board members is crucial in ensuring the right distance from the government.

A further question is whether the tasks of president or board member could be independently exercised by former officials who have served as high-level figures within the bureaucracy of the Ministries of Justice or the Interior. Although, at present, nothing prevents this formally, it remains to be seen if someone with such a professional background can maintain the right distance from the government and, specifically, from the authorities subject to GNPL's monitoring.

The same could be said for individuals who have held important roles, including in Parliament or in other civil society bodies: as noted by the first president of the GNPL, the independence of monitoring authorities must not only be from the executive but also from the Parliament and from non-governmental organisations: independence as equidistance from both politics and organised civil society (Palma, 2009). This is an issue that can be assessed through a comprehensive and careful evaluation of the practices implemented by the NPM, thus in a way that is not merely confined to the scrutiny of relevant legislation.[25]

[25] The following statement by the present president of the GNPL Turrini Vita concerning the denunciation of the current situation in Italian prisons and the related request addressed to Parliament should be welcomed in this sense: "the situation is particularly distressing. It requires immediate measures to alleviate the pressure on prisons. Not only to provide relief to prisoners, but also to show that the exclusion of these people from society should not be considered definitive and permanent. In the democratic history of the Republic, numerous amnesties and pardons have been granted, even after that truly ill-advised constitutional provision that sought to burden the possibility of passing a clemency law with an exorbitant majority. This provision is all the more illogical given that an ordinary law is sufficient to create a crime and increase the penalty. If an ad hoc majority cannot be envisaged, there are other instruments such as the conversion *ope legis* of short periods into probation [...] Together with the Board, we have filed this request with Parliament, the appropriate place" (Martini, 2025b). With regard to the typical practices of the first eight years of activities of the GNPL, see *inter alia* the first seven Reports to Parliament (GNPL, 2017–2023) and the recent book by Palma et al. (2025).

4 The Functions and Methodology of the Italian NPM: Visits and Reports

Turning now to the methods of intervention used by the Italian NPM: these are partly inspired by those of the CPT, as they include regular regional visits, ad hoc visits (to investigate specific and urgent issues), thematic visits (aimed at monitoring specific categories of deprivation of liberty, e.g. detention in special regimes as the one enshrined by art. 41 bis of the Penitentiary Law[26]), and follow-up visits (aimed at monitoring the implementation of recommendations; it should be noted that according to the OPCAT the administrations are in any case obliged to enter into dialogue with the NPM).

After the visits, the GNPL's methodology entails the drafting of reports containing observations and recommendations addressed to the heads of the administrations that manage the various areas of deprivation of liberty, particularly "within" the Ministry of Justice and the Ministry of the Interior.

The report remains confidential for the number of days specified by the GNPL (normally 30 days) and is then published together with any response from the administration concerned,[27] in order to guarantee its right to be heard.

---

[26] The prison regime based on Article 41 bis of the Italian Penitentiary Act is designed to limit interaction between those deemed dangerous because of their ties to an organised criminal group, other inmates and persons outside the prison (see Bondi, 2025).

[27] If the visit is carried out, for example, at a repatriation centre (*Centro di Permanenza per il Rimpatrio* or CPR in Italian), i.e. the main place in Italy where irregular migrants awaiting expulsion are administratively detained, the GNPL report is sent to the competent Ministry of the Interior, which, if it deems it appropriate, responds formally with a note that is published by the GNPL together with the visit report. Similarly, if the visit takes place in a prison, it is the Ministry of Justice that receives the report and provides any response—see Article 3(9), GNPL, new Code of Self-Regulation adopted in 2021. This differs from the procedure for CPT visits, where the report is sent to the Italian Interministerial Committee for Human Rights (*Comitato Interministeriale per i Diritti Umani* or CIDU in Italian, that is within the Ministry of Foreign Affairs and is the national mechanism for reporting and follow-up), which is responsible for sending each competent administration the part of the report that concerns it, so that it can examine it and provide a response that will then be included in the overall report prepared by the CIDU, which constitutes Italy's official response to the CPT report. The CPT report and Italy's response are then published when requested by the State—see Articles 10 and 11, European Convention for the Prevention of Torture and Inhuman or Degrading Treatment or Punishment (ECPT).

These activities tie into the broader mandate of the GNPL as a torture prevention body. This mandate is not interpreted narrowly, however. Of course, the main goal—in accordance with the OPCAT—is to prevent torture and other cruel, inhuman, or degrading treatment or punishment. At the same time, it is often stated that the monitoring of the GNPL has the ultimate aim of protecting the rights and dignity of individuals deprived of their liberty, in such a way as to avoid (albeit indirectly) any deprivation of liberty that could be arbitrary or unlawful (Palma, 2022).[28]

Publishing reports on opaque places such as prisons therefore reflects the need to shed light on "dark materials"[29]: in this respect, one would agree with Louis Brandeis, the father of the right to privacy, who famously stated that "sunlight is [...] the best of disinfectants" (Brandeis, 1913).[30]

In order to carry out its monitoring activities, the GNPL has the right to access all places of detention, the right to have private interviews with all persons concerned, including those deprived of their liberty, and the right to access all relevant information.

The areas of deprivation of liberty under the remit of GNPL were originally singled out in Article 7 of Law Decree no. 146 of 2013. The scope of the NPM's mandate was further specified by a Code of Self-Regulation (a set of guidelines) adopted in 2016, subsequently modified and then replaced in 2021 taking into account the gradual regulatory

[28] This is the wording chosen by the GNPL's guidelines in the new Code of Self-Regulation: see Article 3(3) lett. a) which clarifies that the exercise of the powers of the GNPL is aimed inter alia at "supervising that the enforcement of deprivation of liberty orders on detainees, internees, people in pre-trial detention or other forms of restriction of personal liberty, the enforcement of administrative orders or provisions of a medical nature affecting the liberty of persons, and anyhow all forms of deprivation of personal liberty that are not arbitrary and take place in accordance with the norms and principles established by the Constitution, international conventions on the promotion and protection of the rights of persons and of their dignity ratified by Italy, and any law in force".

[29] We borrow this expression from John Milton's Paradise Lost, Book II, p. 916 (Milton, 1882).

[30] The complete quotation is: "Sunlight is said to be the best of disinfectants; electric light the most efficient policeman".

changes and improvements that have taken place in the meantime even in the law establishing the GNPL.[31]

The main areas on which the GNPL has conducted its monitoring from the very beginning are: (1) the penitentiary system, (2) police custody, (3) administrative detention of migrants, and (4) the healthcare sector. Concerning the healthcare settings, the Code of Self-Regulation has made clear that the Guarantor must exercise its functions with respect to: a) psychiatric diagnosis and treatment services within hospital units dedicated to the management of acute and emergency phases of psychiatric disorders as well as any other clinical and hospital facilities where it is possible to implement orders for compulsory health interventions; and b) residential facilities for elderly or disabled persons, adults or minors, also in compliance with the obligations arising from the UN Convention on the Rights of Persons with Disabilities—ratified by Italy in 2009—in order to prevent that constraints on guests and patients result in a *de facto* deprivation of personal liberty (Losito & Pizzo, 2021).

In this way, the GNPL's guidelines rely on (and seem to be in line with) the definition of deprivation of liberty laid down in Article 4 of the OPCAT.[32] The UN definition of deprivation of liberty highlights "the importance of including in the concept of deprivation of liberty not only the situation of those who are not allowed to leave a place or situation voluntarily because they are prohibited from doing so, but also the situation of those who are not able to leave a place or situation voluntarily because they lack the physical or material capacity to do so" (Albano & Di Terlizzi, 2023).[33]

---

[31] See Self-regulatory Code of the National Guarantor for the rights of persons detained or deprived of liberty, adopted by resolution May 31, 2016, updated by resolutions of December 6, 2017, August 29, 2019, and January 8, 2021 as well as the new Code of Self-Regulation of the National Guarantor for the rights of persons deprived of liberty, adopted by resolution March 30, 2021, www.garantenazionaleprivatiliberta.it.

[32] The OPCAT definition has been developed and detailed in the SPT's first General Comment on the correct interpretation of Article 4 of the OPCAT, to which the Italian NPM contributed significantly both in writing and by participating in events such as the *Day of General Discussion on the draft General Comment on Article 4* (GNPL, 2023b).

[33] The period in quotation marks has been translated by us into English from the original Italian, in the publication cited above, namely Albano and Di Terlizzi (2023). Actually, the concept was expressed in English by the GNPL's head of international relations at the *Day of General Discussion on the Draft General Comment on Article 4* organised in Geneva by the

In practice, this notion has allowed the GNPL to broaden its scope of intervention to cases that fall within a grey area, covered by the law establishing the GNPL through reference to the OPCAT.[34]

These powers implied by the designation as NPM have been recognised in practice since 2016, thanks in part to the recommendations of the UN Committee on the Rights of Persons with Disabilities (CRPD) which were followed by the Italian Government.[35] This framework emerged in practice and has subsequently informed the Guarantor's own guidelines.

The GNPL took a pragmatic approach and found that, based on a systematic reading of the OPCAT and the ECHR, its mandate included the scrutiny of non-conventional, and often temporary, places of deprivation of liberty. To complement its monitoring of migration detention, the GNPL extended its visits to ships that cannot disembark rescued migrants because harbours have been closed as well as so-called quarantine ships (where migrants are held on public health grounds). A further expansion of the GNPL's remit took place during the COVID-19 pandemic: the quarantine facilities, including places like cruise ships and "Covid" hotels, were thought to fall within the mandate of preventive mechanisms.[36]

SPT on 8 June 2023. In both situations, the person "cannot" leave a certain place or context: German and English have different verbs to express the two different situations: in the first case, "*dürfen*" in German and "may" or "to be allowed" in English; on the other hand, in the second sense in German we use "*können*" and in English "to be able to". See also Cordero (1986, p. 16).

[34] Article 7 of Decree Law No. 146 of 2013 explicitly refers through its reference to the OPCAT and the provisions contained therein, including Article 4 itself, thus including all four areas of deprivation of liberty, both *de jure* and *de facto*.

[35] See CRPD, *List of issues in relation to the initial report of Italy* (CRPD/C/ITA/Q/1), 29 April 2016, Par. 16; CRPD, *List of issues in relation to the initial report of Italy. Addendum. Replies of Italy to the list of issues* (CRPD/C/ITA/Q/1/Add.1), 14 June 2016, Par. 33; CRPD, *Concluding observations on the initial report of Italy* (CRPD/C/ITA/CO/1), 6 October 2016, Par. 42, according to which "The Committee recommends that the national preventive mechanism immediately visit and report on the situation in psychiatric institutions or other residential facilities for persons with disabilities, especially those with intellectual and/or psychosocial disabilities".

[36] This was made clear early in 2020 by the SPT itself. The SPT first expressed an opinion on extending the mandate of NPMs to places of compulsory quarantine for reasons of public health protection and therefore also to those for COVID-19: SPT, *Advice of the Subcommittee on Prevention of Torture to the National Preventive Mechanism of the United Kingdom of Great*

The GNPL's guidelines have been redrafted accordingly and now make clear that visits may encompass "any place that, due to a contingent emergency, holds persons who are not authorised to leave such a place at their own will".[37]

With this in mind, we conclude this section with a few details on the practical implications of the visits. First, where, during a visit or monitoring of forced repatriation, it considers that the situation may constitute a violation of Article 3 of the ECHR, as interpreted by the ECtHR, or of the protections established by the Constitution for the dignity and inviolability of the person,[38] the Guarantor shall promptly inform the competent authority so that immediate action may be taken in order to stop the violation, while at the same time notifying the judicial authority so that it may take the necessary measures. Secondly, following the visits the notes are shaped in a structured manner and included in the report which, after a short period of *embargo* decided by the GNPL itself, may be published along with the observations and recommendations as well as the relative observations made by the organs involved in their possible responses to the report.

In keeping with the preventive nature of its functions, the action of the GNPL may be oriented, as much as possible, to avert violations. Therefore, recommendations may address criticisms of a given place of detention even when there are no apparent infringements of fundamental rights, but the implementation of practical adjustments, as suggested in the recommendation, would reduce the likelihood of a violation (Albano & Di Terlizzi, 2023).

Britain and Northern Ireland regarding compulsory quarantine for Coronavirus, adopted at its 40th session (10 to 14 February 2020), www.ohchr.org. The SPT subsequently adopted a more general opinion addressed to all Member States on how the Subcommittee itself and the various NPMs should continue to exercise their mandate during the emergency situation caused by the global spread of COVID-19: SPT, *Advice of the Subcommittee on Prevention of Torture to States Parties and National Preventive Mechanisms relating to the Coronavirus Pandemic*, adopted on 25 March 2020 in www.ohchr.org (see also SPT, 2021).

[37] See the Code of Self-Regulation: Article 3(2) lett. f).

[38] In particular art. 2 and 3 of the Italian Constitution.

5 Other Functions of the Italian NPM: Relationships with the Parliament and the Judiciary

In this section, we turn to some additional features of the GNPL which may highlight some specificities that stand out in a comparative context. Arguably, these peculiar features will appear more clearly if one looks at them through the lens of the relations between the NPM and the legislative or judicial branch of power.

As for the legislative branch, what stands out is the NPM's duty to present a yearly report of its activities to Parliament: this duty reflects underlying reasons of accountability and transparency of the Guarantor's action (Scomparin, 2014). To date reports have been discussed in both houses of Parliament, the Senate and the Chamber, on alternate years and have normally been submitted between March and June of the following year. The practice of presenting annual reports to Parliament continued uninterruptedly until 2023.

Then, in January 2024, the new Board officially began its term, but unfortunately the second President passed away at the end of August of the same year. At the end of October, the third President was appointed. This annual report for the year 2024 has not yet been published. At the time of writing, in early 2026, the current President of the GNPL stated in an interview that the publication of the report and its presentation to Parliament will take place in the near future (Martini, 2025b). Everything suggests that the report to Parliament for 2025 will also be published in 2026, so that the Guarantor can once again fulfil this crucial and annual legal obligation.

Another critical factor is the general decrease in the number of documents reporting on the current activities of the GNPL made available on the website,[39] which—according to some—has made the work of

[39] To give an example, on 9 March 2026, a report" was published on the GNPL website (www.garantenazionaleprivatiliberta.it) showing 82 visits to prisons in 2024, 62 visits in 2025 and 14 visits in 2026, along with the corresponding number of kilometres travelled, respectively 70,000, 30,647 and 4444 km. On the same website, as of 10 March 2026, four reports have been published on visits to four adult prisons, one report on a visit to a juvenile detention

the NPM less effective, accountable and transparent (De Vito, 2025).[40] However, this cannot be said for some areas of activity, such as monitoring in the area of deprivation of liberty concerning migrants. In fact, in this area, "...inspections have been and continue to be thorough, with detailed reports that cause difficulties for the Ministry of the Interior" (Grignetti, 2025).[41]

The dynamics of power vis-à-vis the legislature must also include the NPM's competence to submit proposals and observations on existing or draft legislation, as provided for in Article 19(c) of the OPCAT. In its 2016 report, the SPT pointed out that this power had not been explicitly enshrined in law. This initial weakness in the legal basis was highlighted by those who observed that the NPM's power to comment on legislation affecting the rights of persons deprived of their liberty must be recognised by law in order to avoid the risk of marginalisation in practice (Manca, 2016).

It is true, however, that this prerogative has been regularly exercised in practice, also on the basis of an interpretation that considered the OPCAT requirements on NPMs applicable within national law (as endorsed by the National Guarantor's Code of Self-Regulation since its first version in 2016). This approach was confirmed in 2020 when the law establishing the GNPL was amended to explicitly provide for the applicability of Articles 4 as well as Articles 17 to 23 of the OPCAT and therefore also of Article 19(c).

In this regard, it is worth mentioning the recent ruling by the Italian Council of State[42] annulling the Decree of the Minister of the Interior of 4 March 2024—which approved the tender specifications for the

centre, one report with recommendations on juvenile detention centres, a report with recommendations on the special regime provided for in Article 41-bis of the Prison Law, and a report with recommendations on the application of an administrative circular from the Prison Administration.

40 See also Unione delle Camere Penali Italiane—an association of criminal lawyers—*La necessità di un intervento istituzionale per l'ufficio del Garante dei detenuti*, www.camerepenali.it, 14 August 2025, according to which "the periodic publication of analyses and statistical data" may, in part, allow, "in an era of poor transparency, the analysis of certain specific critical issues in the [...] prison system."

41 Also as of 10 March 2026, the GNPL website (again for the period 2024–2026) contains nine reports published on 11 visits to administrative detention centres and facilities for migrants.

42 N. 7839/2025, published on 7 October 2025.

management and operation of the Centres for Repatriation of Migrants (CPR)—partly because the Ministry had not carried out a complete investigation, having failed, among other things, to consult the GNPL, which should have provided its necessary expertise, also in view of its powers under Article 19 of the OPCAT. The Council of State's decision also cites the GNPL's letter to the Minister of the Interior dated 11 June 2024, in which the NPM inter alia emphasised that it should have been involved in the decision-making process pursuant to Article 19(c) of the OPCAT.

Turning now to the relations with the judiciary, it is worth noting that the legal framework of the GNPL still reflects its primordial role as a body specialised in the protection of the rights of persons detained by the criminal justice system. Article 7 of Law Decree 146 of 2013 and Art. 35 of the Penitentiary Law include the National Guarantor among the bodies that can receive complaints of all kinds from prisoners.[43]

When adjudicating on these complaints the NPM exercises a non-judicial function and can issue non-binding recommendations to the administration concerned (usually prison authorities). It follows that the GNPL have some prerogatives in common with the judge supervising the enforcement of sentences (Cesaris, 2016)[44]: both can receive complaints from prisoners and can issue recommendations to the prison administration when the complaint is well founded.

Importantly, this is not the only preventive remedy that prisoners can avail themselves of: as of 2014, in the aftermath of the *Torreggiani* ruling, the judiciary has much more power and is now also allowed to issue

[43] The Penitentiary Law (Law no. 345 of 1975) allows the local guarantors and the GNPL to carry out visits without the need for authorisation from the penitentiary administration. Accordingly, both non-centralised guarantors and the GNPL may receive and adjudicate on the complaints filed by prisoners even if only the GNPL has the power to make specific recommendations to the administration concerned, if it finds that the complaints submitted pursuant to Article 35 of the Penitentiary Law are well-founded.

[44] In Italy (similarly to other continental legal systems, e.g. Belgium and France) the enforcement of a sentence is subject to the judicial review of a specialised tribunal composed of four members (two of them being expert-members, usually psychologists, forensic psychiatrists and criminologists). This judicial panel (and, in first instance, a single-judge body whose member is also a component of the territorially competent panel) has the power to rule on the protection of fundamental rights of persons on pre-trial detention or serving a custodial sentence in prison; the judge's mandate extends to persons deprived of liberty in the execution of a post-trial security measures (i.e. based on a prognosis of social dangerousness).

binding judicial orders to force a prison administration to put an end to any violation of fundamental rights in prison. In other words, the two sets of complaints (those filed before the Guarantor and those that can give rise to a binding judicial order) are somehow complementary.

It should also be noted here that in 2020, obligations arising from the execution of another judgement of the ECtHR against Italy[45] required the legislator to introduce a corresponding provision establishing the possibility of complaints to the National and local Guarantors also by migrants in administrative detention, again attributing the power of recommendation solely to the GNPL (Albano, 2021b).

With regard to the judicial branch of power, it seems relevant that the National Guarantor is entitled to appear as an offended party or civil party in criminal proceedings concerning cases of serious ill-treatment or the suicide of a person deprived of liberty.

In addition, the GNPL takes part in the judicial process by interacting with the decisions of apex courts, at least when their role pertains to fundamental rights falling within its remit. Hence, under the current regulatory framework, the Guarantor is allowed to submit opinions to the Constitutional Court as *amicus curiae* and it can do the same when a case of the same content is pending before the ECtHR.

On a different note, it is worth emphasising that, in some instances, the GNPL can team up with the judiciary to obtain information or documents from the relevant administrations in charge of the places of detention that the Guarantor is monitoring.

If the administration concerned does not provide an answer within 30 days from the initial request, the National Guarantor can file a complaint with the judge (in particular, the competence to make a decision falls with the court that would be territorially competent for the monitoring of the execution of sentences).[46]

These features describe how the GNPL may interact with the judiciary to fulfil its mandate, thereby laying bare the hybrid nature of the Italian NPM. On the one hand, the GNPL works as a cooperative body and

---

45 *Khlaifia and Others v. Italy*, ECtHR App. no. 16483/12, G. C., 15 December 2016.

46 Arguably this mechanism is applicable also in cases in which the GNPL requests information from administrative organs that are responsible for place of detention beyond the criminal justice system.

can collaborate with the administration to avert and redress a current or potential violation of rights in a consensual manner; on the other hand, it may need to take an adversarial approach vis-à-vis the administration (thus applying for a judicial order) if the concerned administrative organs fail to collaborate with it.

6 The GNPL as a Centralised NPM and the Local Monitoring Bodies

Finally, a few words are in order about the relationship between the GNPL and its regional and local counterparts. As said, the bottom-up movements of criminal justice reform have seen local monitoring bodies—mostly dealing with prisoners' rights—flourish across Italy.

At present, the GNPL coincides with the Italian NPM. This, however, was not the government's original intention when it designated the NPM. In the context of the ratification of the OPCAT, Italy aimed at the creation of an NPM network including both the GNPL and the local monitoring bodies.

On 25 April 2014, Italy designated as its NPM a network of guarantors of various kinds: these included territorial guarantors (regional, provincial, municipal bodies) plus the newly established National Guarantor, as the network coordinator. The model initially devised by the *note verbale* sent to the UN contemplated a division of labour between the national authority (the GNPL) and its local counterparts: while the former would address its recommendations to the central government, the latter would do the same with the regional and local authorities.[47]

In sum, according to this initial approach the NPM would coincide with the system of monitoring bodies as a whole. Subsequently, however,

[47] The verbal note sent to Geneva reads as follows: "The new Guarantor for the rights of persons detained or deprived of personal liberty, established by law n. 10/21 February 2014, will coordinate the net of local Guarantors, formed by institutions already in place or to be set up at regional Authorities, while the national Guarantor will submit recommendations to central Government. The whole system will constitute the National Preventive Mechanism pursuant to the Optional Protocol of CAT."

the GNPL entered into tight discussions with the international monitoring committees in Geneva (most notably the CAT and the SPT) for the sake of verifying the accreditation of territorial guarantors in line with the requirements of the OPCAT.

In this context, the GNPL gathered an initial group of eight regional guarantors which appeared more in line with international standards, to have them recognised as nodes of the NPM network. The reason for doing so was the existence of regional statutes that a) allow for the appointment of the monitoring body by an elected assembly, b) stipulate that nomination cannot be revoked if not due to serious non-compliance with their duties and c) secure that their mandate is not limited in length to the time in office of the assembly which nominated them.

The CAT agreed that these territorial guarantors showed a "normative compliance" with UN standards. At the same time, however, the CAT noted a lack of "operational compliance" in the sense that those guarantors did not fully adopt the CPT's operating methods (Albano, 2018),[48] namely the publication of reports on visits containing observations and recommendations (Albano, 2021a).[49]

The Italian legislator took note of these limitations and, in 2020, with two following Law Decrees—converted into laws in June and December[50]—decided to take a different direction and adopted a new legal framework.[51]

Within it, the GNPL is the only body designated as NPM.[52] Yet, there is still a possibility to resort to the network of territorial guarantors, although on a subsidiary basis (Albano, 2021a).

[48] We can say that, with regard to preventive mechanisms, the CPT represents the "archetype". Its positive experience was fully taken up by the United Nations system in early 2000, with some additions and adaptations.

[49] See also GNPL, 2018.

[50] Law Decree No. 28 of 30 April 2020, converted into Law No. 70 of 25 June 2020, and Law Decree No. 130 of 21 October 2020, converted into Law No. 173 of 18 December 2020.

[51] For the sake of understanding the relationship of the NPM with Parliament (see the previous section), this is a good example of a National Guarantor's opinion that was almost totally accepted by Parliament and enshrined by law (GNPL 2020).

[52] Contrary to prior wording of the law which did not make any explicit reference to this (and, more strikingly, at odds with the content of the *note verbale* directed to the UN in 2014) the new version of the GNPL's legal basis makes it explicit that the NPM coincides exclusively with the National Guarantor.

In fact, the GNPL may delegate its powers to the local monitoring bodies but only in the less traditional areas of deprivation of liberty, namely the administrative detention of migrants and the health sector (mainly, with respect to psychiatric services and social care homes).

From their side, local guarantors have always viewed the natural[53] coordinating role of the GNPL with some suspicion, fearing that it could undermine their autonomy, even though such coordination was crucial in order to exercise the most effective powers attributed to NPMs. There was probably an inherent underlying difficulty for the territorial guarantors—who often felt as representatives of autonomous local authorities—in allowing full and complete coordination by a national authority (GNPL, 2018, 2020). This situation also had a certain influence on the subsequent phase of formal delegation by the GNPL.[54]

At the same time, it must be said that the areas in which this delegation has been envisaged by the law are those in which the mentioned territorial organs are less experienced, their core activity being traditionally concerned with detention in the criminal justice system.

The main issue, in this respect, is that the new status of local bodies—in respect of delegation and therefore the possibility of exercising the powers conferred on the NPM—seems to cast their role as limited to the monitoring of places of deprivation other than those of the criminal justice system.

Drawing on these new provisions, some commentators have suggested that it would even be contrary to the Constitution to bestow local monitoring bodies with the power to inspect prisons and other places of detention within the criminal justice system, as these prerogatives could not be exercised by a regional lawmaker and are exclusive competence of the national legislature (Picozzi, 2021).

[53] In a multiple NPM composed of a national body and a variable number of bodies with different territorial competences, it is self-evident that the coordinating role falls to the body with the broadest competence.

[54] At present, the NPM has exercised its powers only in the area of deprivation of liberty of migrants, on four occasions, and in all four cases the delegation conducting the visit was mixed, composed of the territorial guarantor as head of delegation and members of the NPM office. Following the visits, four reports were published, plus a fifth summary report. See GNPL (2023a).

This brushing interpretation would mean a loss of the expertise of the widespread network of bodies which constitute a specific feature of the Italian model of independent oversight and torture prevention. After all, as far as the prison system is concerned, the Italian penitentiary law makes it explicit that the local guarantors have some prerogatives in common with the GNPL, in accessing the penitentiaries and conducting interviews with inmates (the main difference being in the prerogatives vis-à-vis prisoners under the 41 bis regime).

7 Conclusion

To date the activity of the GNPL has seen ups and downs, partly due to some weaknesses in the legal framework regulating it. The shortcomings pointed out by the SPT as to the independence of the national authority have not been addressed entirely.

The main challenge that threatens the autonomy of the Italian NPM is the appointment process of the president and the board. The ultimate selection of these top officials, eventually, falls with the executive. The decision made by the Council of Ministers is ratified by the President of the Republic and can be effectively counteracted only if the parliamentary committees carry out an insightful scrutiny.[55]

Another problematic question, in this respect, concerns the independence of the personnel of the GNPL's technical body, being recruited entirely within the bureaucracy of the ministries (mostly the Ministry of Justice and the Ministry of Interior). The possibility for the NPM's

[55] Which is, of course, less likely to happen when the political majority in Parliament coincides entirely with the political forces and coalition which are part of the government. On the other hand, according to some, the issue of the autonomy of many 'independent' authorities in Italy deserves more in-depth consideration, not least because even the procedures laid down for the composition of similar institutions (e.g. the data protection authority), which traditionally entrust the power to appoint its member to the Presidents of the two Chambers, no longer seem suitable for ensuring the objective. This latter method does not seem to guarantee the desired independence, given that, for a long time now, the Presidents of the two Assemblies have been the expression of the political forces of the majority alone. The issue of independence in the appointment process therefore deserves to be addressed in a broader context of reviewing the composition of 'independent' authorities (Ruotolo, 2025).

staff of returning to the administration of origin, upon their secondment to the NPM, is not flanked by adequate counterweights to prevent negative repercussions both for their work of monitoring organs of the same administration to which they belong and for them at the time of a possible return to that controlled administration.

In this respect, the former members of the board recently pointed out the intrinsic fragility of an office whose staff is not employed in a stable and specific role. Although any return of staff members to the administrations to which they belong can only take place by decision of the board and not by recall of the administration itself,[56] this working position exposes the members of the office to the vicissitudes of the political world and to the lesser or greater ability of the board itself to resist these (Palma et al., 2025).

At the same time, the said legal structure has allowed the National Guarantor to become operational in less than a month in March 2016. Still, the issues mentioned above are sticking points that will need to be addressed in the near future, as the 'umbilical cord' which ties the NPM to the executive must be severed once and for all.

In this respect, a further challenge that deserves attention is the high turnover that has led to almost 40 people changing in almost ten years, in a workforce that should have 25 people. One of the reasons why CPT has become much more established than SPT lies in the resources available to it, starting from its strong and well-established Secretariat, which has always ensured the continuity of the institution.[57]

Two further issues must be considered. First, the failure to present annual reports to Parliament between 2023 and 2025 has raised many eyebrows (Ruotolo, 2025). Although the circumstances in which the NPM operated could have been easier, the lack of reports and some quarrels between the members of the board regarding the GNPL's stance taken vis-à-vis some statements made by the Ministry of Justice (with

[56] Art. 2 (4) DPCM No. 89 of 10 April 2019.

[57] For example, one can remember that Trevor Stevens headed the CPT secretariat continuously from 1989 to 2015, as did many other members of the secretariat who have worked there for a long time up to the present day.

respect to the number of suicides committed in prison in 2025)[58] would warrant closer scrutiny on the part of UN competent bodies.

Second, with regard to the call made by the SPT in 2016 to pass legislation explicitly mentioning the prohibition of reprisals against persons interviewed by the NPM (in accordance with Article 21 of the OPCAT) Italy introduced in 2020 a reference to this article into the law establishing the Guarantor, specifying that the latter body, in its capacity as NPM, exercises the powers, benefits from the guarantees and fulfils the obligations also referred to in Article 21. This is a step in the right direction, though possibly not a final one as no legal provision has been adopted that prevents an identification of interviewed prisoners, not even when needed to protect their safety and ability to be heard during follow-up visits.

In a time where the multilateral order of state relations and international law go through their most severe crisis since World War II, one cannot overstate the ability of a young institution such as the NPM to navigate the authoritarian turn and the rule of law backsliding in Europe and elsewhere (Levitsky & Ziblatt, 2019) and no stone should be left unturned to avert the risk of a neutralisation of its role.

---

[58] After the GNPL published an update on the registered number of suicides in prison in 2025 (48, between January and August), the Ministry of Justice released a statement contesting the wording chosen by press agency AGI about the data issued by the NPM (which spoke of "alert"), adding that the number of suicides was lower than the average of previous years. A few hours after the Ministry's press release, the GNPL published a rectification ("*precisazioni*" in Italian) which refutes the interpretation of data on suicide "in line with the findings of the Ministry of Justice" and reports "a significant decrease in the number of suicides in Italian prisons compared to the same period last year". On this matter see the press release from the GNPL published on 11 August 2025 (Precisazioni del GNPL, www.garantenazionaleprivatilibe rta.it), the reaction of Mario Serio, member of the Board, to this press release (Martini, 2025a) and the subsequent press release of the Unione Camere Penali Italiane published on 14 August 2015 (www.camerepenali.it).

Bibliography

Albano, A. (2018, July 24). Il sistema NPM Italiano. *News–Garante regionale dei diritti delle persone sottoposte a misure restrittive della libertà—Puglia.* https://garantedetenuti.consiglio.puglia.it/-/il-sistema-npm-italiano-di-alessandro-albano.-responsabile-relazioni-nazionali-internazionali-e-studi-del-garante-nazionale

Albano, A. (2021a). Sviluppo del paradigma preventivo. L'esperienza del Garante nazionale dei diritti delle persone private della libertà personale. *Studium Iuris, 27*(10), 1161–1169.

Albano, A. (2021b). Sviluppo del paradigma preventivo. L'esperienza del Garante nazionale dei diritti delle persone private della libertà personale. *Studium Iuris, 27*(11), 1299–1308.

Albano, A. (2024). La cooperazione in tema di sviluppo e diritti umani: l'esempio del Garante delle persone private della libertà. In M. Nicoletti & M. Lunardini (Eds.), *Politica estera e diritti umani* (pp. 97–114). Donzelli.

Albano, A. (2026). Le Istituzioni di prevenzione della tortura e il contributo delle Organizzazioni non governative (NGO). *Ordine internazionale e diritti umani,* to be published.

Albano, A., & Di Terlizzi, V. (2023), Privazione della libertà e diritti fondamentali nel contesto pandemico. In G. Colaiacovo (Ed.), *Carcere e COVID. Riflessioni giuridiche a margine dell'emergenza* (pp. 117–145). Cacucci.

Anastasia, S. (2023). I garanti dei detenuti nel sistema penitenziario. *Revista De Direito Brasileira, 13*(4), 217–225.

Bexelius, A. (1965). The Ombudsman for civil affairs. In D. C. Rowat (Ed.), *The Ombudsman. Citizen's defender* (pp. 22–44). Toronto University Press.

Bondi, G. (2025). Italy's '41 bis' special prison regime for leading organised crime figures in view of European Court of Human Rights' case law and international prison standards. In A. Schloenhardt, B. Weißer, M. Stempkowski, & G. Ege (Eds.), *Organised crime, criminal procedure, and prisons* (pp. 170–192). Routledge.

Brandeis, L. D. (1913). What publicity can do. *Harper's Weekly for December 20, 1913,* 10–13.

Caputo, A., & Ciuffoletti, S. (2018). Journey to Italy: The European and UN monitoring of Italian penal and prison policies. *Crime, Law and Social Change, 70*(1), 19–35.

Ceresa Gastaldo, M. (2014). Una "Authority" di Cartapesta per i diritti dei detenuti. *La Legislazione Penale, 34*(4), 413–423.

Cesaris, L. (2016). Quali garanzie per il garante dei detenuti? *Archivio Penale, 47*(2), 543–559.

Cogliano, C. (2000). *Diritti in carcere. Il difensore civico nella tutela dei detenuti.* I quaderni di Antigone.

Cordero, F. (1986). *Guida alla procedura penale*. Utet.

Cliquennois, G., & Snacken, S. (2018). European and United Nations monitoring of penal and prison policies as a source of an inverted panopticon? *Crime, Law and Social Change, 70*(1), 1–18.

CRPD. (2016a, April 29). *List of issues in relation to the initial report of Italy* (CRPD/C/ITA/Q/1).

CRPD. (2016b, June 14). *List of issues in relation to the initial report of Italy. Addendum. Replies of Italy to the list of issues* (CRPD/C/ITA/Q/1/Add.1).

CRPD. (2016c, October 6). *Concluding observations on the initial report of Italy* (CRPD/C/ITA/CO/1).

Della Casa, F. (2003). Per un più fluido (ed esteso) monitoraggio delle situazioni detentive: il Difensore civico della libertà personale. *Politica Del Diritto, 34*(1), 69–82.

De Vito, R. (2025, July 8). Sguardo libero e occhi aperti. La reale indipendenza del Garante nazionale dei diritti delle persone private della libertà personale. *Questione Giustizia.*

European Commission. (2025, July 8). EU Rule of Law Report, Country Chapter on the rule of law situation in Italy. Accompanying the 2025 Rule of Law Report on the rule of law situation in the European Union, Strasbourg, SWD (2025) 912 final.

GNPL. (2017). *Relazione al Parlamento.*

GNPL. (2018). *Relazione al Parlamento.*

GNPL. (2019). *Relazione al Parlamento.*

GNPL. (2020). *Relazione al Parlamento.*

GNPL. (2021). *Relazione al Parlamento.*

GNPL. (2022). *Relazione al Parlamento.*

GNPL. (2023a, March). *Documento di sintesi sui Cpr e sul Centro di prima accoglienza di Isola di Capo Rizzuto.*

GNPL. (2023b, June 8). *La definizione Onu di privazione della libertà.*

GNPL. (2023c). *Relazione al Parlamento.*

Grignetti, F. (2025, November 12). Il garante per la Privacy non si dimette e arriva un ruolo sui richiedenti asilo. Il governo stanzia dieci milioni per il monitoraggio in hotspot e questure. *La Stampa.*

Levitsky, S., & Ziblatt, D. (2019). *How democracies die*. Penguin.

Losito, G., & Pizzo, C. (2021). Genealogia di una nuova competenza. Il Garante nazionale dei diritti delle persone private della libertà e la disabilità. *Materiali per una storia della cultura giuridica, 10*(2), 445–457.

Manca, L. (2016). Il garante nazionale dei diritti dei detenuti e delle persone private della libertà. Alcune riflessioni alla luce del diritto internazionale. *Federalismi, 4*(3), 1–23.

Martini, E. (2025a, August 13). Carcere, il Garante: "Nordio contro la nostra autonomia". *il Manifesto.*

Martini, E. (2025b, December 13). Turrini Vita: "Carceri stremate, servono amnistia e indulto". *il Manifesto.*

Mellano, B., & Scomparin, L. (2020). Garantire i diritti di chi non ha libertà. *Il Piemonte Delle Autonomie, 7*(1), 1–15.

Milton, J. (1882), *Paradise lost* (G. Doré, Ill.; H. C. Walsh, Ed.). John W. Lovell Company.

Palma, M. (2009). Le figure di garanzia nella legislazione internazionale. Le esperienze europee, *I garanti e l'esecuzione della pena: quali prospettive? Atti del 2° Convegno Nazionale Coordinamento dei Garanti dei diritti delle persone private della libertà personale territoriali* (pp. 109–113).

Palma, M. (2022). Il Garante nazionale dei diritti delle persone private della libertà personale. *Rivista della Corte dei Conti—Quaderno n. 1/2022—Le Autorità Amministrative Indipendenti* (pp. 149–162).

Palma, M., de Robert, D., & Rossi, E. (2025). Il filo e il fuso. Editoriale scientifica. *Caro Parlamento,* 283–316.

Picozzi, F. (2021). I Garanti regionali dei detenuti nel riparto di competenza legislativa fra Stato e Regioni. *Queste Istituzioni, 20*(4), 45–60.

Ruotolo, M. (2025). Il rilievo costituzionale del Garante nazionale dei diritti delle persone private della libertà personale. *Caro Parlamento,* Editoriale scientifica, 1–12.

Scomparin, L. (2014). Dai garanti locali al garante nazionale. *Il Piemonte Delle Autonomie, 1*(3), 1–15.

Stella, V. (2025, November 11). Circolare del Dap, la più alta barriera tra dentro e fuori. *Il Dubbio.*

The Dutch NPM: A New Horizon for the Prevention of Torture and Other Cruel, Inhuman or Degrading Treatment or Punishment in the Netherlands?

Pauline Jacobs

1 Introduction

People who have been deprived of their liberty by the government find themselves in a dependent and vulnerable position vis-à-vis that government and the authorities of places of detention. Independent monitoring to prevent torture and inhuman or degrading treatment or punishment in such places is therefore of crucial importance. In 2010, the Netherlands took an important step towards promoting independent monitoring of deprivation of liberty by ratifying the Optional Protocol to the Convention against Torture and Other Cruel, Inhuman

The content of this chapter was finalised on 30 March 2026. This chapter is a revised version of the article Jacobs (2026) titled 'Het nationaal preventiemechanisme: een nieuwe horizon voor toezicht op vrijheidsbeneming in Nederland?' in the Dutch Journal for Human Rights (*Nederlands Tijdschrift voor Mensenrechten*, NTM), no 51–2.

P. Jacobs (✉)
Tilburg University, Tilburg, The Netherlands
e-mail: p.jacobs@tilburguniversity.edu

T. Daems et al. (eds.), *Preventing Torture and Monitoring Places of Detention*,
https://doi.org/10.1007/978-3-032-28285-9_6

or Degrading Treatment or Punishment (hereinafter: OPCAT) of the United Nations (hereinafter: UN).[1]

Following ratification of the OPCAT by the Netherlands in December 2011, the State Secretary for Security and Justice announced how the NPM would take shape. According to the State Secretary, there was no need to establish a new body, as monitoring at national level was already guaranteed by various existing inspectorates and supervisory committees.[2] It was therefore decided not to create a new NPM, but to organise the NPM in the form of a network, involving several existing monitoring and advisory organisations. Initially, there were six such organisations,[3] but after some changes, three bodies ultimately remained as designated NPMs: the Council for the Administration of Criminal Justice and Youth Protection (*Raad voor Strafrechtstoepassing en Jeugdbescherming*, RSJ), the current Health and Youth Care Inspectorate (*Inspectie Gezondheidszorg en Jeugd*, formerly the Youth Care Inspectorate and the Health Care Inspectorate) and the current Justice and Security Inspectorate (*Inspectie Justitie en Veiligheid*, formerly the Security and Justice Inspectorate). The coordination of the NPM was assigned to the Inspectorate for Justice and Security, which also made it responsible for consultation between the NPM partners. In addition, four bodies were mentioned that did not receive NPM status but participated in the NPM consultations as associate observers: the Commission of Oversight for Penitentiaries, the Commission of Oversight for Police Cells, the Commission of Oversight for Military Detention and the National Ombudsman. These associate observers would complement the work of the NPM, ensuring wide coverage of places of detention. While not officially holding NPM status, these observers were given the mandate

---

[1] Trb. 2010, 273, November 2010. The UN General Assembly in New York adopted the OPCAT on 18 December 2002.

[2] Letter 'Aanwijzen Nationale Preventie Mechanismen (NPM's) op basis van VN-OPCAT', 20 December 2011.

[3] These were the Inspectorate for the Enforcement of Sanctions (*Inspectie voor de Sanctietoepassing*, ISt), the Commission for Integral Supervision of Return (*Commissie Integraal Toezicht Terugkeer*, CITT), the Inspectorate for Public Order and Safety (*Inspectie Openbare orde en Veiligheid*, IOVV), the Inspectorate for Health Care (*Inspectie voor de Gezondheidszorg*, IGZ), the Inspectorate for Youth Care (*Inspectie Jeugdzorg*, IJZ) and the Council for the Administration of Criminal Justice and Youth Protection (*Raad voor Strafrechtstoepassing en Jeugdbescherming*, RSJ).

to participate in NPM meetings and to communicate concerns to the NPM.[4]

The letter also states that designation as an NPM does not entail any new powers for the organisations concerned and that no additional resources will be made available for the performance of NPM tasks (Jacobs & van Kalmthout, 2015; Schellekens et al., 2022).[5]

Since the designation of the Dutch NPM, it has received much criticism. In the literature, Van Gerven-Mandjes (2011) stated that the monitoring authorities involved did not (all) meet (all) the OPCAT requirements. In addition, she concluded that the content and design of the monitoring was lacking in a number of areas and did not seem to provide for adequate monitoring in all situations (Van Gerven-Mandjes, 2011).[6] In the years that followed, other authors in the literature also concluded that the Dutch NPM is problematic in light of the requirements set by the OPCAT for the NPM (Fernando, 2016; Jacobs & van Kalmthout, 2015). As a result of the NPM's inadequate functioning, the National Ombudsman announced in September 2014 that it would withdraw from the NPM.[7] The Council for the Administration of Criminal Justice and Youth Protection followed in 2016 announcing that it was no longer able to fulfil the original instruction to participate in the NPM.[8] In addition, criticism also came from international and European monitoring bodies, such as the SPT and the Council of Europe's Committee for the Prevention of Torture and Inhuman or Degrading Treatment or Punishment (hereinafter: CPT).[9] The criticism focused on, among other things, the poor safeguarding of the independence of the

---

[4] SPT, Report on the visit of the SPT to the Netherlands for the purpose of providing advisory assistance to the national preventive mechanism: recommendations and observations addressed to the State party, *UN Doc.* CAT/OP/NLD/1, 3 November 2016.

[5] Letter 'Aanwijzen Nationale Preventie Mechanismen (NPM's) op basis van VN-OPCAT', 20 December 2011.

[6] As places lacking adequate monitoring were identified detention rooms ('ophoudkamers'), police cells and court cells.

[7] Letter from the National Ombudsman, 24 July 2014, ref. no. 2014 0273.

[8] Letter from the RSJ to the organisations involved in the National Preventive Mechanism, 10 November 2014, ref. no. RSJ/100/2306/14/AvB/HE.

[9] SPT, Report on the visit made by the SPT for the purpose of providing advisory assistance to the National Preventive Mechanism of the Kingdom of the Netherlands, *UN Doc.* CAT/OP/NLD/R.1, 16 March 2016; CPT/Inf (2012) 21, para. 9.

NPM, its lack of visibility, its lack of financial resources and staff, and the fact that the NPM and its tasks are not legally defined.

After all this criticism, the Dutch NPM was in a state of deadlock for a long time. Since 2019, an investigation has been conducted into whether the current structure of the NPM is still the best one.[10] In 2021, the Ministry of Justice and Security commissioned the consultancy firm Berenschot to investigate the possibility of placing the NPM mandate within the Netherlands Institute for Human Rights (hereinafter: the Institute) (Schellekens et al., 2022).[11] Finally, on 27 September 2023, outgoing Minister Weerwind (Legal Protection) informed the House of Representatives of the cabinet's decision to designate the Netherlands Institute for Human Rights (*College voor de Rechten van de Mens*) as the NPM as of 1 April 2024.[12] This is in line with the choice made by the vast majority of OPCAT ratifying States Parties, which have designated their national human rights institutions as (part of) the NPM (Fernando, 2016).

The new NPM was launched on 1 April 2024. Six NPM visit reports have been published to date. The first annual report for 2024 of the new NPM was published in July 2025, which elaborates on its visits and reflects on its activities, working methods, background and future of the NPM. The NPM published a thematic report on segregation and isolation in forensic psychiatric centres (FPCs) and penitentiary psychiatric centres (PPCs) in January 2026 where it also makes recommendations to actors other than the institutions already visited, as stated in the annual report.[13] Now it is time to take stock. Does the 'new NPM' meet the requirements of the OPCAT? In this contribution, I will first consider the requirements that apply to NPMs as set out in the OPCAT. I will

---

[10] NPM, Annual Report 2021, p. 4.

[11] The possibility of involving the Netherlands Institute for Human Rights in the Dutch NPM network that existed at the time was already explored by Fernando (2016).

[12] Parliamentary Papers II, 2023/24, 33,826, no. 52.

[13] Penitentiary Psychiatric Centres (PPCs) are parts of a penitentiary institution where prisoners with psychiatric problems are housed. Forensic Psychiatric Centres (FPCs) are closed judicial institutions with a high security level, where patients stay who have been sentenced to compulsory treatment. NPM, Report on isolation in FPCs and PPCs, 29 January 2026, https://publicaties.mensenrechten.nl/publicatie/32ab7229-0455-44c2-8125-27776a4a8031; NPM, Annual Report 2024, p. 6.

then discuss the structure, organisation and activities of the new NPM. I will then consider these in light of the requirements set by the OPCAT. I will conclude with conclusions and recommendations.[14]

2 The Requirements Imposed on the NPM Under the OPCAT

The requirements imposed on the NPM are set out in the OPCAT. The standards set out in the OPCAT have been further elaborated in guidelines issued by the SPT[15] and the Association for the Prevention of Torture (hereinafter: APT).[16] The SPT has noted that these guidelines are not intended to repeat what is already stated in the text of the OPCAT, but to provide greater clarity about the SPT's expectations regarding the establishment and operation of NPMs.[17]

The OPCAT provides for a preventive system of periodic visits to persons deprived of their liberty with a view to strengthening the protection of these persons against torture and other cruel, inhuman or degrading treatment or punishment, where necessary (Article 4, paragraph 1). Article 4(2) of the OPCAT stipulates that this applies to any place where persons are or may be detained under the jurisdiction and influence of the Member State, either by order or at the instigation of the public authorities or with their consent or acquiescence (hereinafter

[14] In order to gain a clear understanding of the activities and working methods of the current NPM, this chapter draws on an interview conducted for this contribution with Anne van Eijndhoven, team leader of the Dutch NPM, in addition to the desk research. This semi-structured interview took place on 8 October 2025. Anne van Eijndhoven also provided feedback on an earlier version of this contribution. The author is very grateful for her willingness to share her insights and to provide feedback.

[15] SPT, Guidelines on National Preventive Mechanisms, *UN Doc.* CAT/OP/12/5, 9 December 2010.

[16] APT, The Optional Protocol Implementation Manual, 2010, revised edition. The APT is an international non-governmental organisation that focuses on preventing torture and other acts considered cruel, inhuman or degrading treatment.

[17] SPT, Guidelines on National Preventive Mechanisms, *UN Doc.* CAT/OP/12/5, 9 December 2010, under 3. In addition, the SPT has developed an analytical self-assessment tool for NPMs: SPT, Analytical self-assessment tool for National Prevention Mechanisms (NPM), 25 January 2016, *UN Doc.* CAT/OP/1/Rev.1.

referred to as places of detention). The OPCAT thus contains a broad definition of deprivation of liberty and therefore covers more than just criminal detention. Furthermore, the aforementioned places of detention are not only places where persons are actually deprived of their liberty, but also places where persons may be deprived of their liberty. This means that the power to monitor also exists when there is a suspicion that people are being detained in a place. This definition also recognises that deprivation of liberty can take place in both public and private institutions (Van Gerven-Mandjes, 2011).[18]

Based on Article 3 of the OPCAT, each Member State shall establish, designate or maintain at the national level an NPM for the prevention of torture and other cruel, inhuman or degrading treatment or punishment. The NPM should complement existing monitoring systems and should not replace them or prevent the establishment or functioning of other such complementary systems.[19] Under Article 17, Member States are required to establish an NPM no later than one year after the entry into force or ratification of the OPCAT. This does not necessarily mean that a new body has to be established; existing mechanisms may also be designated as NPMs, as stated in the second sentence of this article.[20]

Although the OPCAT does not prescribe a specific form for the NPM, Articles 18–20 of the OPCAT require the NPM to meet certain criteria and have certain powers with regard to its mandate.

In order to effectively prevent torture and other cruel, inhuman or degrading treatment or punishment, it is essential that NPMs are independent. Article 18 contains provisions to ensure that the NPM can carry out its tasks without government interference. Furthermore, Article 18(4) contains a specific reference to the principles relating to the status of national institutions for the promotion and protection of human rights of the UN, known as the 'Paris Principles'.[21] The Paris Principles

---

[18] SPT, General Comment No. 1 (2024) on Article 4 of the Optional Protocol (Places of Deprivation of Liberty), *UN Doc.* CAT/OP/GC/1, 4 July 2024.

[19] SPT, Guidelines on National Preventive Mechanisms, *UN Doc.* CAT/OP/12/5, 9 December 2010, under 5 ('basic principles').

[20] Whichever form is chosen, the starting point is that the NPM must be fully in line with the requirements set out in the OPCAT. APT, The Optional Protocol Implementation Manual, 2010, revised edition, p. 86.

[21] Paris Principles, UN Doc. GA Res 48/134, 20 December 1993.

set out conditions that institutions for the promotion and protection of human rights must meet. The APT has indicated that the requirements for NPMs, as laid down in Article 18, should be interpreted with the Paris Principles in mind.[22] Under Article 18, the Member State must guarantee the functional independence of the NPM, as well as the independence of NPM staff. In practice, functional independence means that NPMs must be able to act independently and without interference from public authorities. The SPT has emphasised that the NPM must enjoy full financial and operational autonomy in carrying out its tasks under the OPCAT.[23] An important aspect of independence is that NPMs are perceived as independent from public authorities.[24] Therefore, NPM members should be appointed through a public procedure, in consultation with relevant stakeholders, and the SPT recommends that an NPM be established by means of a constitutional or legislative text describing its main elements, including the mandate and powers of the body, the appointment procedure for staff and members, the term of office, funding and accountability.[25]

Article 18(3) also stipulates that the States Parties shall take the necessary measures to ensure that the experts of the NPM have the required skills and professional knowledge. It is obvious that this refers to knowledge of the relevant international human rights, but given the mandate and the fact that the NPM may visit many different places of detention, including (forensic) psychiatric institutions, nursing homes and hospitals, this may also refer to expertise in the field of medical care, psychology and psychiatry. The Member State shall take all necessary measures to ensure that the experts of the NPM have the required capacities and professional knowledge. A balanced gender distribution and adequate representation of ethnic and minority groups in the country shall also be sought (paragraph 2). The SPT guidelines clarify on this

---

22 APT, The Optional Protocol Implementation Manual, 2010, revised edition, p. 89.

23 SPT, Guidelines on National Preventive Mechanisms, *UN Doc.* CAT/OP/12/5, 9 December 2010, under 12.

24 APT, The Optional Protocol Implementation Manual, 2010, revised edition, p. 89.

25 APT, The Optional Protocol Implementation Manual, 2010, revised edition, p. 89, with references.

point that the NPM must ensure that its staff have the necessary diversity of backgrounds, skills and professional knowledge to properly fulfil its NPM mandate.[26]

Under Article 18(3), the Member State must provide the necessary resources for the functioning of the national preventive mechanisms. Sufficient financial, human and logistical resources are essential for the effective performance of the NPM's preventive tasks. In line with the Paris Principles, financial autonomy is seen as a fundamental condition for independence: without financial autonomy, NPMs cannot exercise operational autonomy or independence in decision-making.[27]

In order to be able to carry out its monitoring tasks properly, Article 19 stipulates that the NPM must at least have the power to (a) periodically visit persons deprived of their liberty with a view to strengthening their protection against torture and other cruel, inhuman or degrading treatment or punishment, where necessary; (b) make recommendations to the relevant authorities with a view to improving the treatment and conditions of persons deprived of their liberty and preventing torture and other cruel, inhuman or degrading treatment or punishment, taking into account the relevant UN standards; and (c) submit proposals and comments on existing or draft legislation.

With regard to the monitoring power referred to in (a), the OPCAT does not specify how often visits should take place. NPMs can therefore tailor the frequency of visits to the challenges in the national context.[28] In this light, the SPT has emphasised that the NPM should plan its activities and use its resources in such a way that places where deprivation of liberty occurs are visited in such a manner and with sufficient frequency as to make an effective contribution to the prevention of torture and other cruel, inhuman or degrading treatment or punishment.[29]

---

[26] SPT, Guidelines on National Preventive Mechanisms, *UN Doc.* CAT/OP/12/5, 9 December 2010, para. 20.

[27] APT, The Optional Protocol Implementation Manual, 2010, revised edition, p. 91, with references.

[28] APT, The Optional Protocol Implementation Manual, 2010, revised edition, pp. 92–93.

[29] SPT, Guidelines on National Preventive Mechanisms, *UN Doc.* CAT/OP/12/5, 9 December 2010, para. 34.

As a result of the provision under (b), NPMs are authorised to make recommendations to the relevant authorities in order to improve the treatment and conditions of persons deprived of their liberty and to prevent torture and other cruel, inhuman or degrading treatment or punishment. This means that NPMs are not only authorised to identify shortcomings within places of detention, but also to identify any structural weaknesses or gaps in legislation relating to the protection of persons deprived of their liberty. The provision to make recommendations is therefore not limited to observations made after a visit to a place of detention.[30] According to the SPT guidelines, NPMs should further engage in a follow-up process with the national authorities to implement the NPM's recommendations.[31]

The preventive approach to torture and other cruel, inhuman or degrading treatment or punishment is further strengthened by the NPM's power under provision (c) to review existing and proposed legislation relating to places of detention and persons deprived of their liberty. For example, an NPM may review legislation against international standards to determine whether it adequately promotes the protection of persons deprived of their liberty.[32] In order to exercise the power referred to in (c), the SPT has included in the guidelines for NPMs that the state must inform the NPM of any draft legislation under consideration that is relevant to its mandate and must enable the NPM to make proposals or comments on any existing or proposed policy or legislation.[33]

The fact that the OPCAT system attaches great importance to monitoring at the national level is evident from the fact that the mandate of the NPM is very similar to that of the SPT (as described in Article 14 of the OPCAT). In order to adequately fulfil its mandate, Article 20 of the OPCAT requires the Member State to provide the NPM with:

---

30 APT, The Optional Protocol Implementation Manual, 2010, revised edition, p. 93.

31 SPT, Guidelines on National Preventive Mechanisms, *UN Doc.* CAT/OP/12/5, 9 December 2010, under 13.

32 APT, The Optional Protocol Implementation Manual, 2010, revised edition, pp. 93–94.

33 SPT, Guidelines on National Preventive Mechanisms, *UN Doc.* CAT/OP/12/5, 9 December 2010, para. 28.

a. access to all information concerning the number of persons deprived of their liberty in the Member State, as well as the number of establishments and their location;
b. access to all information concerning the treatment of those persons and the conditions of detention;
c. access to all places of detention and their facilities and equipment;
d. the opportunity to hold confidential conversations without witnesses with persons deprived of their liberty, either in person or through an interpreter if deemed necessary, as well as with any other person whom the national preventive mechanism considers could provide relevant information;
e. full freedom to choose the places they wish to visit and the persons they wish to interview.

In addition, the NPM has the right to maintain contact with the SPT, to send it information and to meet with it (under f).

The guarantees provided by Article 20 are fundamental to the effective functioning of NPMs. They enable NPMs to conduct thorough and comprehensive investigations of domestic preventive frameworks without interference from public authorities, and to build up an accurate picture of the level of protection afforded to persons deprived of their liberty.[34] The SPT guidelines state, with regard to NPM visits, that the state must ensure that the NPM can carry out visits in the manner and with the frequency determined by the NPM itself. This includes the possibility of conducting confidential interviews with persons deprived of their liberty and the right to make unannounced visits at any time to all places where deprivation of liberty occurs, in accordance with the provisions of the OPCAT.[35]

The mandate and working methods of the NPM, as set out in the provisions of the OPCAT, are very similar to those of the Council of Europe's CPT. The CPT's task is to prevent violations of Article 3 of

[34] APT, The Optional Protocol Implementation Manual, 2010, revised edition, p. 95.

[35] SPT, Guidelines on National Preventive Mechanisms, *UN Doc.* CAT/OP/12/5, 9 December 2010, para. 25.

the ECHR, the prohibition of torture, inhuman and degrading treatment and punishment in cases of deprivation of liberty. To this end, the CPT visits establishments where people are deprived of their liberty in the member states of the Council of Europe. An important part of this working method is the (random) examination of prisoners' files, talking to prisoners and investigating the activities offered to prisoners. Cross-checking information is of great importance in this regard (Jacobs & Van Kalmthout, 2015).

On the basis of Article 22 of the OPCAT, the competent authorities of the member state must examine the recommendations of the national preventive mechanism and engage in dialogue on possible implementation measures. Under Article 23, the State Party is also obliged to publish and disseminate the NPM's annual reports. Reports following the visit, including the recommendations made, may be published without the prior consent of the national authorities. This is in contrast to the reports of the CPT and the SPT, which are confidential in nature and whose publication is decided by the national authorities themselves (Jacobs & Van Kalmthout, 2015).

3 The New NPM—Structure and Working Methods

As stated earlier, since 1 April 2024, the NPM tasks have been performed by the Netherlands Institute for Human Rights. The decision to designate the Netherlands Institute for Human Rights as the NPM was explained on 27 September 2023 by the outgoing Minister for Legal Protection, Weerwind, in a letter to the House of Representatives.[36] This letter states that the minister has deliberately chosen to assign the NPM task to a single party, because this party has the entire mandate, rather than opting for a form in which several parties have part of the

[36] Parliamentary Papers II, 2023/24, 33,826, no. 52, p. 2.

mandate. According to the minister, this also better guarantees independence, which he states is an important requirement for the proper performance of the NPM task.[37]

The minister further states that there are several arguments in favour of assigning the NPM mandate to the Netherlands Institute for Human Rights. Firstly, the tasks of the NPM—monitoring compliance with a human rights treaty—are in line with the existing statutory tasks and activities of the Netherlands Institute for Human Rights. The Netherlands Institute for Human Rights also has considerable expertise in the field of assessing actual cases against human rights. Furthermore, the Netherlands Institute for Human Rights already has almost the entire legal mandate required for the NPM, including visiting locations, requesting the desired information and speaking to all persons it deems necessary for the investigation. Finally, the Netherlands Institute for Human Rights enjoys A status in accordance with the UN Paris Principles. This means that the Netherlands Institute for Human Rights is entitled to participate in all consultations on human rights at the UN and that it meets the UN's requirements for independence.[38] In the letter it is furthermore stated that a member with specific expertise in the field of the NPM will be appointed to the Netherlands Institute for Human Rights and that a team will be set up to support this member. An amendment to the Netherlands Institute for Human Rights Act (*Wet College voor de rechten van de mens*)[39] will also be prepared in order to explicitly mention the NPM task in the Act and to regulate a number of additional powers. Pending the amendment to the Act, the Netherlands Institute for Human Rights can already start working as an NPM, because the NPM task fits within the current tasks and powers of the NPM. Nevertheless, the Minister has opted for an amendment to the

[37] Parliamentary Papers II, 2023/24, 33,826, no. 52, pp. 1–2.

[38] Parliamentary Papers II, 2023/24, 33,826, no. 52, p. 2. The fact that the Netherlands Institute for Human Rights has A status was an important argument in favour of assigning the NPM tasks to the Netherlands Institute for Human Rights rather than to the National Ombudsman, who had expressed a preference for assigning the NPM to the Ombudsman himself. Parliamentary Papers II, 2023/24, 33,826, no. 52, Decision memorandum accompanying the letter to Parliament concerning the National Prevention Mechanism, p. 2.

[39] This law entered into force on 17 December 2011, Stb. 2011, 573.

Act in order to properly safeguard the task within the Netherlands Institute for Human Rights.[40] In addition, based on the exploratory study, a budget for the NPM has been agreed with the Netherlands Institute for Human Rights. The costs are approximately 900,000 euros per year and the necessary funds have already been reserved in the budget of the Ministry of Justice and Security, the Minister indicates.[41]

Within the Netherlands Institute for Human Rights, the NPM currently is a separate team with staff members working solely for the NPM. The NPM has an independent position in the governance structure of the Institute and it has a designated budget that is not used for other activities. The member of the Institute that is appointed for the NPM is independently authorised to deal with NPM-related matters, including providing guidance on the NPM task, deciding on the main lines of policy regarding the NPM, holding consultations with relevant stakeholders (departments, other bodies, etc.) and signing agreements with third parties on behalf of the Institute regarding the NPM. The NPM member informs the executive board (*dagelijks bestuur*) and the general board (*algemeen bestuur*) of the Institute about relevant developments that affect the Institute's overall strategy and policy, or that may influence the organisation's positioning and image. The member also ensures sufficient coordination with the executive board regarding the relationship between NPM and other tasks of the Institute, in order to guarantee policy consistency.

With regard to the recruitment and selection of NPM members, it should be noted that the NPM, as part of the Netherlands Institute for Human Rights, operates on the basis of the Paris Principles. A number of factors were therefore explicitly taken into account in the recruitment and selection of a member for the NPM within the Netherlands Institute for Human Rights and the team members. For example, the vacancies were made public and widely advertised in order to reach as many potential candidates as possible. Efforts were also made to ensure diversity in

[40] Parliamentary Papers II, 2023/24, 33826, no. 52, p. 2 and Parliamentary Papers II, 2023/24, 33826, no. 52, Decision memorandum accompanying the letter to Parliament concerning the National Prevention Mechanism, p. 2.

[41] Parliamentary Papers II, 2023/24, 33,826, no. 52, Decision Memorandum accompanying the Letter to Parliament on the National Prevention Mechanism, p. 2.

terms of backgrounds and experience, so that the team could work in a multidisciplinary manner. This has resulted in a dedicated NPM team of 7 persons[42] (not all working full-time) which, despite its limited size, consists of professionals with different educational backgrounds, knowledge and experience. For example, members of the team have experience as a practitioner, in monitoring and academia. The team has methodological expertise and medical and legal knowledge. Nevertheless, the team is small and it is impossible to have all the relevant knowledge and experience within the team. The team has therefore set aside a budget for hiring knowledge and expertise to supplement the team where necessary, which can also be used for translation.[43] In addition, the NPM draws on expertise from the rest of the Institute, such as the communications officer, who for a small part of his appointment does NPM work.

According to the website, the scope of the Dutch NPM appears to extend to all places where persons are deprived of their liberty, as the website states that 'Our NPM task concerns situations of deprivation of liberty. This may involve prisons or police detention centres, but also immigration detention or secure care facilities'.[44] Although the OPCAT itself does not mention locations where only certain departments or rooms are places of deprivation of liberty (e.g. within a health care facility, such as a facility for elderly or a psychiatric ward within a psychiatric wing, where a part is open and a part is closed), this situation is also explicitly included in the NPM's mandate, according to the website.[45] Anne van Eijndhoven, team leader of the Dutch NPM, indicates that if a location is (temporarily) empty at the time (e.g. detention cells at a local police station where no suspects are present at the time of the visit), the NPM will still visit it if deemed useful, in accordance with the broad definition of deprivation of liberty as used in the OPCAT.

---

[42] Currently, the NPM team consists of one member of the Institute that is appointed for the NPM, one coordinator, three senior advisors, one advisor and one project officer.

[43] NPM, Annual Report 2024, pp. 22–23, https://publicaties.mensenrechten.nl/publicatie/5b6df4b9-e75d-44ea-bb3f-ddc945475900.

[44] NPM, *Which institutions do we supervise?*, https://www.mensenrechten.nl/themas/vrijheidsbeneming.

[45] NPM, *Which institutions do we supervise?*, https://www.mensenrechten.nl/themas/vrijheidsbeneming.

According to the 2024 annual report, the Dutch NPM considers the periodic investigation of the treatment of persons deprived of their liberty to be a core part of the work of an NPM.[46] To date, the NPM has completed twelve site visits, resulting in six visit reports.[47] In July 2025, the annual report for 2024 was published, which also reflects on the findings at the five institutions visited in 2024.[48] Besides, the NPM published a thematic report in January 2026.[49]

During the site visits, the NPM decided to focus on Penitentiary Psychiatric Centres (PPCs) and Forensic Psychiatric Centres (FPCs).[50] In addition to the general conditions at each location, during the first series of visits, the NPM chose to focus specifically on the manner and conditions of segregation and isolation. The choice of the theme of segregation arose from the fact that people who are placed in segregation are particularly vulnerable and dependent on others for almost everything.[51] In addition, a recent study (Shalev, 2024) had been conducted on prison isolation (solitary confinement) practices in the Netherlands, and the authorities were still in the process of implementing the recommendations from that study. By looking at the theme of segregation in different locations, the NPM was able to examine the similarities and differences, make recommendations for improvement and highlight the good examples it found.[52]

---

[46] NPM, Annual Report 2024, p. 4.

[47] Reports published following visits to Forensic Psychiatric Centre Rooyse Wissel in April 2024, Penitentiary Psychiatric Centre Haaglanden in September 2024, Zwolle Penitentiary Psychiatric Centre in June 2024, Forensic Psychiatric Centre Pompestichting in October 2024, Penitentiary Psychiatric Centre Vught in June 2024, Forensic Psychiatric Centre Van der Hoeven Clinic in February 2025 and August 2025. These reports, along with an easy read (a translation of the report into language that is as understandable as possible (B1 level)) and an English translation of some reports, have been published on the website https://www.mensenrechten.nl/themas/vrijheidsbeneming/npm-rapporten.

[48] NPM, Annual Report 2024, available at https://publicaties.mensenrechten.nl/publicatie/5b6df4b9-e75d-44ea-bb3f-ddc945475900.

[49] NPM, Report on isolation in FPCs and PPCs, 29 January 2026, https://publicaties.mensenrechten.nl/publicatie/32ab7229-0455-44c2-8125-27776a4a8031; NPM, Annual Report 2024, p. 6.

[50] NPM, Annual Report 2024, p. 4.

[51] NPM, Annual Report 2024, p. 4.

[52] NPM, Annual Report 2024, p. 4 and 22.

The approach taken by the NPM when conducting visits is reported in the 2024 annual report. This report indicates that a conscious decision was made not to conduct any unannounced visits this year. The annual report notes both advantages and disadvantages to unannounced visits. Unanticipated visits can have the advantage that the visited institution does not have time to make any adjustments before the visit, and sends the signal that inspections can take place at any time. However the NPM notes that unannounced visits limit the opportunities for both the NPM and the location to prepare properly, which means that the visit may be less efficient or less effective. Additionally, there is a high risk that relevant persons will not be present or available in the case of unscheduled visits, and it may provoke resistance at the location if the lack of notice is not necessary. These disadvantages have motivated the NPM's choice not to carry out unannounced visits this year. At the institutions visited, the NPM assessed that the likelihood of last-minute changes or adjustments due to the announcement was small to nil. And that if such changes did occur, the NPM would hear about them in conversations with patients. Moreover, the NPM is still working on building name awareness and the possibility to request information in advance benefited the quality of the investigation, according to the NPM.[53]

While conducting the on-site investigations, the NPM gathered information about the situation at the location of deprivation of liberty in question, including by looking around, talking to staff and talking to people deprived of their liberty. Prior to the visit, the NPM requested documents such as house rules, policies and relevant evaluations, as well as other information that could be relevant to the NPM. The NPM also had an information sheet about the NPM's mandate and the visit to the location posted in relevant departments in advance. In this way, the arrival of the NPM was announced and patients had the opportunity to contact the NPM on their own initiative and speak to them. In consultation with the institution concerned, the NPM indicated in advance which job groups it wanted to speak to during the visit. Prior to the

[53] NPM, Annual Report 2024, p. 5.

interview, these employees received an information leaflet explaining the NPM and the purpose of the interview.[54]

During the visit, the NPM spoke to the management of the location and was given a tour of relevant parts of the location. The NPM spoke to as many patients as possible and held several group discussions with employees. The NPM also visited various departments and, where present, the segregation ward. During several visits, the NPM reviewed patient files. The conversations with people deprived of their liberty were conducted in private, something that is mentioned as an important principle in the annual report. This meant that staff of the facility were not present or could not listen in on the conversations, unless the patient themselves preferred this. The location of the conversations varied: sometimes they took place in a consultation room on or near the wards, sometimes in a consultation room in the visiting area or in another separate room.[55]

After the visit, the NPM held a meeting with the institution to discuss the findings, approximately 6 to 8 weeks after the visit. These meetings focused on what was going well and on ways to reduce or eliminate risk factors for inhumane treatment. A summary of each visit report was also published in accessible language ('easy read') so that the findings would be accessible to as wide an audience as possible. The NPM distributed this 'easy read' version to patients at the relevant locations. English translations of the visit reports on FPC de Rooyse Wissel, PPC Zwolle and PPC Haaglanden have been published. The NPM also asked the management to formulate a written response to the recommendations within three months of the visit report's publication. On this basis, the NPM will continue to engage in dialogue with the institution about the steps taken or to be taken with regard to the recommendations. Following the visits carried out, a thematic report on segregation and isolation in FPCs and PPCs was published in January 2026. In the report, the NPM sets out eight key findings, along with corresponding recommendations and best practices.

[54] NPM, Annual Report 2024, p. 5.
[55] NPM, Annual Report 2024, p. 5.

In total, the NPM made 42 recommendations to the five locations it visited in 2024. The NPM has received an initial response to the recommendations from all institutions. In their responses to most of the recommendations, the institutions indicated that they would take steps to implement improvement measures. In order to keep its finger on the pulse, the NPM will discuss the progress made on these recommendations with the management teams approximately one year after the visit.[56]

Currently, NPM staff sometimes contribute to advice issued by the Netherlands Institute for Human Rights (which is not only the NPM, but also, for example, the monitoring body for the implementation of the UN Convention on the Rights of Persons with Disabilities). So legislative advice does take place, although this is mainly done by the Netherlands Institute for Human Rights, and is not explicitly put forward as legislative advice coming from the NPM. Anne van Eijndhoven indicates in this respect that the NPM's limited capacity is currently mainly focused on site visits and the resulting recommendations.

The 2024 annual report also covers the NPM's activities in the field of information and education. In the first year, the focus was on providing information about the NPM's mandate and tasks. To this end, various activities were undertaken to raise awareness of the NPM and share knowledge with relevant parties. An initial exploration was also conducted into educational opportunities for professionals who work with people who have been deprived of their liberty. In addition, the NPM held various discussions with the various national monitoring authorities, such as the Inspectorate of Justice and Security, the Inspectorate of Health and Youth Care and the Council for the Administration of Criminal Justice and Youth Protection, the National Ombudsman, the National Centre for Monitoring Committees on the Care of Detainees, and the core group of supervisory committees. The discussions focused on both procedural coordination—such as the exchange of data and locations of planned visits—and substantive exchange.[57] The NPM also had

---

56 NPM, Annual Report 2024, p. 16.

57 Until now, the NPM has not published any joint reports or press releases.

contact with the relevant ministries and various civil society organisations, among others.[58] International exchanges took place with other foreign NPMs and there was contact with the SPT and CPT.[59]

The 2024 annual report also reflects on the development of the NPM. It notes that the NPM is continuously evolving and that the first year was dominated by its establishment. Because the NPM consists of a relatively small team, choices have to be made about the focus of the NPM's attention. To this end, the NPM has established a number of criteria on the basis of which it sets priorities. It considers the seriousness of the problem (based on the seriousness of the (potential) infringement or violation, the size of the target group and/or the vulnerability of the target group), the added value of the NPM's activities compared to the work of other relevant actors, and the expected impact of the NPM's activities. Factors that may play a role here include whether there are developments that the NPM can link up with and how promising certain recommendations are. At the same time, the NPM may decide, on principle, to also develop activities where it does not expect short-term impact.[60]

In 2025, the NPM continued to build on its informative task and (further) invest in awareness-raising, among other things by engaging in a dialogue with professionals in the field about humane treatment and segregation; writing relevant publications, for example by giving lectures at seminars. In addition, the NPM held discussions with training institutes for professionals who work with people who have been deprived of their liberty. In 2025, the NPM conducted various preliminary explorations into different themes and sectors. Based on the assessment criteria that have been drawn up, these preliminary explorations will identify which themes, target groups and sectors should be given priority within the NPM in the coming years.[61]

In addition, it should be noted that the Netherlands Institute for Human Rights has taken on the NPM task, on condition that it is enshrined in the Netherlands Institute for Human Rights Act.

---

[58] NPM, Annual Report 2024, p. 19.

[59] NPM, Annual Report 2024, p. 21.

[60] NPM, Annual Report 2024, p. 22.

[61] NPM, Annual Report 2024, p. 24.

In the annual report, it is noted that a number of extensions of powers are also necessary in order to be able to carry out all NPM tasks in full, including breaking medical confidentiality so that the NPM team members can access all relevant medical information about patients, and being able to enter homes for on-site investigations. Also, the NPM notes that in the current situation the NPM is not authorised to carry out its activities in the Caribbean Netherlands, which results in an unjustified difference in legal protection for residents of the Caribbean Netherlands. The NPM's aim is to apply the OPCAT equally in the European and Caribbean Netherlands.[62]

4 The New NPM in Light of the OPCAT Requirements

By assigning the NPM tasks to the Netherlands Institute for Human Rights, the Minister recognises the added value of the monitoring body created by the OPCAT compared to the existing monitoring bodies. Assigning the NPM tasks to the Netherlands Institute for Human Rights provides better guarantees regarding independence (a much-criticised aspect of the old NPM due to the involvement of the inspectorates in the NPM). This independence is seen as an essential aspect of the NPM which must be emphasised in the NPM's actions and external communications in order to guarantee its (also perceived) independence. This independence seems to be well guaranteed in the current model, as the NPM currently acts as a separate entity and has its own logo. As indicated in paragraph 2, functional independence in practice means that NPMs must be able to act independently and without interference from government agencies. As stated earlier, the SPT has emphasised that the NPM must enjoy full financial and operational autonomy in carrying out its tasks under the OPCAT.[63] An important guarantee of independence would be that also the legal task, mandate and powers of the NPM,

---

[62] NPM, Annual Report 2024, p. 24.

[63] SPT, Guidelines on National Preventive Mechanisms, *UN Doc.* CAT/OP/12/5, 9 December 2010, under 12.

the appointment procedure for staff and members, the term of office, funding and accountability are laid down in law. In this light, it is important to note that currently a legislative proposal is pending to explicitly mention the NPM's tasks in the law and to regulate a number of additional powers. This legislative proposal aims to enable the NPM to carry out its mandate, as set out in Article 20 of the OPCAT, more effectively, primarily by allowing the NPM, without the resident's consent, to enter a residential area where a person is deprived of his liberty (for example, in the case of a residential area within a care institution) and, secondly, it enables the NPM to request information and documents that are relevant to the fulfilment of the NPM's duties. In the current situation, the NPM can only access medical records with the consent of patients, who are not always willing or able to give their consent (e.g. due to their mental state). The legislative proposal provides that, where necessary for the performance of the NPM's duties, medical confidentiality may be breached in order to access (medical) records. Such a power to inspect the files of clients held in places of detention was already enshrined in law for the SPT and CPT as of 1 July 2025.[64] This power would enable the NPM to conduct a thorough and comprehensive investigation into the treatment of persons deprived of their liberty, as envisaged by the OPCAT. The extension of the power to visit a residential area where a person is deprived of his liberty without his consent must also be viewed in this light. In its advice on the legislative proposal, the Council for the Administration of Criminal Justice and Youth Protection noted that further safeguards are required to ensure the responsible use of the new powers and has made a number of recommendations relating primarily to the scope of the new powers for the NPM, and has emphasised that the powers should only be used when strictly necessary.[65]

The working method used by the NPM before, during and after visits to places of detention is very much in line with the requirements set out by the OPCAT. This working method is characterised by an approach

---

[64] *Kamerstukken I 2024/25,* 36 579, *A.*

[65] Council for the Administration of Criminal Justice and Youth Protection, *Advies Wijziging van de Wet College voor de rechten van de mens ten behoeve van de verankering van de taak en bevoegdheden van het College voor de Rechten van de Mens als Nationaal Preventie Mechanisme*, d.d. 10 February 2026, p. 5.

that prioritises the preventive identification of risks of torture and other cruel, inhuman or degrading treatment or punishment. This is done by visiting places of detention, where meetings and conversations with detainees play an important role and the available protocols, policy documents and systematically recorded information about the detainees are consulted. By issuing a report following the visit, asking the management to formulate a written response to the recommendations within three months of the visit report's publication, and continuing to engage in dialogue with the institution about the steps taken or to be taken with regard to the recommendations, the NPM provides a follow-up procedure that encourages the sustainable embedding of the recommendations in policy and practice.

5 Conclusions and Recommendations

The Dutch NPM has been in a dormant state for years. By choosing to assign the NPM task to the Netherlands Institute for Human Rights, the way has been paved to exploit the potential of the monitoring body at the national level as envisaged in the OPCAT.

Since 2024, the NPM has demonstrated its commitment to its task by conducting six visits to PPCs and FPCs, during which, in addition to the general conditions at each location, specific attention was paid to the manner and conditions of segregation. This is an important theme, as people who are isolated and separated are vulnerable to human rights violations, and there is a focus at European and international human rights level on reducing this in the prison system, due to the harmful effects it has on the mental and physical health of prisoners.[66] By choosing this theme, the NPM has explicitly opted for an an approach that ties in with changes already underway at the national level to take a (more) critical look at the practice of segregation in Dutch prisons. The NPM has also chosen a theme that lies at the intersection

[66] See, among others, Shalev (2008). The increased attention to this theme is evident, among other things, in the most recent revision of the European Prison Rules, which devotes considerable attention to the solitary confinement of prisoners, as evidenced by the inclusion of Articles 53A to 53D and 60.6. For more information, see Jacobs (2021).

of security and care, a theme that is well suited to the multidisciplinary approach reflected in the composition of the NPM. The reasons for this thematic approach are therefore easy to understand. A question can be whether such thematic focus is in line with what a NPM should do in light of the broad mandate that NPMs have on the basis of the OPCAT. If in the future (also) a thematic approach is chosen, from an (international) human rights perspective, the choice could be made to focus on high-security regimes in the prison system, closed youth care facilities, life imprisonment and immigration detention. These aspects of Dutch detention have been criticised in recent years by national and international advisory and monitoring bodies. However, such a thematic approach that is based on risks carries the risk that certain institutions or departments will not be visited, or will be visited very rarely, if such risks are not yet known or identified in those places. In addition, it may be obvious for the NPM to focus on issues that have not (yet) received much attention from other monitoring bodies, such as deprivation of liberty within elderly care. It will therefore be interesting to see whether the NPM will maintain its thematic approach and, if so, on which issues or sectors the NPM will focus in the coming years.

As stated earlier, the working method used during the visits clearly reflects the working method derived from the OPCAT, with the international standards framework serving as a guide. Conducting visits, which the NPM rightly describes as a core part of its task, has become a reality. It should be noted, however, that so far these have always been announced visits, which can be explained by the NPM's efforts in raising its profile. In order to be able to carry out unannounced visits successfully, the existence of the NPM must be well-known nationally among institutions that may be visited. Once the existence of the NPM is well-known nationally, it would be beneficial to start carrying out unannounced visits (as well), because of their potential preventive effect.

What distinguishes the NPM from other national monitoring bodies and makes it unique is its assessment framework, in which the international human rights framework plays a prominent role, its preventive nature by identifying risks of torture and other cruel, inhuman or degrading treatment or punishment, the multidisciplinary team that can make both announced and unannounced visits to all places where people are deprived of their liberty, with meetings with detainees playing an important role during the visit, and the consultation of all available systematic information about the detainees.

The OPCAT has created a unique triangular relationship in international law between the SPT, the NPM and the State Party (Van Gerven-Mandjes, 2011). However, the question arises as to what role the CPT plays in this context. In principle, the CPT falls outside this triangular relationship, but it has a mandate and preventive role similar to that of the NPM. The CPT's refined standards framework and the reports following its visits provide states with concrete tools for improving situations involving deprivation of liberty. Given that the CPT is only able to visit each member state once every four to five years, it would be interesting to examine more closely whether and, if so, what role the NPM could play in monitoring compliance with the CPT's recommendations. In addition, the future will tell whether the NPM will be able to give shape and substance to another task arising from the OPCAT, namely submitting proposals and comments on existing or draft legislation. Currently, NPM staff occasionally contribute to advice issued by the Netherlands Institute for Human Rights (which is not only the NPM, but also, for example, the monitoring body for the implementation of the UN Convention on the Rights of Persons with Disabilities). Accordingly, legislative advice does take place, although this is not explicitly put forward as legislative advice coming from the NPM, and the NPM's contribution is not explicitly mentioned in the legislative advice. If consideration is given to implementing this NPM task (further), the question of the added value of the NPM's advice compared to that of the Council for the Administration of Criminal Justice and Youth Protection should also be explicitly addressed, given that the Council for the Administration of Criminal Justice and Youth Protection already advises (upon request or on its own initiative) on public policy subjects and proposed legislation, on subjects such as the prison system, the forensic care system, youth protection and the probation and aftercare service.

The working method and unique mandate mean that the arrival of the NPM has opened up new horizons for the monitoring of deprivation of liberty in the Netherlands. The NPM has great potential to contribute to improving detention conditions in the Caribbean Netherlands.

It is therefore encouraging to see that the current legislative proposal aims to amend the Netherlands Institute for Human Rights Act to extend the application of the act to the public entities of Bonaire, Saba and Sint Eustatius. It is to be recommended that in the coming time efforts are being made to apply the OPCAT equally in the European and Caribbean Netherlands to (further) broaden the horizon for the prevention of torture and other cruel, inhuman or degrading treatment or punishment.

References

Fernando, R. (2016). Het Nederlandse nationaal preventiemechanisme: Herstructurering gewenst? De rol van het College voor de Rechten van de Mens bij de waarborging van de OPCAT-normen. *NTM/NJCM-Bulletin, 4*, 429–449.

Jacobs, P. (2021). De Europese Gevangenisregels zijn vernieuwd: Oude wijn in nieuwe zakken of inspiratie voor verandering? *Sancties*, 2, 95–105.

Jacobs, P. (2026). Het nationaal preventiemechanisme: een nieuwe horizon voor toezicht op vrijheidsbeneming in Nederland? *Nederlands Tijdschrift voor Mensenrechten*, 51(2), 214–229.

Jacobs, P., & van Kalmthout, A. M. (2015). Toezicht op vrijheidsbeneming in Nederland. CAT in de zak? *Nederlands Juristenblad, 12*, 752–757.

Schellekens, G., van den Hoef, J., Valks, R., Boot, J., & Stockmann, E. (2022). *Meer dan de som der delen? Verkenning NPM*. Berenschot.

Shalev, S. (2008). *A sourcebook on solitary confinement*. Mannheim Centre for Criminology, London School of Economics.

Shalev, S. (2023). *'Iso': Perspectives on prison isolation in the Netherlands*. University of Oxford.

Van Gerven-Mandjes, S. (2011). Het Nederlandse nationaal preventiemechanisme langs de opcat-lat. De resultaten van een onderzoek naar de implementatie van het Facultatief Protocol bij het Verdrag tegen foltering en andere wrede, onmenselijke of onterende behandeling of bestraffing in Nederland. *NTM/NJCM-Bulletin, 8*, 849–865.

The United Kingdom's National Preventive Mechanism: Lessons in Coordination and Collaboration

Sam Gluckstein and Sarah Rennie

1 Introduction

In the United Kingdom, torture is broadly defined as the subjection of a person to severe physical or mental suffering.[1] This is not limited to extreme interrogation tactics, rather torture and ill-treatment can arise out of conditions or treatment in places of deprivation of liberty, such as excessive time in-cell, excessive time without human contact, poor fabric of buildings and insufficient access to food, water, healthcare and advocacy or information. These factors can amount to violations of the fundamental rights set out in the Convention against Torture and

[1] Section 134, Criminal Justice Act 1988, https://www.legislation.gov.uk/ukpga/1988/33/contents.

S. Gluckstein (✉) · S. Rennie
UK NPM, London, UK
e-mail: Sam.Gluckstein.OIP@outlook.com

S. Rennie
e-mail: sarah.rennie@hmiprisons.gov.uk

T. Daems et al. (eds.), *Preventing Torture and Monitoring Places of Detention*,
https://doi.org/10.1007/978-3-032-28285-9_7

Other Cruel, Inhuman or Degrading Treatment or Punishment. The UK NPM works to proactively prevent this treatment in all settings of deprivation of liberty in line with the Optional Protocol to the United Nations Convention against Torture (OPCAT). It seeks to drive standards and improvements for detained people and works independently, but constructively, with decision-makers to challenge poor treatment and bring a voice to some of the most vulnerable in society.

The UK NPM is the largest and most complex NPM structure in the world, with 21 statutory bodies, which brings both challenges and opportunities to effectively implement the mandate. Adding to this complexity, the UK is made up of nations with their own parliaments and executives. Across the country, justice and health portfolios are devolved to varying extents in Scotland, Northern Ireland and Wales. Immigration and military detention remain reserved matters and are monitored across the UK by the England and Wales bodies.

The UK's deprivation of liberty landscape is one of continuing and deepening concern. In too many settings, the same systemic problems recur, and conditions that fall far short of international and domestic human rights standards have become normalised.[2] In the prison estate, overcrowding and decay have deepened, with staff and local leaders striving against impossible odds to maintain safety and decency. In immigration detention, violence, self-harm and indefinite detention have all increased significantly, with growing evidence of poor mental health and deteriorating safety for detainees. In secure mental health establishments, we are seeing individuals detained for years in settings that are neither therapeutic nor appropriate. The UK NPM's preventive mandate is needed now more than ever to safeguard the rights of people in places where they are most vulnerable and least visible.

This chapter explores the UK NPM's unique structure, examining how its complexity shapes both opportunities and obstacles in fulfilling its preventive mandate. It highlights the collaborative approach at the heart of the UK NPM's work, demonstrating how 21 statutory bodies coordinate across jurisdictions and settings to safeguard rights in places of

[2] UK NPM, Monitoring Places of Detention—16th Annual Report of the United Kingdom's National Preventive Mechanism, 2025, https://nationalpreventivemechanism.org.uk/document/sixteenth-annual-report-2024-25/.

deprivation of liberty, and details the challenges of a multi-body NPM, and how the UK NPM works to mitigate these.

2 The UK NPM: Origins and Structure

The UK ratified the OPCAT in December 2003 and established the NPM in March 2009. The UK NPM is a complex, multi-body structure designed to fulfil the preventive obligations enshrined in OPCAT.

Upon designating an NPM, the UK had an already established network of national oversight bodies whose statutory mandates aligned with the preventive functions envisaged under the OPCAT. Scrutiny of some places of detention pre-existed the ratification of the OPCAT, and so in establishing the NPM the UK had to consider how to embed and grow the preventive mandate envisaged by the OPCAT with bodies that had long oversight histories. Rather than constructing an entirely new national institution, the UK adopted a distributed model, selecting these pre-existing bodies as members of the UK NPM. This approach recognised that the existing powers and responsibilities of these bodies, particularly their authority to carry out unannounced visits to places of deprivation of liberty, met the requirements set out in Articles 19 and 20 of the OPCAT. At its formation, the UK NPM comprised 18 bodies, which were officially designated by the UK Government. Three new designations to the UK NPM were made in 2013, one being a merger of two existing bodies, and in 2017, the final NPM body was formally designated, consolidating NPM membership at 21 bodies.

As of November 2025, the UK NPM remains a 21-body mechanism with an estimated network of 3500 people (including staff and volunteers) carrying out the OPCAT mandate across the various jurisdictions within the UK. Each NPM body is endowed with its own powers to independently inspect or monitor places of deprivation of liberty and, collectively, these bodies cover an array of detention settings, including prisons, young offender institutions (YOIs), police and court custody, secure accommodation for children, deprivation of liberty in mental health and social care settings, as well as detention under mental health legislation, immigration detention, military detention and detention under terrorism legislation.

3 Governance

Governance within the UK NPM is structured to ensure accountability, coordination and strategic coherence across its 21 bodies. The UK NPM is led by the Head of the UK NPM, who is supported by a small central team responsible for facilitating collaboration between bodies and implementing agreed priorities and workstreams. This team exists as an Arm's Length Body and works to support and lead the NPM component parts in their execution of their OPCAT obligations. Oversight is provided by a Chair, elected from one of the 21 bodies for a 3-year term, and a Steering Group, which functions as a non-executive board and operates under a formal constitution that defines its relationship with the central team. The Chair appoints the Head of the UK NPM, who in turn appoints the team in line with equality recruitment principles. This governance framework ensures that the central team remains accountable to the wider membership of the UK NPM.

National subgroups provide a platform for regional collaboration and allow bodies to address issues that are devolved to Scotland and Northern Ireland. The Scotland Subgroup was established in 2014 and is comprised of designated UK NPM bodies operating in Scotland, while the Northern Ireland Subgroup was launched in 2023, with Northern Ireland's designated bodies. These subgroups aim to deliver the UK NPM's mandate under the OPCAT in Scotland and Northern Ireland, enabling more focused work on emerging regional issues. The subgroups also facilitate engagement with devolved governments and local stakeholders, ensuring that preventive efforts are contextually relevant.

Since 2023, the UK NPM has convened various Task and Finish groups to address priority issues. The *Menopause in detention* group produced a dedicated toolkit to support inspectors and monitors in identifying risk factors and impacts associated with perimenopause, menopause and post menopause in settings of deprivation of liberty. The *Definition of deprivation of liberty* group developed and published a

UK-specific definition of deprivation of liberty,[3] responding to a general comment by the SPT that emphasised the need for NPMs to exercise autonomy and functional independence in determining whether a particular place constitutes a place of deprivation of liberty.[4] A third group focused on improving collection and analysis of mental health transfer data, aiming to strengthen transparency and oversight of pathways for individuals in custodial settings requiring specialist care. Deaths in detention also emerged as a cross-cutting theme addressed by both the Scotland and Northern Ireland subgroups. As of November 2025, a new Task and Finish group has been launched to examine the implications of artificial intelligence in scrutiny, including its potential to enhance preventive monitoring.

The UK NPM operates within a framework shaped by four strategic objectives, as well as four guiding principles and the functions of NPMs as set out by the SPT.[5] These strategic objectives underpin all aspects of the UK NPM's work, providing a coherent basis for its activities. In line with its mandate, the UK NPM is committed to (1) supporting and leading NPM members in delivering their responsibilities under the OPCAT, (2) undertaking collective work and taking joint action to prevent ill-treatment of detained people in the UK, (3) promoting awareness and understanding of the OPCAT principles and the work of the UK NPM, and (4) working with international mechanisms and organisations with a mandate to prevent ill-treatment of detained people.

Embedded within all UK NPM activities are four guiding principles: a detainee-focused approach, independence, a commitment to human rights and collaboration. These principles also ensure that the mechanism's work remains consistent, credible and aligned with international standards and obligations.

---

[3] UK NPM, *Definition of deprivation of liberty*, 2025, https://nationalpreventivemechanism.org.uk/document/places-of-deprivation-of-liberty-uk-npm-definition/.

[4] SPT, General Comment No. 1 (2024) on Article 4 of the Optional Protocol (Places of Deprivation of Liberty), *UN Doc*. CAT/OP/GC/1, 4 July 2024, https://www.ohchr.org/en/documents/general-comments-and-recommendations/catopgc1-general-comment-no-1-2024-article-4.

[5] OHCHR, Preventing Torture: The Role of National Preventive Mechanisms—A Practical Guide, *UN Doc*. HR/P/PT/21, 2018, https://www.ohchr.org/sites/default/files/Documents/Publications/NPM_Guide_EN.pdf.

4 Composition of the UK NPM

The strength of the UK NPM lies in its very composition, each body operating under its own statutory mandate, inspection or monitoring powers and ways of working. This diversity enables the UK NPM to effectively monitor a wide range of detention settings, while requiring careful coordination to maintain consistency. Examining the membership of the UK NPM is critical to understanding how preventive monitoring is implemented in practice, how expertise is distributed across sectors and how governance operates within a multi-body NPM. Each of the four UK nations has different levels of devolved powers that influence how the various detention settings are overseen, adding a further complexity to this landscape. When carrying out an inspection or monitoring visit, UK NPM mandate holders operate without security escort and take the keys to the establishment and individual cells. This allows for stronger preventive monitoring by ensuring inspectors and monitors have unrestricted and independent access to all areas and individuals without relying on the establishment's staff. This reduces the risk of influence or interference. Given the complexity of the NPM model in the UK, we have taken the time to elucidate the approach across jurisdictions below.

Prisons

Scrutiny of prisons is undertaken through a dual model of inspection and monitoring, combining inspectorates with monitoring organisations across all jurisdictions. When we refer to inspection, we mean the oversight role of the NPM which involves periodic deep and lengthy visits to places of detention with large professional teams. Monitoring refers to more regular visits by a cadre of volunteers who build a picture of an establishment over time.

In England and Wales, His Majesty's Inspectorate of Prisons (HMIP) leads on formal inspections, assessing conditions and treatment of prisoners. This scrutiny is underpinned by the Prison Act 1952. While this legal mandate predates the ratification of the OPCAT, it is interpreted to create powers and duties which conform to the OPCAT standards.[6] HMIP operates on a cyclical basis, inspecting all prisons and YOIs, unannounced, at least once every five years, with most visited every two to three years. HMIP also publishes detailed inspection reports, thematic reviews and annual reports, which include key areas of concern and examples of positive practice. HMIP also carries out Independent Reviews of Progress (follow-up inspections) or issues Urgent Notifications to the Secretary of State of Justice after negative inspections, enabling a following-up of concerns highlighted. The standards that HMIP applies in inspections are based on international human rights standards and are used to examine all aspects of life in detention. While these standards vary depending on the type of setting inspected, broadly they consist of a series of thematic judgements or "healthy establishment tests": safety, respect, purposeful activity and rehabilitation and release planning. HMIP inspectors also use "Expectations" to guide them on inspection. These set out what establishments are expected to be doing, providing a list of indicators that may help to show that an establishment is achieving an expectation.[7]

Independent Monitoring Boards (IMBs) across England and Wales provide continuous monitoring of the prison estate through weekly visits by over 1,500 volunteers, also under the Prison Act 1952. Each prison has its own IMB. IMBs report annually to the Secretary of State for Justice through a written report which examines conditions and treatment of prisoners in the establishments they monitor. IMBs produce setting-specific annual reports, reporting on a summary of findings from across the Boards, and thematic reports when there are key issues that need to be highlighted.

Comparable arrangements exist in devolved nations. In Northern Ireland, Criminal Justice Inspection Northern Ireland (CJI) conducts formal prison inspections, though also carries out inspections of all criminal justice settings (including court custody, police custody and probation services) in Northern Ireland, doing so on a regular basis

[6] Sections 5A and 43, Prison Act 1952, https://www.legislation.gov.uk/ukpga/Geo6and1Eliz2/15-16/52/contents.

[7] HMIP, *How we inspect*, https://hmiprisons.justiceinspectorates.gov.uk/how-we-inspect/.

in proportion to their significance and role within the system. CJI's mandate is written out in the Justice (Northern Ireland) Act 2002.[8] The Independent Monitoring Board for Northern Ireland (IMBNI) undertakes regular, weekly monitoring of prisons, as per the Prison Act (Northern Ireland) 1953.[9] Similarly to the IMBs in England and Wales, IMBNI produces annual reports for the three prisons in Northern Ireland which detail the conditions and treatment of detainees within them.

In Scotland, His Majesty's Inspectorate of Prisons for Scotland (HMIPS) assumes responsibility for both inspection and monitoring visits (as set out in the Prisons (Scotland) Act 1989[10] and the Public Services Reform (Inspection and Monitoring of Prisons) (Scotland) Order 2015,[11] respectively), though the latter is still carried out by volunteer Independent Prison Monitors. HMIPS's programme follows a similar approach to HMIP's and CJI's, with prisons being formally inspected every few years but being monitored by volunteers weekly. Both inspection and monitoring visits can be announced or unannounced. HMIPS also produces thematic reviews and has published Standards for Inspecting and Monitoring Prisons in Scotland, which guide its methodology and ensure consistency across inspections.[12] The nine Standards[13] articulate what is expected of a well-run prison and contain clear statements identifying what is important and what will be monitored and inspected. At their very core is the upholding of human

[8] Section 46, Justice (Northern Ireland) Act 2002, https://www.legislation.gov.uk/ukpga/2002/26/contents.

[9] Section 10, Prison Act (Northern Ireland) 1952, https://www.legislation.gov.uk/apni/1953/18/contents#pt1-ch1-l1g9.

[10] Sections 6A and 7, Prisons (Scotland) Act 1989, https://www.legislation.gov.uk/ukpga/1989/45/contents.

[11] Section 7, Public Services Reform (Inspection and Monitoring of Prisons) (Scotland) Order 2015, https://www.legislation.gov.uk/ssi/2015/39/made.

[12] HMIPS, Inspecting and Monitoring Standards for Inspecting and Monitoring Prisons in Scotland, 2018, https://prisonsinspectoratescotland.gov.uk/publications/inspecting-and-monitoring-standards-inspecting-and-monitoring-prisons-scotland.

[13] Lawful and Transparent Custody; Decency; Personal Safety; Effective, Courteous and Humane Use of Authority; Respect, Autonomy and Protection against Mistreatment; Purposeful Activity; Transitions from Custody into the Community; Organisational Effectiveness; Health and Well-being.

rights of those deprived of their liberty. Each Standard has a number of Quality Indicators which inform the grade for the Standard overall. Quality Indicators themselves are split into features (a brief overview of the themes and key areas of interest), specification (a detailed description of evidence that could demonstrate an achieved outcome) and legal standards (relevant sections of domestic and human rights law).

Immigration Detention

Oversight of conditions and treatment in immigration detention is not a devolved matter. Therefore, HMIP and the IMBs also hold the power to inspect and monitor places of immigration detention across the UK jurisdictions. These powers are set out in the Prison Act 1952[14] and the Immigration and Asylum Act 1999.[15] Immigration detention establishments include both short-term holding facilities (including those at the France-UK borders) and immigration removal centres. The former allows for individuals to be held for a short period for up to seven days, while awaiting their entry to be processed or awaiting transfer or release, whereas individuals can be detained for longer periods in the latter as they await removal or the outcome of an asylum claim. Similarly to the prison inspections, HMIP inspects and reports on findings in immigration detention on a cyclical basis, while IMBs again provide continuous monitoring, as well as annual (setting- and establishment-specific) and thematic reports to highlight systemic issues. HMIP also conducts inspections on escorts and removals (deportation flights) to various countries worldwide.

Military Detention

At the request of the Ministry of Defence, HMIP also inspects places of military detention, including the Military Corrective Training Centre

[14] Section 5A, see note 2.

[15] Section 152, Immigration and Asylum Act 1999, https://www.legislation.gov.uk/ukpga/1999/33/contents.

and other service custody facilities nationwide. These establishments hold military personnel who have been detained or imprisoned. Inspections of military facilities are conducted every few years and only by agreement and invitation from the military. This constitutes a gap in the UK NPM's OPCAT compliance, as there is no legal basis for unannounced entry or inspection.

Police Custody

Scrutiny of police custody in the UK follows a similar dual model to prison and immigration oversight. As set out in the Police Act 1996,[16] His Majesty's Inspectorate of Constabulary and Fire & Rescue Services (HMICFRS) is the principal body responsible for inspecting police custody in England and Wales. HMICFRS carries out police effectiveness, efficiency and legitimacy (PEEL) inspections that assess the performance of police forces in England and Wales, including whether they provide a safe and lawful custody environment. Compliance with the Police and Criminal Evidence Act 1984[17] is also assessed through HMICFRS' inspection reports.

The Independent Custody Visiting Association (ICVA) carries out frequent monitoring of police custody by volunteers. ICVA represents over forty geographical schemes across England and Wales. Scotland (Independent Custody Visiting Scheme in Scotland, ICVS) and Northern Ireland (Northern Ireland Policing Board Independent Custody Visiting Scheme, NIPBICVS) also have their own schemes. ICVA is mandated under the Police Reform Act 2002.[18] As well as monitoring the general custody environment, Independent Custody Visitors (ICVs) monitor special "TACT" cells, which hold individuals suspected of terrorism or terrorism-related offences under the Terrorism Act 2000. ICVs produce local annual reports, as well as thematic reports.

---

[16] Section 54(2), Police Act 1996, https://www.legislation.gov.uk/ukpga/1996/16/contents.

[17] Police and Criminal Evidence Act 1984, https://www.legislation.gov.uk/ukpga/1984/60/contents.

[18] Section 51, Police Reform Act 2002, https://www.legislation.gov.uk/ukpga/2002/30/contents.

The Police and Fire and (Scotland) Act 2012[19] sets out His Majesty's Inspectorate of Constabulary in Scotland's (HMICS) powers to formally inspect police custody settings in Scotland. Under the same legislation, ICVS has the power to monitor these settings on a continual basis. HMICS produces reports on all custody inspections, which are done by geographic cluster, and ICVS, like the ICVA schemes, produces an annual report based on findings from monitoring visits. ICVS also has the power to visit TACT cells, certain facilities at the request of Border Force, as well as Legalised Police Cells (LPCs). LPCs are regulated police holding cells that are authorised to hold both remanded and sentenced detainees, which derive from a historic inaccessibility of the Scottish courts in certain districts and islands.

As mentioned, CJI has the mandate to inspect all criminal justice settings, including police custody. The NIPBICVS, again similarly to ICVA and ICVS, carries out frequent monitoring of police custody under the Police (Northern Ireland) Act 2000,[20] and of detainees being held on suspicion of terrorism under the Coroners and Justice Act 2009.[21] Inspections by CJI are done every few years, while NIPBICVS visits are more frequent and findings published in annual reports.

Court Custody

Some of the aforementioned bodies, namely HMIP, HMIPS, and CJI, that scrutinise prisons also inspect court custody facilities, as well as detainee escorts between settings and establishments.[22] In England and Wales, the Lay Observers also carry out a voluntary monitoring function similar to the IMBs, as set out in the Criminal Justice Act 1991.[23] Lay

[19] Police and Fire Reform (Scotland) Act 2012, https://www.legislation.gov.uk/asp/2012/8/contents.

[20] Section 71, Police (Northern Ireland) Act 2000, https://www.legislation.gov.uk/ukpga/2000/32/contents.

[21] Section 117, Coroners and Justice Act 2009, https://www.legislation.gov.uk/ukpga/2009/25/contents.

[22] See footnotes 4, 5, 7.

[23] Section 81, Criminal Justice Act 1991, https://www.legislation.gov.uk/ukpga/1991/53/contents.

Observers visit court custody cells and observe the transfers of detainees. Visits normally occur multiple times a month. Lay Observers produce annual monitoring reports, as well as thematic reports that highlight key issues in an often-overlooked part of the detention process.

Secure Mental Health

Scrutiny of secure mental health settings (including low, medium and high secure settings) is a devolved matter between the four nations, and the oversight of these establishments is carried out by different bodies in each nation. In England, this is the Care Quality Commission (CQC). CQC was created by the Health and Social Care Act 2008,[24] and its statutory functions are also laid out in the Health and Social Care Act 2012.[25] CQC also retains specific powers and duties to monitor psychiatric detention under the Mental Health Act 1983 (MHA).[26] Inspection reports are published by each NHS Trust—organisations providing healthcare services at a local level in England and Wales—and rate establishments from inadequate to outstanding using an assessment framework made up of five key questions.[27] CQC assesses whether the inspected service is safe, effective, caring, responsive to people's needs and well-led. Preventive methodology is embedded into this assessment framework. CQC also publishes annual assessments of health and social care and the use of the MHA in England and Wales.

In Northern Ireland, this inspection work is done by the Regulation and Quality Improvement Authority (RQIA). The Health and Personal Social Services (Quality, Improvement and Regulation) (Northern Ireland) Order 2003[28] sets out RQIA's statutory mandate, as does

[24] Health and Social Care Act 2008, https://www.legislation.gov.uk/ukpga/2008/14/contents.

[25] Health and Social Care Act 2012, https://www.legislation.gov.uk/ukpga/2012/7/contents.

[26] Mental Health Act 1983, https://www.legislation.gov.uk/ukpga/1983/20/contents.

[27] CQC, *Assessment Framework*, 2025, https://www.cqc.org.uk/guidance-regulation/providers/assessment/assessment-framework.

[28] The Health and Personal Social Services (Quality, Improvement and Regulation) (Northern Ireland) Order 2003, https://www.legislation.gov.uk/nisi/2003/431/contents/made.

the Mental Health (Northern Ireland) Order 1986.[29] In addition to inspecting secure mental health settings, RQIA also inspects healthcare in prisons in Northern Ireland.

Under the Mental Health (Care and Treatment) (Scotland) Act 2003[30] and the Adults with Incapacity (Scotland) Act 2000,[31] Mental Welfare Commission for Scotland (MWCS) carries out visits of secure mental health settings, as well as mental health provision in Scottish prisons. As well as visiting individuals in these settings, MWCS instigates full-scale investigations where care or treatment have gone wrong. MWCS produces local visit reports, as well as thematic reports. In Wales, Healthcare Inspectorate Wales (HIW) leads on inspecting secure mental health settings. This power is set out in the Health and Social Care (Community Health and Standards) Act 2003.[32] HIW also carries out reviews of organisations or services in response to concerns or incidents.

Secure Children's Homes

Oversight of the secure children's estate is also shared among the four UK nations. The Office for Standards in Education, Children's Services and Skills (Ofsted) carries out inspections of secure children's homes, the secure training centre and the secure school. Secure Children's Homes are run by local councils, taking children from ages 10 to 17. Though there is now only one in operation, Secure Training Centres have historically either been run by the Youth Custody Service or private companies, for children aged 12–17. Both environments should provide 30 hours of education and training a week, though findings show that, in practice, this is rarely achieved. Oasis Restore, the only Secure School in the UK, is designed to provide high-quality education and training for children.

[29] Sections 85 and 86 of the Mental Health (Northern Ireland) Order 1986, https://www.legislation.gov.uk/nisi/1986/595/contents.

[30] Mental Health (Care and Treatment) (Scotland) Act 2003, https://www.legislation.gov.uk/asp/2003/13/contents.

[31] Adults with Incapacity (Scotland) Act 2000, https://www.legislation.gov.uk/asp/2000/4/contents.

[32] Health and Social Care (Community Health and Standards) Act 2003, https://www.legislation.gov.uk/ukpga/2003/43/contents.

This is a new model, opened after the 2016 Taylor Review suggested that the youth justice system would rehabilitate young people more effectively if education was at its heart.[33] Envisaged as "smaller custodial establishments of up to 60–70 places", Secure Schools should bring together the essential services (education, health and offender desistence programmes) to rehabilitate children.[34] Ofsted's inspections are mandated under Part 8 of the Education and Inspections Act 2006[35] and Section 31 of the Care Standards Act 2000.[36] These inspections can take the form of a Monitoring Visit, an interim check-in to assess progress, or a Full Inspection, which is a full evaluation of the service with a formal grading. Ofsted has different inspection standards for secure children's homes,[37] secure training centres[38] and secure schools,[39] which place care and human rights at their centre.

In Scotland, the Care Inspectorate (CI) inspects secure accommodation services (the Scottish legal term for secure establishments holding children) under the Public Services Reform (Scotland) Act 2010.[40] CI can carry out inspections on a regular basis, but also has the power to investigate specific incidents or causes for concern.

Oversight of providers of social care services in Wales, including the one secure children's home, is carried out by Care Inspectorate Wales (CIW) under the Regulation and Inspection of Social Care (Wales) Act

---

[33] Taylor, C., *Review of the Youth Justice System in England and Wales*, 2016, https://assets.publishing.service.gov.uk/media/5a80b2b540f0b62305b8ca3f/youth-justice-review-final-report.pdf.

[34] Ibid., p. 40.

[35] Part 8, Education and Inspections Act 2006, https://www.legislation.gov.uk/ukpga/2006/40/contents.

[36] Section 31, Care Standards Act 2000, https://www.legislation.gov.uk/ukpga/2000/14/contents.

[37] Ofsted, *Social care common inspection framework: secure children's homes*, https://www.gov.uk/government/publications/social-care-common-inspection-framework-sccif-secure-childrens-homes/social-care-common-inspection-framework-sccif-secure-childrens-homes.

[38] Ofsted, *Inspecting secure training centres: framework*, https://www.gov.uk/government/publications/inspecting-secure-training-centres-framework.

[39] Ofsted, Guidance: Secure 16 to 19 academies, https://www.gov.uk/government/publications/secure-16-to-19-academies/secure-16-to-19-academies.

[40] Section 44, Public Services Reform (Scotland) Act 2010, https://www.legislation.gov.uk/asp/2010/8/contents.

2016.[41] Inspection visits are organised based on whether the service requires a routine, early or priority inspection and culminate in inspection reports, though CIW also publishes thematic reports. In Northern Ireland this work is overseen by CJI, which carries out inspections of Woodlands Juvenile Justice Centre, Northern Ireland's youth detention centre, every few years.

Other Settings

There are three remaining UK NPM bodies that are not fixed to any one setting. The Children's Commissioner for England (CCE) promotes and protects the rights of children in all settings in England. The role of the Children's Commissioner was created by the Children Act 2004,[42] and its mandate further strengthened by the Children and Families Act 2014.[43] The Commissioner undertakes a rolling programme of visits to YOIs and secure training centres to keep abreast of issues children in custody are experiencing. Thematic reports are published by the CCE as and when they arise.

The Scottish Commission for Human Rights Act 2006[44] provides the statutory basis for the Scottish Human Rights Commission (SHRC), Scotland's national human rights institution. SHRC promotes awareness and understanding of all human rights in Scotland and may conduct an inquiry (which can include visiting a place of deprivation of liberty) into human rights issues if the rights are contained in human rights conventions (and their protocols) that are ratified by the UK, including the OPCAT.

Despite the Independent Reviewer of Terrorism Legislation's main focus being reviewing the Terrorism Acts 2000[45] and 2006,[46] this also

---

[41] Regulation and Inspection of Social Care (Wales) Act 2016, https://www.legislation.gov.uk/anaw/2016/2/contents.

[42] Children Act 2004, https://www.legislation.gov.uk/ukpga/2004/31/contents.

[43] Children and Families Act 2014, https://www.legislation.gov.uk/ukpga/2014/6/contents.

[44] Scottish Commission for Human Rights Act 2006, https://www.legislation.gov.uk/asp/2006/16/contents.

[45] Terrorism Act 2000, https://www.legislation.gov.uk/ukpga/2000/11/contents.

[46] Terrorism Act 2006, https://www.legislation.gov.uk/ukpga/2006/11/contents.

includes reviewing and monitoring of the conditions of persons detained for more than 48 hours under the Terrorism Act 2000, prompting the IRTL to be designated as the most recent UK NPM body. The IRTL oversees these conditions across all jurisdictions and relevant settings (which include police custody and prisons).

5 A Layered Approach to Monitoring

The multi-body composition of the UK NPM offers distinct advantages over a centralised structure, particularly in terms of reach, expertise and credibility. By drawing on the statutory mandates and inspection powers of 21 separate bodies, the UK NPM is able to visit a wide variety of places of deprivation of liberty through legislative provisions and Memoranda of Understanding, ensuring compliance across diverse settings. This structure also enables the application of a "breadth and depth" model to oversight of particularly high-risk places of deprivation of liberty in the UK, like prisons and police custody. Breadth is achieved through frequent, routine monitoring visits that capture the day-to-day realities of life and provide continuous observation. Complementing this, depth comes from periodic, organised inspections that involve detailed scrutiny of processes and systems. Together, these approaches create a layered monitoring system that combines snapshots of individual establishments, with a longitudinal picture of systematic trends over time, enabling both immediate responses and sustained improvement over time (Fig. 1).

The diversity of backgrounds, operational cultures, and professional expertise within the UK NPM strengthens its capacity to identify risks and share intelligence across sectors, enhancing preventive impact. Peer learning among members fosters continuous improvement and methodological consistency, and this exchange of intelligence supports early identification of emerging concerns. Furthermore, the multi-body model allows for a higher frequency of visits overall than a single centralised body could achieve, ensuring that monitoring remains dynamic and responsive. Collectively, these features create a mechanism that is not only comprehensive in scope but also in expertise. This is an essential

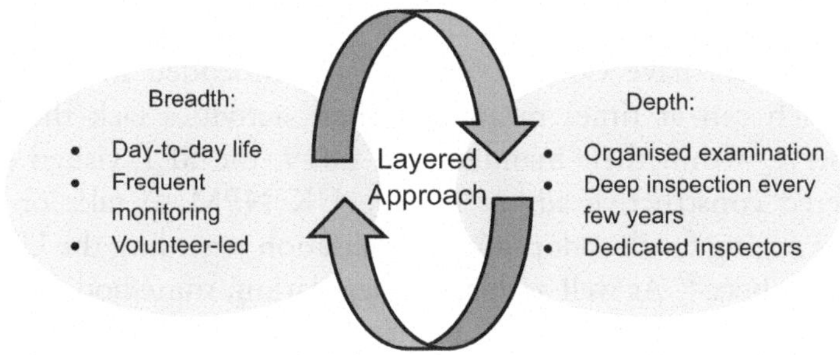

Fig. 1 Layered approach to monitoring

foundation for effective preventive monitoring in a complex, multi-jurisdictional environment. The UK NPM central team connects the dots between the 21 bodies and leverages decision-makers to amplify findings and drive systemic improvements in conditions and treatment in detention. This is achieved through an Annual Conference for heads of agencies, as well as quarterly Steering Group meetings. Additionally, in 2025, the UK NPM hosted its first "all mandate-holder" conference for all 3,500 staff members who work within the NPM network, and launched its Reporting Dashboard, which collates all NPM body outputs into a publicly accessible single source.

6 Challenges of a Multi-body NPM

The multi-body structure of the UK NPM presents unique challenges that distinguish it from single-body counterparts. Comprising over twenty organisations with diverse mandates and ways of working, the UK NPM must navigate issues of coordination and consistency.

Primarily, the UK NPM has no separate legal identity nor a formal legislative text establishing the mechanism, which has long been a matter of concern. This absence of legislation has long been recognised as a significant barrier to the UK NPM's effectiveness and credibility and raises concerns about full compliance with the OPCAT. Without a clear statutory framework, the powers, functions and responsibilities remain undefined in law. Furthermore, the statutes and legislations of individual bodies do not adequately reflect their NPM-related duties—at present, only two bodies have OPCAT obligations embedded in their legislation—which can at times mean that these activities lack the priority they deserve within their mandates. In 2019, the SPT visited the UK and offered constructive advice for the UK NPM to take on board, including urging for the adoption of legalisation regarding the UK NPM and its members.[47] As well as a lack of legislation, some bodies are regulatory bodies (that is, while these bodies do inspect places of deprivation of liberty, they also hold legal duties for their regulatory compliance) and for this reason, OPCAT-specific work may be difficult to distinguish. To address this, the UK NPM created induction and prevention training, which the Head of UK NPM and Steering Group required to be embedded for all individuals within the NPM network, allowing for a better understanding of the OPCAT mandate within individual bodies.

While the UK NPM's structure, as described, minimises gaps in monitoring due to its comprehensive coverage of distinct settings, the SPT warned that this may also create risks of duplication and inconsistencies in findings.[48] To be effective in preventing ill-treatment, strong coordination is essential. Without this, monitoring can become fragmented and undermine the UK NPM's work. Stronger collaboration and consistency are especially needed, as many stakeholders and detained persons do not recognise the UK NPM as one being, rather as its individual organisations. This challenge is compounded by the distinct political appetites of bodies, leading to diverging approaches and desire to influence legislation. There are also differences in how bodies perceive the preventive mandate and the importance of it in their work. The UK NPM's collective voice can therefore lack clarity on key legislative issues, potentially undermining its obligation under the OPCAT to promote laws and practices that prevent ill-treatment. However, efforts to strengthen collaboration must be carefully balanced against the principle of independence—a key tenet of the OPCAT mandate. As well as an obligation,

[47] SPT, Report to the NPM on the visit of the SPT to the United Kingdom of Great Britain and Northern Ireland, *UN Doc.* CAT/OP/GBR/RONPM/1, 16 December 2020, para 73., p. 8.
[48] Ibid., p. 12.

independence is a practical safeguard that ensures monitoring remains impartial and responsive to the unique risks across detention settings.

The UK NPM recognises many of its own challenges not mentioned in the SPT report. For example, with 21 bodies of varying size and capacity, a unique challenge for representation is created. Larger bodies can sometimes dominate national discussions and outputs, making it difficult to ensure that all jurisdictions and sectors are equally reflected in our collective work. Achieving balanced participation and influence across the UK NPM remains a priority. Principal responsibility for ensuring fair representation of bodies sits with the National Chair and Steering Group. The UK NPM has made progress in the appointment of a Chair (for the first time) from a smaller body and, a non-prison monitoring body.

Fair representation is also a challenge within the UK NPMs volunteer base. Volunteers are invaluable to delivering the OPCAT mandate, particularly in prisons, immigration detention, and police custody settings. However, the demographic profile of volunteers is limited. The significant time commitment required for effective preventive monitoring means that volunteering is often accessible only to individuals with certain privileges—typically those who are older, retired or financially secure. This lack of diversity can affect perspectives and the inclusivity of the UK NPM's work, especially considering the demographic of those within the establishments monitored.

The complexity and size of the UK NPM model raises questions about whether obligations under the OPCAT mandate truly reach all 3500 staff and volunteers across the UK. This is not simply a matter of awareness, but also of embedding preventive principles into every layer of work, especially since all pre-existing bodies joined the UK NPM with their own priorities, culture and aims. Each body has undertaken significant work to interpret their methodology under a preventive lens and adapt strategy where necessary over the NPM's sixteen-year existence. To address this, the UK NPM hosted its first annual "all mandate-holder" conference in 2025, inviting everyone that carries out the OPCAT mandate to attend. The conference reinforced the importance and relevance of all roles within the UK NPM network, including those who do not actively inspect or monitor but work in business support or communications. Attendees heard directly from staff within establishments monitored by the UK NPM, providing valuable insights into how joint efforts can lead to better outcomes for those deprived of liberty.

7 Successes: Collaboration and International Engagement

Working closely across its 21 bodies and engaging with external and international partners, the UK NPM strengthens its capacity to monitor places of deprivation of liberty effectively and align itself with global normative standards. These collaborative relationships have enabled knowledge exchange, joint action and the development of consistent approaches to preventing ill-treatment.

Internal Collaboration

The UK NPM continues to coordinate effective joint working between its bodies. One of the most tangible examples of this collaboration is its joint inspections and reporting, which allow different bodies to combine perspectives, expertise and resources for more holistic and comprehensive assessments of settings of deprivation of liberty. Combining this approach with the depth and breadth model of inspecting and monitoring strengthens the UK NPM's ability to effectively prevent ill-treatment. For instance, HMIP frequently works alongside CQC, HIW and Ofsted during inspections of prisons and YOIs, producing inspection reports that examine healthcare provision and education services more concretely. Similarly, CJI often collaborates with RQIA during inspections, and HMIPs and HMICS work with Healthcare Improvement Scotland, an associate member of the Scotland Subgroup.[49] Additionally, SHRC has supported HMIPS in creating a human rights-based approach to prison inspections, and in joint work by the UK NPM

[49] For examples of joint inspections, see reports on the UK NPM's Reporting Dashboard, https://npm-reporting.powerappsportals.com/Reports/.

central team, HMIP and HMICFRS, human rights-based expectations for police custody inspections were developed, and joint visits were carried out for the first few years of the programme.

Beyond joint inspections and reporting, UK NPM bodies also collaborate on thematic work. In 2023, CI and HMIPS undertook a joint thematic review of prison-based social work, revealing that many detained individuals reported limited contact with and visibility of social workers.[50] HMIP, working with CQC, produced a thematic review of delays in the transfer of mentally unwell prisoners,[51] calling for fundamental and patient-centred change to a growing problem. For a thematic review of work and training provision in adult prisons in 2025, HMIPS and Ofsted joined forces, concluding that too many detainees are spending their time out of education or work and are often suffering drug addictions caused by a lack of purposeful activity.[52] These partnerships demonstrate how combining specialist knowledge strengthens analysis, raises awareness of critical issues, and promotes cross-sector learning and coordinated preventive strategies.

Further, findings from UK NPM bodies' inspections do not remain isolated. Any findings or concerns that are fed into inspection, monitoring or thematic reports are then shared publicly and throughout the UK NPM network. The UK NPM central team analyses and synthesises these reports and findings, highlighting national systemic issues in the UK NPM Annual Report. Reporting is therefore mixed, with NPM bodies reporting on local matters establishment-by-establishment and the UK NPM reporting on systemic issues. The central team also engages with authorities and alerts treaty bodies where obligations are unmet, ensuring that local evidence drives national accountability. This cycle demonstrates how internal collaboration, between UK NPM bodies and the central team, amplifies impact and creates a unified voice, with

---

[50] CI and HMIPS, Prison-based social work: thematic review, 2023, https://www.careinspectorate.com/images/documents/7524/Prison-based%20social%20work%20thematic%20review.pdf.

[51] HMIP, The long wait: A thematic review of delays in the transfer of mentally unwell prisoners, 2024, https://hmiprisons.justiceinspectorates.gov.uk/hmipris_reports/the-long-wait-a-thematic-review-of-delays-in-the-transfer-of-mentally-unwell-prisoners/.

[52] HMIP, 'Just passing time': A review of work and training provision in adult prisons, 2025, https://hmiprisons.justiceinspectorates.gov.uk/hmipris_reports/just-passing-time-a-review-of-work-and-training-provision-in-adult-prisons.

the UK NPM acting as the connective tissue between national and international prevention of ill-treatment and torture.

Case Study—UK NPM Internal and External Collaboration

A clear example of the UK NPM's collaborative ability can be found from the outcome of concerns raised at HMPYOI Cornton Vale, Scotland's previous national facility for young and adult women. In 2015, HMIPS conducted an inspection at Cornton Vale and found aspects of the conditions there to be unacceptable (including issues of hygiene, safety and segregation).[53] Following this inspection, UK NPM bodies worked together to escalate these concerns internationally, briefing the European Committee for the Prevention of Torture (CPT) on major ongoing concerns. In October 2018, the CPT visited the UK and spent time at HMPYOI Cornton Vale. In the subsequent visit reports, the CPT raised "serious concerns about the treatment of women prisoners held in segregation at Cornton Vale Prison", especially those who needed urgent care and treatment in a psychiatric facility.[54] The CPT made a follow-up ad hoc visit in October 2019 and noted continued concern.[55]

The NPM commissioned a follow-up report on progress since the 2018 and 2019 CPT visits, published in 2021,[56] while HMIPS commissioned a review of segregation in Scottish prisons, published in 2023, which investigated the concerns raised by the CPT.[57] This report concluded overall that segregation was overused in Scottish prisons, and

---

[53] HMIPS, Report on HMP YOI Cornton Vale Full Inspection, 2015, https://prisonsinspectoratescotland.gov.uk/publications/report-full-inspection-hmp-yoi-cornton-vale-28-sept-7-oct-2015.

[54] CPT, Executive Summary (Ad hoc visit: 17/10/2018–26/10/2018), CPT/Inf (2019) 29, 2019, https://rm.coe.int/1680982a01.

[55] CPT, Executive Summary (Ad hoc visit: 14/10/2019–18/10/2019), CPT/Inf (2020) 28, 2020, https://rm.coe.int/16809fdebd.

[56] UK NPM, Scotland's progress in the prevention of ill-treatment in places of detention, 2021, https://cloud-platform-e218f50a4812967ba1215eaecede923f.s3.amazonaws.com/uploads/sites/23/2023/07/Full-report-on-Scotlands-progress-in-the-prevention-of-ill-treatment-in-places-of-detention.pdf.

[57] HMIPS, A Thematic Review of Segregation in Scottish Prisons, 2023, https://prisonsinspectoratescotland.gov.uk/publications/thematic-review-segregation-scottish-prisons.

increasingly used as a place of safety for prisoners who were mentally unwell, echoing CPT findings. These actions demonstrate how internal collaboration among UK NPM bodies and external engagement with the CPT created sustained pressure for change. Following these combined efforts, HMPYOI Cornton Vale formally closed in 2023, being replaced by HMPYOI Stirling, which opened the same year and received a "satisfactory" rating for its segregation practices in a 2024 inspection (the second-highest rating possible as per HMIPS's assessment marker).[58] The design of the new HMPYOI Stirling was heavily focused on mental well-being and a trauma-informed and gender-specific approach.

External Collaboration

The UK NPM has also developed strong partnerships internationally. A key relationship exists with both the SPT, which provides technical guidance, and the CPT. These relationships ensure that UK monitoring aligns with international standards, and that findings from UK NPM bodies inform the global dialogue surrounding prevention of ill-treatment.

The UK NPM actively participates in Council of Europe forums, contributing to thematic discussions and sharing good practice with other European NPMs. Beyond Europe, the UK NPM has supported the establishment and strengthening of NPMs globally, including in Kyrgyzstan, Australia, Ireland and South Korea, offering advice on governance, methodology and independence.

Collaboration also extends to external partners, including civil society organisations or academic institutions. Throughout 2025, the UK NPM has worked closely with the University of Edinburgh on the issue of environmental conditions of detention, examining how factors like light, temperature, sound and air impact detainee well-being. Presented at a conference with South American NPMs in September 2025, this work reflects the UK NPM's drive to collaborate externally in order to influence international standards for the prevention of ill-treatment.

---

[58] HMIPS, Report on HMP YOI Stirling Full Inspection, 2024, https://prisonsinspectoratescotland.gov.uk/publications/report-full-inspection-hmp-yoi-stirling.

Through these key external relationships, the UK NPM does not only strengthen its own practice, but also plays a leading role in shaping global standards for the prevention of torture and ill-treatment.

8 Successes: Shared Monitoring and Research Outputs

As a large, multi-body NPM, its work spans an extensive range of activities, far too broad to capture in full, however, some notable examples illustrate this approach.

Preventive Guidance and Training

The preventive guidance is designed to deepen thinking about how the monitoring and inspection process can be strengthened to better prevent ill-treatment, both at managerial level and at the frontline of monitoring. It provides practical strategies that help bodies move beyond compliance towards proactive prevention. Complementing this guidance, the UK NPM commissioned and produced preventive training which operationalises this guidance. The project aimed to embed consistency and coherence across UK NPM monitoring, while respecting the legislative diversity of individual bodies. Together, these resources provide the first published work on how to apply a preventive mandate in practice, and a shared foundation for this work, equipping monitors with the tools and knowledge to identify risks early and influence systemic change.

Annual Report and Thematic Outputs

The UK NPM's sixteenth Annual Report offers a consolidated view of detention monitoring across the UK. Drawing on findings from all 21 bodies, the report provides a level of systemic analysis that individual reports cannot achieve. It identifies recurring concerns, highlights emerging trends and maps patterns that cut across jurisdictions and detention settings. The Annual Report provides a single source of truth of all monitoring activity each year and offers a big-picture view of the state of detention in the UK.

The report showcases good practice, offering practical examples that can be adapted elsewhere. This dual focus on risks and solutions makes the Annual Report a valuable resource for UK NPM bodies, policymakers and practitioners seeking to strengthen safeguards against ill-treatment. Its findings inform parliamentary debate, shape policy discussions and contribute to international dialogue on preventive standards, ensuring that UK NPM monitoring has impact beyond national borders.

The UK NPM also works collaboratively to produce its own thematic outputs when there are particular areas of concern. For example, a recurring issue in immigration detention is the length of time that detainees are detained in these settings, due to the UK not having a statutory time limit on the duration of immigration detention—the only country in Europe lacking this safeguard. In light of this, the UK NPM produced a briefing on indeterminate detention across different settings.[59] Indefinite detention in the immigration estate (and elsewhere) can last years, with little information for detainees on case progress, causing profound effects on detainee well-being. This issue was also raised by the UK NPM in its evidence to the UK Committee on Human Rights' 140th Session in 2024.[60] The UK NPM highlighted an increase in the unlawful use of immigration detention, calling for the creation of statutory time limit and its use as a last resort.

Reporting Dashboard

One of the UK NPM's most significant recent outputs is the launch of its Reporting Dashboard, an analytical tool that consolidates findings from all 21 UK NPM bodies into a single, accessible platform. Due to

[59] UK NPM, Indeterminate detention regimes, 2025, https://nationalpreventivemechanism.org.uk/document/uk-npm-briefing-indeterminate-detention/.

[60] UK NPM, Concluding Observations of 140th session, examination of the UK, 2024, https://nationalpreventivemechanism.org.uk/document/uk-npm-briefing-on-the-human-rights-committee-concluding-observations-july-2024/.

its multi-body nature, the UK NPM makes thousands of recommendations annually, though these have historically been dispersed across individual reports, making it difficult to identify systemic issues, see the bigger picture or share effective solutions. The Dashboard was designed to address this challenge, providing a centralised, real-time repository of data, enabling users to track trends, highlight recurring concerns and monitor progress on preventive measures. This development marks a global first, offering public access to collective insights on conditions across the UK's places of deprivation of liberty. At present, the Reporting Dashboard has been populated with data from 2020 to October 2025, totalling over 23,000 records. This includes 18,049 recommendations and 5,116 examples of good practice.

The Reporting Dashboard was designed for a broad audience, including UK NPM bodies, but also civil society organisations, policymakers and anyone else seeking to prevent ill-treatment in places of deprivation of liberty. Its functionality extends beyond data collection; it facilitates knowledge exchange by allowing users to access recommendations and examples of good practice from across the UK. For instance, a prison governor could quickly review strategies implemented elsewhere to address similar challenges, encouraging the adoption of proven approaches and fostering continuous improvement.

Consolidating findings from multiple bodies, the Dashboard promotes transparency and consistency in recommendations. It also strengthens collaboration within the UK NPM, enabling organisations to review each other's observations and refine their own. The Reporting Dashboard represents a transformative step in preventive monitoring, as it not only improves access to information, but also drives systemic change by supporting the production of informed, accessible recommendations that may help to prevent ill-treatment.

The UK NPM continues to use the Reporting Dashboard as a central tool for identifying trends and systemic risks and is producing a series of papers based on the data collected. These papers highlight areas of good practice across different settings and themes and provide practical insights that can support the work of UK NPM bodies and the establishments they inspect or monitor. For example, following a recent SHRC's report on Access to Justice for Prisoners,[61] the central team developed a thematic paper on good practice relating to complaints handling across all settings and jurisdictions. Taken together, these resources enable establishments and monitoring bodies to learn from effective strategies already in place elsewhere, adopt proven approaches to their own context and strengthen consistency in safeguarding detainee rights. By linking data-driven analysis with real-world examples of good practice, the UK NPM ensures that its monitoring work translates into actionable improvements across the UK.

9 Conclusion

Lessons from the UK NPM show us that an effective NPM requires more than just compliance with international obligations; it demands a strategic approach that places prevention at the heart of organisational design and practice. For the UK NPM, collaboration has also been a defining strength, but has also presented challenges that require ongoing effort to overcome. Managing diverse mandates, methodologies and priorities across 21 bodies is complex, and achieving coherence without compromising independence demands consideration. As well as navigating a complex structure across four nations, the UK NPM must also navigate a landscape marked by persistent and troubling findings across all settings of deprivation of liberty. However, there are important examples of good practice that deserve recognition. In recent months, progress has been evident across all settings in areas such as well-being support and the quality of staff–detainee relationships, for example, demonstrating that positive change is possible even in difficult circumstances.[62]

[61] SHRC, Access to Justice for Prisoners: The Complaints System, 2025, https://www.scottishhumanrights.com/media/3055/pdf-mainreport-spotlights-accesstojusticeforprisonerscomplaints-2025.pdf.

[62] UK NPM, 2025, Monitoring Places of Detention—16th Annual Report of the United Kingdom's National Preventive Mechanism, pp. 51–53.

The UK NPM continues to work collaboratively to protect the rights of those deprived of their liberty, by continuing its extensive monitoring and driving standards through constructive challenge, but also by producing important outputs and embedding the preventive role across the UK NPM network. Internationally, the UK NPM continues to play a leading role within the global preventive community. By working closely with other national mechanisms and international partners, it is helping to strengthen the OPCAT implementation worldwide and promote a culture of prevention that protects the rights and dignity of all those deprived of liberty. These efforts reflect the UK NPM's commitment to meeting its core obligations under the OPCAT: to prevent ill-treatment through independent monitoring and constructive engagement.

15 Years of the Swiss National Preventive Mechanism: Reflecting on Impact and the Boundaries of Deprivation of Liberty

Jean-Sébastien Blanc

1 Introduction

Fifteen years after its creation, the National Commission for the Prevention of Torture (NCPT), Switzerland's National Preventive Mechanism (NPM), has accumulated both notable achievements and ongoing challenges. Understanding its development requires situating the Swiss NPM within its historical and institutional context, particularly the country's deeply rooted federalist tradition. This article explores the evolution of the NPM through the lens of the various places and forms of deprivation of liberty that have shaped its mandate and activities over time. By examining the rationale behind the NPM's decisions to monitor deportation flights, federal asylum centres, and nursing homes, it reflects on how deprivation of liberty can be understood in a broader and more nuanced

J.-S. Blanc (✉)
National Commission for the Prevention of Torture—Swiss NPM, Bern, Switzerland
e-mail: jean-sebastien.blanc@unige.ch

T. Daems et al. (eds.), *Preventing Torture and Monitoring Places of Detention*,
https://doi.org/10.1007/978-3-032-28285-9_8

sense, shedding light on both the practical and conceptual dimensions of the NPM's preventive work.

2 The Choice of a Centralised NPM in a Federal State

Following its signature of the Optional Protocol to the Convention Against Torture and Other Cruel, Inhuman or Degrading Treatment or Punishment (OPCAT) in 2004, Switzerland took five years to ratify the Optional Protocol. The law establishing the NPM—the "National Commission for the Prevention of Torture" (NCPT)—was adopted by the Federal Assembly in March 2009 and the NPM started its activities in early 2010, after its first 12 members were designated by the federal government (*Federal Council*) in October 2009. Unlike several other federal States that have chosen to establish local preventive mechanisms under the umbrella of a central committee (such as Brazil or Argentina), Switzerland decided to create a single institution responsible for the monitoring of all places of deprivation of liberty under Swiss jurisdiction.

Federalism is a strong component of both the Swiss collective identity as well as its legal order. Subsidiarity is a core principle enshrined in the federal Constitution (art. 5), whereby political and legislative powers are distributed in a way that grants the greatest possible autonomy to the 26 Cantons and approximately 2.000 municipalities (*communes*). The Cantons are sovereign—except to the extent that their sovereignty is limited by the Constitution (art. 3)—and therefore act as constituent states. They have their own parliaments, governments, and courts.[1] Furthermore, they are responsible for important issues, such as the school system, policing, and the execution of criminal sanctions, while the Confederation has an overall responsibility for national security and foreign policy. The country has a federal Criminal Code since 1942, but its unified Code of Criminal Procedure (CPP) only came into force in 2011, ending a complex legal system comprising 26 different CCP.

[1] Some Cantons also have their own Constitution, in addition to the Swiss Federal Constitution.

Given its strong federalistic culture, Switzerland could have opted for decentralised entities. In fact, during the official consultation with Cantons and political parties before the signature of the OPCAT, the Federal Council considered the option of establishing decentralised mechanisms, but eventually concluded that, "in addition to cost savings and efficiency gains", a single federal solution would be more apt to design and apply "uniform examination methods and criteria".[2] It is therefore a combination of costs, efficiency, and a uniform approach that led to the choice of a single institution. However, in practice, the multiplicity of stakeholders represents a challenge for a centralised NPM. For example, in issues related to policing and the prison system, there are 26 local (cantonal) Ministers responsible for justice and police matters, in addition to the Federal Department of Justice and Police. In this context, the local entities have established so-called "conferences" and subregional "agreements" (*concordats*) to discuss policy issues that are relevant beyond the cantonal level. While these forums therefore represent prime venues to discuss State practices, policies, and regulations, the NPM nevertheless strives to maintain bilateral relationships at the cantonal level.

3 Composition and Independence

The Swiss NPM is composed of twelve members "with the necessary professional and personal expertise, particularly in the medical, psychiatric, legal and intercultural fields and in matters relating to deprivation of liberty and visits to places of deprivation of liberty[3]", assisted by a small secretariat based in the capital city Bern. The NPM's members perform their duties in their personal capacity[4] and do not carry out this function on a full-time basis. Members typically hold professional

---

[2] *Message relatif à un projet d'arrêté fédéral portant approbation et mise en œuvre du Protocole facultatif se rapportant à la Convention contre la torture et autres peines ou traitements cruels, inhumains ou dégradants du 8 décembre 2006 (06.105)*, (*hereafter*: Message 2006 (06.105), p. 262) (all translation are by the author).

[3] Federal Law on the National Commission for the Prevention of Torture (*hereafter*: L-NCPT), art. 5.

[4] Art. 4 L-NCPT.

positions in a field closely related to the NPM's area of activity or are retired. The SPT has expressed criticism regarding the part-time status of its members.[5] Although during the consultation stage, the number of members was considered sufficient to ensure that the NPM could conduct between 20 and 30 visits every year, several stakeholders suggested establishing a larger body.[6] The members are appointed by the Federal Council for a four-year term, with the possibility of being reappointed twice.[7]

The OPCAT foresees that State Parties "shall strive for a gender balance and the adequate representation of ethnic and minority groups in the country".[8] In view of the above-described prominence of federalism, this provision is particularly relevant for Switzerland, and the NPM law—in line with the OPCAT—stipulates that both gender and the country's linguistic regions must be adequately represented.[9] Since its inception, the NPM has ensured good gender balance and representation of the main linguistic regions. However, some other minorities are underrepresented, particularly those with migration backgrounds. It should also be noted that the members, the staff of the secretariat, and any persons whose services the NPM calls upon are bound by official secrecy.[10]

[5] "The Subcommittee is concerned that the 12 members of the National Commission for the Prevention of Torture perform their duties on a part-time basis and without remuneration, in keeping with the State party's tradition of part-time public service (milice), even though that tradition is an integral part of the country's custom of participation, which is practised in a range of fields, including the political and social spheres. The Subcommittee noted that, despite the commendable efforts of the members of the Commission and their strong commitment to preventing torture, there is a de facto limit on their availability, which hampers their ability to carry out their mandate properly, particularly with regard to the number, duration and regularity of visits and the conduct of unannounced or urgent visits with the requisite speed". SPT, *Visit to Switzerland undertaken from 27 January to 7 February 2019: recommendations and observations addressed to the State party*, CAT/OP/CHE/ROSP/1, March 2021, para. 33–34, p. 6.

[6] Message 2006 (06.105), p. 267 and p. 271.

[7] Art. 6, para. 3 L-NCPT.

[8] Art. 18, para. 2 L-NCPT.

[9] Art. 5, para. 3 L-NCPT.

[10] Art. 11 L-NCPT.

Independence is a cornerstone of torture prevention. The OPCAT therefore requires that States Parties "guarantee the functional independence of the national preventive mechanisms as well as the independence of their personnel".[11] In Switzerland, the NPM is administratively attached to the Federal Department of Justice and Police, which also provides its annual budget. The NPM's budget is therefore included within the overall budget of the Department's General Secretariat and does not appear anywhere as a stand-alone entity, which undermines transparency and traceability.[12] Although the law foresees that the NPM carries out its tasks independently,[13] several entities have criticised the NCPT for not being fully independent,[14] not only because of administrative attachment to the Federal Department of Justice and Police, but also because of the nomination of its members by the Federal Council. Following its visit to Switzerland in February 2019, the SPT stressed the authorities to "sever the links" between the NPM and the Federal Department of Justice and Police so that the NPM "can function with complete independence, both institutional and operational, and carry out all its activities and tasks separately from those of the Federal Department of Justice and Police, by having its own structure[15]".

Pursuing its reasoning, the SPT also recommended that the Swiss authorities provide the NPM with a "budget separate from that of the Federal Department of Justice and Police" so that it can be "financially autonomous and, as a result, operationally independent".[16] An additional criticism relates to the nomination process of the NPM members, who are appointed on the recommendation of the Federal Department of Justice and Police and the Federal Department of Foreign Affairs.[17]

[11] OPCAT, art. 18.

[12] Rapport d'activité de la Commission nationale de prévention de la torture (CNPT) 2017, p. 43.

[13] Art. 4, para. 1 L-NCPT.

[14] The Swiss NPM itself tasked two experts to issue an expert opinion on legal aspects of the independence of the NCPT: see Kälin and Nowak (2017) in CNPT (2017).

[15] SPT, *Visit to Switzerland undertaken from 27 January to 7 February 2019: recommendations and observations addressed to the State party*, CAT/OP/CHE/ROSP/1, March 2021, para. 24, p. 5.

[16] *Ibid.*, para. 27, p. 5.

[17] Art. 6, para. 1 L-NCPT.

Although the law provides that non-governmental organisations may propose candidates,[18] the question of the recruitment procedure remains debatable in view of the independence of the NCPT. Despite these criticisms, the NPM considers that its members can carry out their mandate independently from the authorities and the NPM has never suffered any interference in its work. The authorities also stress the respect for the NPM's independence in official communications. For example, a former head of the Federal Department of Justice and Police has publicly recognised that the NPM's independence is "important and central", even when "it brings uncomfortable issues to light".[19]

4 NPM's Mandate and Dialogue with the Authorities

The law establishing the NPM rests mostly on the provisions included in the OPCAT, notably with regard to the NPM's task. It is responsible for regularly monitoring the situation of persons deprived of their liberty and for inspecting the places where such persons are or may be held.[20] Monitoring visits involve a qualitative assessment of places of deprivation of liberty to ensure the protection of the fundamental rights of persons held therein. While the NPM is legally empowered to undertake unannounced visits,[21] it also conducts visits that are notified in advance.[22] Visiting delegations—composed according to expertise, availability, and regional representation—assess the situation of individuals subject to measures restricting their liberty through interviews and the examination of all relevant documents and records. These include internal regulations, administrative instructions, disciplinary sanctions and other security measures, decisions regarding medical treatments administered

[18] Art. 5 L-NCPT.

[19] Official reply by Federal Councillor Simonetta Sommaruga to "Motion Streiff-Feller Marianne", N° 11.3222, 2012: https://www.parlament.ch/fr/ratsbetrieb/amtliches-bulletin/amtliches-bulletin-die-verhandlungen?SubjectId=20613.

[20] Art. 2, al. a L-NCPT.

[21] Art. 8, para. 2 L-NCPT.

[22] Art. 8, para. 2 L-NCPT.

without consent, execution plans for sentences or therapeutic measures, treatment plans, and similar materials. Each visit concludes with an initial oral debriefing, during which the delegation communicates its preliminary findings to the management of the institution.

Following its visits, the NPM makes recommendations to the relevant authorities.[23] It may also make proposals and comments on existing legislation or draft legislation.[24] Finally, it must draw up an annual report that is accessible to the public,[25] which the Federal Council must ensure is published and disseminated.[26] It is sometimes said that the lack of enforcement powers is the main weakness of both the SPT and the NPMs (McGregor, 2017). Recommendations and dialogue with authorities are in fact their main means to achieve change. It is therefore of particular relevance that the Swiss law includes an obligation for the authorities to examine "the proposals submitted to them by the commission and issue an opinion on their implementation".[27] This provision, which did not exist in the preliminary draft law but was included during the consultation process, is crucial in that it engages directly the authorities' responsibility for considering and implementing the recommendations. In practical terms, the Swiss NPM shares confidentially, upon completion of a visit, its report with the relevant authorities and often holds a meeting on that basis to discuss possible diverging views and correct factual errors. Following this exchange, the NPM report is published on its website, together with the authorities' response. This is now a standard procedure.

Without a constructive dialogue, such a process would be deemed to fail, and this is the reason why the OPCAT foresees the State's obligation to enter into a dialogue with the NPM on possible implementation measures.[28] In practice, dialogue goes beyond the follow-up exchanges specific to each visit. Given Switzerland's federal structure, there is a

[23] Art. 2, al. b L-NCPT.

[24] Art. 2, al. c L-NCPT.

[25] Art. 2, al. d L-NCPT.

[26] Art. 9, para. 1 L-NCPT.

[27] Art. 9, para. 2 L-NCPT.

[28] Art. 9 OPCAT.

considerable number of stakeholders and the NPM relies notably on so-called inter-cantonal conferences[29] as platforms to sustain its dialogue with the authorities. That is notably the case when the NCPT holds discussions in connection with the publication of its thematic reports (broader in scope than the visit reports). The NPM also interacts with the Federal Parliament, notably in hearings before various committees and cantonal parliaments.

The NPM also maintains an ongoing dialogue with both the SPT and the CPT, as enshrined in its legislation.[30] Furthermore, the CPT consults with the NPM prior to its visits and invites NPM representatives to participate in its concluding meeting with the Swiss authorities. During its sole visit to Switzerland to date, the SPT carried out one joint visit with the NPM.[31]

5 Preventing Torture in a Variety of Detention Settings: How the Swiss NPM Seeks to Achieve Changes in Specific Areas

One of the cornerstones of the OPCAT lies in its very broad definition of deprivation of liberty (art. 3) which has been further elaborated upon in the first SPT's General comment, whereby both the SPT and NPM shall have an "autonomous decision-making"[32] with regard to defining what should be considered a place of deprivation of liberty.

[29] For the criminal justice system, there is a Conference of Cantonal Prison Service Heads at the administrative level and a Conference of Cantonal Justice and Police Department Directors at the political level. There are also similar structures at the subregional level. The same goes for other areas, such as migration or health.

[30] The NPM "liaises with the Subcommittee on Prevention and the European Committee for the Prevention of Torture, provides them with information and coordinates its activities with theirs" (Art. 2, al. e L-NCPT).

[31] SPT, *Visit to Switzerland undertaken from 27 January to 7 February 2019: recommendations and observations addressed to the national preventive mechanism - Report of the Subcommittee*, CAT/OP/CHE/RONPM/1 22 March 2021, p. 14.

[32] SPT, *General comment No. 1 (2024) on article 4 of the Optional Protocol (places of deprivation of liberty)*, CAT/OP/GC/1, para. 59, p. 13.

The law on the Swiss NPM adopts the terminology of the OPCAT regarding deprivation of liberty and does not include lists of places falling under the NPM's mandate.[33] The NPM carries out its mandate in a broad range of places of deprivation of liberty and has diversified the type of detention settings monitored over the years. In addition to prisons, juvenile correctional facilities, police stations, psychiatric institutions (focusing primarily on persons with a compulsory treatment order), and administrative detention centres,[34] the NPM also carries out visits to federal asylum centres and nursing homes, although these are not *stricto sensu* places of deprivation of liberty. Furthermore, since 2012, the NPM has systematically monitored all forced deportations on chartered flights (so-called special flights), as well as selected forced deportations on commercial flights. With the exception of constraints related to human and financial resources and to expertise, there are no substantive limits on the types of places that the NPM may visit. The scope of such visits may therefore expand in the future to include, for example, institutions for persons with disabilities.[35]

The diversity of places of deprivation of liberty monitored by the Commission over the years, as well as the fact that the NPM—since its inception—has had limited funding to carry out its mandate, constitutes a significant challenge in guaranteeing "regular" monitoring, as required by Swiss law and by the OPCAT. There is no comprehensive mapping of all places of deprivation of liberty across the country. However, for reference, there are 90 prisons, over 40 federal asylum centres, and approximately 1.000 nursing homes. For these reasons, the Swiss NPM has defined strategic priorities over the years, based primarily on the vulnerability and risks faced by persons deprived of their liberty. In the following sections, specific areas of work of the NPMs will be further explored. The rationale for selecting these areas relies on the fact that they all relate to non-traditional places of deprivation of liberty and/

33 Art. 3 L-NCPT.

34 Under Swiss law, administrative detention can be ordered by an administrative authority to detain someone with the sole purpose to secure its subsequent forced deportation from the country.

35 See for example: CNPT, *Rapport d'activités,* 2018, p. 8.

or situations that question more narrow definitions of deprivation of liberty.

Forced Deportation Flights Under Scrutiny

Deportation refers to the practice of forcibly expelling people whose asylum request has been rejected. In the Swiss context, it can also apply to foreigners who have committed specific offences that carry a mandatory expulsion upon completion of the sentence.[36] While deportation is a procedure and not a place of deprivation of liberty *per se*, people who are forcibly deported are deprived of liberty by a public authority. Furthermore, the process of deportation itself, whereby force and restraints are often used (see below), entails heightened risks of ill-treatment. The Order on the use of coercion and police measures in areas falling within the jurisdiction of the Confederation clarifies how these deportations should take place in practice, notably through a system of levels of coercion depending on the persons' behaviour.[37] Accordingly, persons who have agreed to return independently may be escorted by the police until boarding, but continue their journey alone (level 1), persons who have not agreed to return independently may be escorted during the flight by plainclothes police officers and, if necessary can be handcuffed (level 2), or other physical force may be used (level 3). Finally, persons who are likely to resist using strong physical force may be transported on so-called special flights (level 4).

Public scrutiny over deportation practices drastically increased in 2010, when Joseph Ndukaku Chiakwa, a Nigerian national, died on the tarmac of Zurich airport after being restrained by the police. Following public outrage, the State Secretariat for Migration (SEM), the entity

---

36 The criminal codes foresee that "the court shall expel foreign nationals from Switzerland for a period of 5–15 years if they are convicted" to a range of offences (art. 66 CC). This provision stems from a so-called popular initiative "For the Criminal Foreigners' Deportation", launched by the Swiss People's Party (SVP/UDC). Initially thought as targeting persons convicted for serious crimes, the law also includes minor misdemeanours such as frauds related to social insurance or social assistance.

37 Art. 28 Order (*ordonnance*) on the use of coercion and police measures in areas falling within the jurisdiction of the Confederation (OLUsC, 364.3).

responsible to oversee deportations, opened a call for tenders to ensure that an independent entity would be present to monitor deportation procedures. The Swiss NPM was awarded the mandate and is therefore paid directly by the authority (SEM) for this specific task. Although this mode of funding raises legitimate questions regarding the NPM's impartiality, in practice the NPM has never self-censored nor experienced any form of pressure from the SEM. This situation nevertheless underscores the structural vulnerability of the NPM's financing. Given the resource-intensive nature of this particular mandate, the NPM has established a pool of monitors—comprising five to ten human rights experts—to support its members in carrying out this function.

Since 2012, the NPM monitors all "special flights" and, more recently, has also started monitoring the apprehension and transfer to the airport for forced removals by commercial flights. Monitors from the Swiss NPM may also be present in so-called Frontex flights, whereby several States organise together deportation operations under the umbrella of the EU's European Border and Coast Guard Agency, if the flight is organised by Switzerland. The Swiss NPM is one of the few to carry out this type of monitoring in such a systematic way, while many NPMs have not included such practice in their monitoring activities. In 2024 (most recent thematic report published to date), the NPM monitored 53 forced deportation flights (level 4). A total of 460 persons were thus removed by special flight, including 46 families with 88 children. The NPM also observed 13 forced removals at enforcement levels 2 and 3, involving a total of 26 persons, including 5 families with 9 children.[38]

Monitoring forced deportations differs from the NPM's other monitoring activities in many regards and raises specific challenges. In fact, monitors often observe situations of active use of force and restraints; they are often on their own and not part of a team, and they may be faced with specific moral dilemma (Blanc, 2022). However, the rationale of monitoring bodies—including the CPT which sometimes also monitors deportation flights—is based on the conviction that scrutiny is always a better option than deportations taking place "behind closed

---

[38] CNPT, *Résumé du rapport de la Commission nationale de prévention de la torture (CNPT) relatif au contrôle des renvois en application du droit des étrangers - Janvier à décembre 2024*, pp. 1–2.

doors". The monitoring of deportation flights undertaken by the NPM over more than a decade has enabled significant changes in police practices. In particular, the use of restraints has become more aligned with the principle of proportionality and the use of full restraints[39]—a highly criticised method by the NPM—is used in exceptional cases. Inhuman and degrading practices, including the prohibition of accessing toilets while on board (and the subsequent use of diapers[40]) or the administration of sedatives without the person's consent have also been abolished.

Nevertheless, every year, the NPM continues to observe problematic situations, such as the use of restrains on a pregnant woman while breastfeeding her younger child (2021), the use of restraints on children, or the separation of family members, to name a few. During the COVID-19 pandemic, the NPM—alongside other stakeholders, including from the medical profession—failed to fight against the entry into force of a legal provision that enabled to subject deportees to forced testing. Nevertheless, the fact that the NPM is present during the flights is an illustration of the double dimension of torture prevention: deterrence (police officers may refrain from resorting to questionable practices because of the mere presence of an independent observer) and longer-term improvement thanks to a regular dialogue with the SEM and cantonal police forces. Furthermore, the NPM has been participating in police training to sensitise police officers on its recommendations. In a context of

[39] Full restraints are a combination of handcuffs (on the wrists, sometimes in front, sometimes behind the back), ankle restraints, restraint belts or harness and, in some cases, additional restraints connecting the wrists, the belt, and the ankles. Some cantons used to systematically apply full restraints to all persons subject to deportation, regardless of their behaviour (see for example: CNPT, *Rapport au Département fédéral de justice et police (DFJP) et à la Conférence des directrices et directeurs des départements cantonaux de justice et police (CCDJP) relatif au contrôle des renvois en application du droit des étrangers de juillet 2012 à avril 2013*, para 24, p. 10).

[40] In its first thematic report on deportation flights (covering 2010 and 2011), published in November 2011, the NPM observed the following: "On certain flights, and for security reasons, returnees were not permitted to leave their seats for the entire duration of the journey. Being unable to access the toilets, they were required to relieve themselves using devices such as 'Travel-John,' a situation that those concerned quite rightly experienced as humiliating. This immobilization, which can last several hours, also increases the risk of thromboembolism" (pp. 5–6).

harsher immigration policies across Europe,[41] the NPM can act as a guardian and reminder of the importance of human rights in every facet of migration phenomena.

Monitoring Federal Asylum Centres: Restriction of Movement in Focus

Federal asylum centres (FACs) are an example of places that are not *stricto sensu* places of deprivation of liberty, but where there are restrictions of movements. FACs have therefore been included in monitoring activities undertaken by the Swiss NPM. In Switzerland, migration issues are dealt with both centrally through the SEM and locally by the Cantons. Asylum proceedings are the responsibility of the SEM and are conducted in six "asylum regions".[42] Each region has a federal asylum centre with processing facilities[43] and several other centres without such facilities.[44] There are approximately 5.000 accommodation places for asylum seekers, but the capacity can be increased to about 10.000 places in case of emergency or sudden influx of migration flows.

During its visits to the FACs, the NPM monitors the housing conditions and adequacy of the infrastructure, particularly with regard to the needs of families with children, the situation of unaccompanied minors, healthcare and support, as well as recreational opportunities. Other important components of its visits relate to the proportionality of disciplinary and security measures that may apply in certain cases, as well as violence prevention. On certain visits, the NPM is assisted by interpreters.

[41] The most recent example is a parliamentary initiative, tabled in 2024, aimed at authorising the use of sedatives instead of restraints if they are deemed necessary to carry out forced deportations.

[42] This division does not correspond to any other administrative division. They are organised as follows: French-speaking Switzerland, Bern, North-Western Switzerland, Zurich, Eastern Switzerland, Ticino, and Central Switzerland.

[43] An asylum application can only be lodged in such centres. Asylum seekers must remain in these centres while their application is processed.

[44] These other centres are mostly used for people who are due to be removed to another Dublin member state under the Dublin Regulation, or whose asylum applications have been rejected.

The NPM has first visited "federal registration and processing centres" (the name of these centres have been changed later on to FACs) between 2011 and 2013 and again regularly from 2018 on, based on the rationale that, although asylum applicants are not formally deprived of their liberty, there are specific hours when they have to be present in the centres (at night). As for deportation flights, the NPM receives specific funding from the SEM to carry out this task.

Considering its most recent visits to FACs, the NPM has notably criticised and made recommendations in relation to: the use of underground facilities (which is primarily for civilian protection during war time) in non-emergency situations, whereby other FACs in the same asylum regions were underused[45]; appalling material conditions (a FAC in the region of Ticino and Central Switzerland was closed shortly after a visit by the NPM[46]); inappropriate reactions by staff to situations of violence among asylum seekers; poor training of security staff hired by private companies; the use of pepper spray or gel; the lack of clarity with regard to the use of security rooms; discrimination faced by groups in vulnerable situations (notably LGBTIQ+ people). The Swiss NPM also monitors FACs located within the international airports of Zurich and Geneva, where asylum seekers are de facto deprived of liberty for a period up to 60 days. At Geneva airport, faced with the situation of an asylum seeker whose stay had largely exceeded the legal duration, the NPM considered that this was not in conformity with the right to liberty and security and recommended, for any similar situation, a transfer to an accommodation offering a greater freedom of movement.

[45] See for example: CNPT, *Rapport de la Commission nationale de prévention de la torture (CNPT) au Secrétariat d'État aux migrations (SEM) sur ses visites dans les centres fédéraux d'asile (CFA) de la région d'asile Suisse romande de février à juin 2024*, para 14, p. 6.

[46] CNPT, *Bericht an das Staatssekretariat für Migration (SEM) betreffend die Überprüfung der Bundesasylzentren (BAZ) der Asylregion Tessin und Zentralschweiz durch die Nationale Kommission zur Verhütung von Folter (NKVF), September 2023 – Januar 2024*.

Safeguarding the Most Vulnerable: Oversight of Nursing Homes

Further expanding the types of places visited, the Swiss NPM started to monitor nursing homes in 2021, with a focus on measures restricting freedom of movement. The NPM considers itself, as a matter of principle, authorised to visit all institutions in the field of eldercare, irrespective of whether they operate closed units. Residents of nursing and residential care facilities are in structurally asymmetric relationships with staff and management, and dependent and older persons are exposed to specific risks, including violence, abuse, and neglect. They therefore fall within the NPM's preventive mandate.[47] Between 2021 and 2024, the Swiss NPM monitored 16 nursing homes across 13 cantons. Almost all these facilities had a closed unit[48] for persons with dementia. The procedure for placement in a secure unit differs from one institution to another. In some cases, the measure is provided for in the care contract[49] signed by the person authorised to represent the patient. In others, placement is ordered in writing—either by an administrative authority or by a medical doctor—as a measure restricting freedom of movement.[50]

The monitoring of nursing homes is a highly complex task, in light of methodological and ethical considerations. Furthermore, such visits pose significant challenges in relation to fundamental rights, notably with regard to persons incapable of discernment. Facing at times contradicting standards between the European Convention on Human Rights (ECHR) and the Convention on the Rights of Persons with Disabilities (CRPD),[51] the NPM commissioned legal experts at the University of Bern to issue a legal opinion on the classification of the placement

---

[47] CNPT, *Rapport d'activité de la Commission nationale de prévention de la torture (CNPT), 2022* p. 8.

[48] A closed unit is an area within a nursing home in which persons with dementia cannot leave freely. The institutions usually refer to "secure" or "protected" units, but in the view of the NCPT, those units are closed.

[49] Art. 382 Swiss Civil Code.

[50] Arts. 428–429 Swiss Civil Code.

[51] For example, while the ECHR permits, under certain conditions, the placement of persons with dementia in closed settings, the CRPD opposes placement without consent, prioritising the autonomy of persons with disabilities.

of persons incapable of discernment in closed units of nursing homes (Künzli et al., 2024). The experts concluded that the placement of persons against their will or without their consent in a closed unit constitutes a deprivation of liberty, since they cannot or would not be able to leave the institution at will without the consent of another person. This type of placement may therefore only be appropriate pursuant to a decision by the authorities ordering placement for assistance purposes due to mental illness and if the person poses a danger to themselves or others. A contract constitutes a sufficient basis for placement in a closed unit, but only if the person is capable of giving his or her consent or has given their prior consent.

During its visits to closed units within nursing homes, the NPM observed that deprivation of liberty is designed in such a way that it applies only to those targeted by the measure. For instance, the entrance doors can only be opened by codes that residents—given their condition—cannot memorise, or doors are made difficult to open (because they are heavy, or tricks and *trompe-l'oeil* are used). In practice, this means that a space can easily be accessed by someone without a medical condition, but not by someone with dementia.

Unlike with bars and knocks, deprivation of liberty is therefore tailored and designed based on a given disability. Although the ground for such measures may be deemed reasonable (preventing residents from leaving the institution on their own and possibly get injured or lost), it is important for the NPM to maintain a critical perspective regarding the procedures enabling placement in closed units (including through advanced directives) and their related safeguards. The NPM also unveiled vocabulary that tends to diminish the fact that these units are *per se* deprivation of liberty. For instance, naming a closed unit "protected" or "with selective accessibility" should not render invisible the fact residents cannot leave their units independently.

6 Conclusion

Fifteen years after its establishment, the Swiss NPM has demonstrated the capacity to exercise its preventive mandate, extending well beyond traditional detention settings. Its work illustrates how a centralised mechanism can navigate a highly federalised system while maintaining functional independence, fostering constructive dialogue with a multiplicity of authorities, and addressing both legal and ethical challenges inherent in monitoring persons deprived of liberty.

Through systematic oversight of diverse sites—from forced deportation flights to federal asylum centres, and more recently, nursing homes—the NPM has highlighted the importance of focusing on the vulnerability of specific populations, whether asylum seekers, children, or older persons with limited autonomy and/or incapable of discernment. At the same time, persistent challenges—limited resources, part-time mandates of its members, and questions surrounding institutional and financial independence—illustrate the ongoing need for structural and operational support to fully realise the preventive potential envisioned by the OPCAT.

Measuring impact is undoubtedly one of the most complex tasks for an NPM. Beyond the effective implementation of its recommendations, it is important to identify secondary forms of impact, for instance when NPM reports are cited by courts to support factual findings.[52] Above all, the preventive culture fostered by the NPM should not be underestimated. Its regular presence in places of deprivation of liberty, the awareness among institutions of potential unannounced visits, ongoing dialogue with authorities and civil society, the exposure of often-overlooked issues related to confinement, and engagement in training and awareness-raising collectively contribute to shaping a culture of torture and ill-treatment prevention in Switzerland.

[52] See, for example, the judgement of the Federal Supreme Court of 12 March 2025: 6B_712/2024 12.03.2025.

References

Blanc, J.-S. (2022). *Monitoring deportation flights: Questionable practices and moral dilemmas*. Border Criminologies, Faculty of Law Blogs, University of Oxford. https://blogs.law.ox.ac.uk/border-criminologies-blog/blog-post/2022/10/monitoring-deportation-flights-questionable-practices

Commission nationale de prevention de la torture [CNPT]. (2017). *Rapport d'activités*. CNPT.

CNPT. (2018). *Rapport d'activités*. CNPT.

CNPT. (2022). *Rapport d'activités*. CNPT.

CNPT. (2011). *Rapport au Département fédéral de justice et police (DFJP) et à la Conférence des directrices et directeurs des départements cantonaux de justice et police (CCDJP) relatif à l'accompagnement par la Commission Nationale de Prévention de la Torture (CNPT) de rapatriements sous contrainte par voie aérienne en 2010 et 2011*. CNPT.

CNPT. (2013). *Rapport au Département fédéral de justice et police (DFJP) et à la Conférence des directrices et directeurs des départements cantonaux de justice et police (CCDJP) relatif au contrôle des renvois en application du droit des étrangers de juillet 2012 à avril 2013*. CNPT.

CNPT. (2022). *Bericht an das Eidgenössische Justiz- und Polizeidepartement (EJPD) und die Kantonale Konferenz der Justiz- und Polizeidirektorinnen und - direktoren (KKJPD) betreffend das ausländerrechtliche Vollzugsmonitoring von April bis Dezember 2021*. CNPT.

CNPT. (2024). *Bericht an das Staatssekretariat für Migration (SEM) betreffend die Überprüfung der Bundesasylzentren (BAZ) der Asylregion Tessin und Zentralschweiz durch die Nationale Kommission zur Verhütung von Folter (NKVF), September 2023–January 2024.*

CNPT. (2024). *Rapport au Secrétariat d'État aux migrations (SEM) sur ses visites dans les centres fédéraux d'asile (CFA) de la région d'asile Suisse romande de février à juin 2024*. CNPT.

Conseil fédéral. (2006). *Message relatif à un projet d'arrêté fédéral portant approbation et mise en œuvre du Protocole facultatif se rapportant à la Convention contre la torture et autres peines ou traitements cruels, inhumains ou dégradants du 8 décembre 2006* (06.105).

Conseil national. (2012). *Motion Streiff-Feller Marianne. Commission nationale de prévention de la torture,* 11.3222.

Kälin, W., & Nowak, M. (2017). *Rechtliche Aspekte der Unabhängigkeit der Nationalen Kommission zur Verhütung der Folter (NKVF)*, Gutachten zuhanden der NKVF [not published]. Cited in CNPT (2017). *Rapport d'activités*. CNPT.

Künzli, J., Bertoni, L., & Stucki, N. (2024). *Die Unterbringung urteilsunfähiger Personen in geschlossenen Abteilungen von Alters- und Pflegeinstitutionen - Gutachten zuhanden der Nationalen Kommission zur Verhütung von Folter (NKVF)*. Universität Bern.

McGregor, J. (2017). The challenges and limitations of OPCAT national preventive mechanisms: Lessons from New Zealand. *Australian Journal of Human Rights, 23*(3), 351–367.

Subcommittee on Prevention of Torture and Other Cruel, Inhuman or Degrading Treatment or Punishment [SPT]. (2021). *Visit to Switzerland undertaken from 27 January to 7 February 2019: recommendations and observations addressed to the State party*, CAT/OP/CHE/ROSP/1, March 2021.

SPT. (2021). *Visit to Switzerland undertaken from 27 January to 7 February 2019: recommendations and observations addressed to the national preventive mechanism*, CAT/OP/CHE/RONPM/1, 22 March 2021.

SPT. (2024). *General comment No. 1 on article 4 of the Optional Protocol (places of deprivation of liberty)*, CAT/OP/GC/1.

The Austrian Ombudsman Board as National Preventive Mechanism: A Unique Approach Combining OPCAT and CRPD Mandates

Kerstin Buchinger and Johannes Carniel

1 Introduction and Historical Background[1]

The Austrian National Preventive Mechanism (NPM) took up its work in the summer of 2012. Its start was preceded by a nine-year-long process from Austria's signature of the Optional Protocol to the Convention against Torture and Other Cruel, Inhuman or Degrading Treatment or Punishment (OPCAT) to the establishment of the monitoring body. During this process, the involved lawmakers have weighed many arguments for the implementation. As the global experience shows, there

[1] Among others cp. Barth (2012), Berka (2018), Bertel (2013), Czech (2016), Klaushofer (2013), Kopetzki (2012), Kucsko-Stadlmayer (2013a, 2013b), Möstl (2017), Pratscher and Carniel (2012) and Vogl (2013) for the basics.

K. Buchinger (✉) · J. Carniel
Austrian Ombudsman Board—Austrian NPM, Vienna, Austria
e-mail: kerstin.buchinger@volksanwaltschaft.gv.at

J. Carniel
e-mail: johannes.carniel@volksanwaltschaft.gv.at

T. Daems et al. (eds.), *Preventing Torture and Monitoring Places of Detention*,
https://doi.org/10.1007/978-3-032-28285-9_9

are several potential models on how to implement an NPM reaching from national human rights commissions to ombuds institutions to new specialised institutions (APT, 2026). Austria is a federal republic consisting of nine states (*Bundesländer*). The legislative and executive powers are divided between the federation and the nine states, and therefore Austria has a federal government and parliament (National Council) as well as nine state governments and nine state parliaments. Accordingly, the competencies concerning the legal and administrative framework relevant for the comprehensive NPM-work are divided between the federation and the states. Considering its constitutional framework, the federal structure and the functioning of its public administration, Austria chose, like many other European states, to vest an ombuds institution, namely the Austrian Ombudsman Board (AOB or *Volksanwaltschaft*) with an additional mandate as NPM. Thereby, the new task could be fulfilled by an existing, highly trusted body with a broad experience of examining public authorities on federal as well as on state level and having the protection of individual complainants at the heart of its work (APA/OGM, 2025).[2,3] Furthermore, the Austrian constitution guarantees the AOB's competencies and prescribes its independence as a highest-ranking institution in the Austrian legal system comparable with the Constitutional Court or the Court of Audit.[4]

During the legislative process for the OPCAT-Implementation Act,[5] civil society organisations, academics and practitioners had been involved in the drafting process and the proposed legal text had been influenced by the various experts' voices. In September 2011, the AOB and Amnesty International participated, for example, in a European 'OPCAT and Ombudsman' seminar in Poland and could get insights into the expertise and experience of other ombuds institutions, SPT and European Committee for the Prevention of Torture and Inhuman or Degrading

[2] The AOB holds the second highest score in institutional confidence ranking.

[3] Besides the classic ombuds individual complaint mechanism, the AOB can initiate examination procedures of its own motion. In addition, the AOB hosts the General Secretariat of the International Ombudsman Institute (IOI) since 2009.

[4] Art. 148 et seq. of the Federal Constitution.

[5] Federal Law Gazette (BGBl.) 1/2012.

Treatment or Punishment (CPT) members, as well as civil society organisations. The AOB shared this knowledge of challenges and chances during the drafting process.

The broad inclusion of stakeholders during the law-making process led to, *inter alia*, the parliament entrusting the AOB and future NPM, uniquely in Europe, also with the mandate of the independent authority to prevent exploitation, violence and abuse for persons with disabilities according to Art. 16 para 3 of the Convention on the Rights of Persons with Disabilities (CRPD).[6] This independent authority has to ensure that all facilities and programmes designed to serve persons with disabilities are effectively monitored in order to prevent the occurrence of all forms of exploitation, violence and abuse; a role that is very important for the AOB and influenced its work as NPM.[7,8] Since the NPM interpreted the term 'places of detention' in Art. 4 OPCAT broadly, not just prisons or other detention centres, police stations, or barracks could be visited, but also the so-called less traditional places of detention like facilities for persons with disabilities, psychiatric institutions, retirement and nursing homes, crisis centres and residential communities for young persons. The overall number of facilities, which were identified to fall under the NPM's mandate amounts to more than 5.300 to date. Although sheltered workshops or organised homes for persons with disabilities fall under the category of less traditional places of detention and can be visited under OPCAT, the CRPD mandate reaffirmed that the NPM can monitor those places. In the latter institutions, the AOB took a comprehensive look at risks for mistreatments and a broad view on what

---

[6] Convention on the Rights of Persons with Disabilities (CRPD) of 12 December 2006, entry into force 3 May 2008.

[7] The SPT, initially, recommended for the NPM-mandate to focus on traditional places of detention and was hesitant to embrace the additional CRPD mandate of the AOB. However, in its General Comment No 1 (2024) on Art. 4 OPCAT, the SPT explicitly called upon a comprehensive interpretation of the term 'places of detention' and listed, for example, nursing homes and centres for persons with disabilities.

[8] In addition, the parliament vested the AOB with the powers to monitor and concomitantly inspect the conduct of police bodies or officers authorised to exercise direct administrative authority to issue orders and enforce coercive measures. While this task is strictly speaking not part of the NPM's work, it was introduced in the same act. In 2025, 10 such activities have been carried out.

may constitute violence. This comprehensive view influenced also the assessment of human right risks in other institutions.

Although the new competencies for the AOB were substantial, the support for the new act was huge and the vast majority of members of parliament across the political spectrum voted in favour of the proposed law and supported the changes to the constitution that were necessary in order to grant the AOB its new mandate.[9]

The implementation of the new mandate caused the biggest restructuring of the AOB since its founding in 1977.[10] Prior to the new mandate, the traditional ombudsman work was carried out by legal experts supported by administrative staff. With the introduction of the NPM mandate, some of those legal experts were, in addition, entrusted with tasks under the OPCAT system and have been carrying out both functions since. This proved valuable, because the experts could partly draw from their complaint experiences and identify potential risk areas for the preventive work.[11]

Following the tasks of the new mandate, the AOB had to extend and further develop its procedures and to incorporate new stakeholders under its roof. The OPCAT-Implementation Act was prescribed for pluralistic visiting commissions (hereinafter referred to as 'Commissions') to monitor places of detention as well as a human rights advisory council. While the Commissions carry out the monitoring visits (possibly accompanied by AOB staff) and report back to the AOB on the findings and preventive risk assessment, the Human Rights Advisory Council (HRAC) has an exclusively advisory mandate in relation to the AOB and the Commissions.

[9] 89% of members of parliament supported the act and voted in favour.

[10] With the OPCAT-Implementation Act, the National Council changed the Federal Constitution, the Ombudsman Act 1982, the Security Police Act and the Penitentiary System Act. In conjunction with the Standing Rules of the AOB and the Allocation of Responsibilities and Duties of the AOB, those laws form the main legal basis for the AOB's exercise as NPM.

[11] As an example: The AOB might learn from individual complaints that for persons with disabilities, there is a severe lack of places in care institutions and therefore waiting lists are long. This means that if a person finally gets a place, they have no choice regarding the place to stay and are, therefore, faced with a situation of power imbalance between the institution and themselves. Such aspects of the living reality of persons with disabilities are important to know when making the risk assessment for the preventive mandate.

Such bodies were not completely new to Austria. Following recommendations of the CPT[12] after a visit to Austria 13 years prior to the OPCAT-Implementation Act, the Federal Ministry of the Interior had already set up a human rights advisory council and six regional visiting commissions to monitor the conditions of detention in police jails.

However, the new NPM bodies have a broader mandate.

The six regional visiting Commissions and the federal Commission for prisons are all headed by eminent experts in the field of human rights.[13] The 60 Commission members[14] are selected and appointed by the AOB following a public tender and have an expert background in the fields of medicine, psychology, sociology, social work, care work, law, pedagogy or disability work.[15] Furthermore, the members represent a segment of the Austrian society that is as pluralistic as possible. The goal behind the pluralistic composition of the Commissions is to identify and assess potential human rights relevant risks in the most comprehensive way and thereby be able to give useful recommendations in order to fulfil the preventive mandate in the best possible way. The selection criteria prescribe for the diversity of backgrounds, capabilities and professional knowledge, and the AOB strives to ensure a gender balance as well as proper representation of different ethnic groups and persons with disabilities. The Commissions also have the possibility to bring in additional (peer-)experts for individual visits in order to guarantee the necessary expertise and diversity. Whenever there is doubt about a person's independence or impartiality, this person is excluded from the Commission's work.

The Commissions' experts are appointed for a six-year period, independent in their capacity, and do not become members of the permanent AOB staff. Instead, they receive a remuneration for each monitoring activity they participate in.

---

[12] CPT, Report to the Austrian Government on the visit to Austria carried out by the CPT from 20 May 1990 to 27 May 1990, CPT/Inf (1991) 10, 3 October 1991, para 87.

[13] Sec 12 Ombudsman Act 1982.

[14] As of January 2026.

[15] Sec 12 and 13 Ombudsman Act 1982 (e.g. 'The AOB shall strive to achieve a balanced gender representation and a reasonable representation of ethnic groups and minorities in the commission as well as an independent, interdisciplinary and pluralistic composition having regard to the duties of the commissions').

As far as the HRAC is concerned, several human rights NGOs, the federal ministries involved and the representatives of the *Bundesländer* have a right to nominate members. The number of members is equally balanced between public authorities (8) and NGOs (8). The AOB freely chooses the chairperson and its deputy.

The HRAC supports the AOB and its Commissions with a view to the methodology of the Commissions' work and advises on which foci might be set in the preventive monitoring of places of detention.[16] It makes proposals for control standards, which are intended to ensure a standardised approach by the Commissions. However, the AOB decides independently in these matters and the HRAC, which serves as a dialogue platform for representatives of public administration, civil society and the AOB, purely issues opinions and advice.

In terms of funding and resources, the Austrian NPM has been relatively well positioned already from the beginning up until now. In order to fulfil the requirements under OPCAT and the CRPD, a budget of EUR 1,947,000 was released for the second half of the year 2012. For 2013, expenditures in the amount of EUR 2,960,000 were budgeted for the initial set-up of the NPM and the implementation of the new monitoring system. Moreover, the AOB was allocated 15 additional permanent positions. In 2024, a total amount of EUR 1,700,000 was budgeted for the heads of Commissions, the Commissions' members and the members of the HRAC (AOB, 2025a, p. 20). This budget had to cover travel expenses, compensation for visits (incl. preparation and follow-up) as well as additional expenses, such as cooperation with the SPT, annual reporting, training or participation in evaluation proceedings with respect to the enactment of legislation. However, the costs for the NPM's legal experts within the AOB are always covered by a separate budget.

As far as cost accounting is concerned, the NPM forms a separate cost unit dedicated exclusively to NPM activities. The use of resources allocated to the NPM's work is determined by the members of the AOB

[16] Those foci are chosen by the NPM after discussions among the AOB, the Commissions and the HRAC on issues which are considered particularly important for risk prevention.

in consultation with the seven Commissions. As a result, full financial independence and operational autonomy of the NPM is guaranteed.

2 Monitoring Framework and Methodology

In order to ensure the best possible outcome, the NPM performs its mandates in line with the most common principles of human rights monitoring. Thus, and in line with international standards[17], the Commissions regularly examine the treatment of persons deprived of their liberty by undertaking regular (planned) visits as well as ad hoc visits (upon urgent incidents) and follow-up visits in cases where the experts had encountered certain problems during a regular visit before. It is the NPM's conviction that only when visits are being undertaken in an adequate frequency, an effective contribution is being made to the prevention of torture, ill-treatment or other human rights violations.

Following the general principle of 'quality before quantity', a high number of visits per year is not the most important factor. As prevention aims at minimising risks and taking anticipatory action to protect human rights, the NPM rather endeavours to undertake only a certain number of targeted visits in *selected* facilities and institutions. However, due to the fact that the Austrian NPM is equipped with sufficient financial and human resources (cp. above), the number of actual monitoring activities per year is still high. The conduct of rather short visits proved useful for the NPM in order to get a comprehensive picture of a high number of institutions within a couple of years. This practice helped influencing the institutions' awareness for human rights issues even before an actual Commission's visit in a specific institution or facility took place.

Given this situation, the Commissions conducted a total of 423 preventive monitoring activities throughout Austria in 2025. In total, 311 visits were conducted to so-called less traditional places of detention[18], such as e.g. homes for elderly people or nursing homes, homes

[17] Art. 19 OPCAT.

[18] Throughout Austria, over 5,300 different such institutions and facilities exist.

for the young or foster homes, institutions for children or adults with disabilities, psychiatric institutions and mental health centres. Out of 311 institutions and facilities, 100 were such for persons with disabilities.

Preparation of Visits

The preparation, conduct and follow-up of visits as such are based on a methodology that was jointly developed by the AOB, the Commissions and the HRAC. This approach helps to counter obstacles or difficulties that arise, e.g. from federal structures. As far as possible, the Commissions apply uniform monitoring procedures and assessment standards nationwide to obtain a high level of data comparability. At the same time, regional necessities or priorities are taken into account where this seems reasonable.

The relevant authorities and/or institutions concerned have to provide the NPM with all necessary information on places where persons are or may be deprived of their liberty, on the number of persons concerned as well as on the conditions of detention in order to facilitate the NPM's tasks.[19] In addition, the NPM collects information on the institutions and facilities to be visited also from other bodies (like e.g. the Child and Youth Advocacy, the Patients' Advocacies or NGOs that are active in the relevant fields) in order to get a bigger picture and a better understanding of the institutions and their potential structural deficiencies.

The NPM can choose freely among the institutions it wishes to visit and inspect. It has unrestricted access to all relevant premises of each place to be visited. Usually, the Commissions carry out their visits to places of detention unannounced. Only when certain monitoring foci (cp. below) demand, e.g. the presence of specialised personnel or the preparation of specific documents or data, visits are preannounced. Moreover, the visiting delegations choose the date, time and duration of each visit freely and according to what they deem useful for the individual institution or facility in question. A half-day visit might make

[19] Sec. 11 para. 3 Ombudsman Act 1982.

sense for a quick follow-up, whereas larger institutions regularly demand two or more days of extensive monitoring.

Setting of Monitoring Foci

When preparing the visits, the Commissions concentrate their efforts on concrete monitoring foci and predefined topics. Such focus areas are being determined jointly by the Commissions' experts and AOB staff, incorporating suggestions from the HRAC. Focusing on suggested topics or priorities, the Commissions decide upon the size and composition of visiting delegations as well as upon the number and planned duration of visits. It is at the Commissions' discretion to include additional experts where this seems useful either due to the type of institution to be visited or to a current monitoring focus. After the COVID-19 pandemic, the NPM intensified its efforts to redefine monitoring foci. Following an internal process of strategy planning, which was started already during the COVID-19 pandemic, the NPM agreed upon a new monitoring focus for the area of psychiatric hospitals and departments in 2020. Special attention was turned on the effective prevention of violent incidents. The monitoring focus was developed in an internal NPM process over several months with experts from all regional Commissions and inputs coming from the HRAC. In course of 2021, the regional Commissions conducted 50 visits focusing on this topic. After having addressed the main findings and observations of each visit to the respective authorities, the results were then published in the AOB's annual report accordingly and led to several recommendations to the relevant authorities of the *Bundesländer* (AOB, 2022, pp. 53 et seq.). Since then, several other monitoring foci had been defined and conducted in all areas of the NPM's mandate.

For the best possible preparation of visits, each of the seven Commissions issues quarterly programmes of visits, taking into account the aforementioned monitoring topics and/or foci.

Consideration of Internal Processes

When performing their work, the visiting delegations have to respect and consider the internal processes of the visited institutions or facilities. Especially in the early stages of the NPM's work, the institutions' management and staff were reluctant to cooperate with the NPM, sometimes hesitated to provide the information asked for and in specific cases even refused access to the relevant premises. Sometimes even the persons deprived of their liberty themselves did not have enough trust to talk to the Commissions' experts. Therefore, it was important to create a trustful image of the NPM and the Commission members. In this context, the 'Do no harm'-principle, which is a guiding principle of the Austrian NPM, proved to be extremely important and indispensable. Over time, the continuous attention to this principle enhanced the trust the persons concerned (e.g. patients in psychiatric institutions, children and juveniles in child and youth welfare facilities, elderly people in nursing homes, etc.) felt for the Commissions' experts, especially in cases where they visited institutions repeatedly.

Composition of Visiting Delegations

Each visiting delegation is composed of no less than two Commission experts in order to provide for 'a second set of eyes' and be able to cross-check any information obtained during a visit. Whenever necessary, the visiting delegations can also make use of interpreters and additional external experts in order to cover a broader spectrum of expertise.

Conduct of Visits

The Commissions are granted access to all areas of the respective premises.[20] Over time it proved useful to start each visit with a conversation with the head of the respective institution. However, since such conversations may take time, it is advisable that one or more experts

[20] Sec. 11 para. 3 Ombudsman Act 1982.

talk to the management while others carry out interviews with persons deprived of their liberty and observe the given situation and atmosphere right away. This is important in order to prevent any covering of visible deficiencies in the institution.

The delegations conduct private interviews with the personnel on site as well as with persons deprived of their liberty and other informants that are willing to communicate. The visiting delegations have a right to be provided with all necessary documents, to check the files and to make copies free of charge. The Commissions' experts cross-check all information obtained during interviews.

Whenever possible, the visiting delegations hold closing meetings with the management or the persons in charge that are present at the time of the visit and provide preliminary oral feedback.

Documentation of Findings

Comprehensive documentation of the Commissions' findings is crucial for the initiation of structural changes and improvements, as any measures taken by State authorities or other parties responsible largely depend on the specificity, traceability and reliability of sources. Therefore, the NPM elaborated a standardised reporting template for internal use in line with general principles of documentation. Every observation is documented in detail by the visiting experts so that appropriate conclusions can be drawn by the AOB. The template allows for a comprehensive human rights assessment of all findings. In addition, the in-depth documentation facilitates the planning of follow-up visits and/or the setting of future monitoring foci.

3 Further Action to Achieve Improvements

After having received a Commission's report on findings and observations during a visit, the AOB assesses the recommendations and confronts the highest administrative body responsible for the supervision and operation of the visited facility in writing. As appropriate, the facility's management is also being informed and consulted. The AOB's written communication regularly contains suggestions on how to remedy the deficiencies that were found and/or how to implement appropriate measures in order to prevent human rights violations (so-called consultation proceeding or confrontation proceeding).

In certain cases of serious findings and upon recommendation by the respective head of Commission or the AOB itself, a joint recommendation in accordance with Article 148c of the Austrian Federal Constitution is drafted. It contains a brief description of the case and any maladministration observed as well as a short summary defining the human rights standards applied and indicating recommended measures to be taken. After having sent the draft recommendation to the HRAC for further advisory remarks, it is then submitted to the responsible supreme administrative body. The body in question is obligated to comply with the NPM's recommendation within a period of eight weeks (and to notify the NPM thereof) or to provide reasons in writing why the recommendations have not been followed. The statement as such (in condensed form) is published on the AOB's website.

In recent years, for example, the NPM had repeatedly found that extramural care options for people with chronic psychiatric illnesses are inadequate throughout Austria (cp. AOB, 2022, pp. 49 et seq. with further references). In 2023, one of the NPM's regional Commissions visited a number of homes for the elderly and came across several rather young people with mental illnesses and/or needs for specific care also living there. The activities and leisure programmes, daily routines and staff training, however, were geared exclusively towards the actual target group of the facilities in question, namely the (very) elderly. After having approached the respective regional government several times, the NPM requested information on the specific steps, measures and considerations taken in recent years (since 2019) to create specialised facilities for younger people dependent on care. The NPM determined a case of maladministration and recommended to present short and medium-term plans for the expansion of appropriate, needs-based and community-based housing support for younger people with care needs, as well as more information on alternative options for support and assistance (AOB, 2024, pp. 65 et seq.).

In cases where the monitored institution is established under private law and entrusted with State functions, its management is informed about the NPM's assessment, with Article 148c of the Austrian Federal Constitution applied with the necessary changes. The competent supervisory authority of the *Bundesland* in question is then being notified accordingly.

Once a recommendation has been adopted, its main content (set out as a guiding principle) is binding for the NPM. The guiding principles defined in such manner help facilitating the preparations for follow-up visits as well as the elaboration of subsequent visit reports. Apart from identifying human rights violations, the guiding principles also help promoting the preventive character of the NPM's mandate.

4 Publication of Results

With Austria being a federal republic, the AOB reports on its preventive human rights monitoring annually to the National Council (being the lower house of Parliament, where Austria's federal legislative is concentrated), the Federal Council (the upper house, representing the nine states at the federal level) and all regional (states') parliaments.[21] In its reports, it highlights the perceived systemic shortcomings that have been identified by the Commissions during the respective reporting periods and issues recommendations for improvements in line with the existing (inter)national standards. Moreover, the AOB makes proposals for corresponding legislative amendments when deemed to be necessary. After

[21] Sec. 3 para. 1 Ombudsman Act 1982.

having been submitted to the National Council and the Federal Council, the AOB has to publish its reports. Also, and in line with its obligations under OPCAT, the AOB submits its annual reports to the SPT.[22]

5 Dialogue and Communication Within the NPM

An open, intensive and continuous dialogue between the AOB and the Commissions, where ideas and experiences are shared, also increases the effectiveness of the NPMs work. Therefore, the AOB regularly provides for information about relevant developments on the international, European and national level and special trainings in all thematic fields within the NPMs mandate. Moreover, a two-day event for all members of the NPM's Commissions as well as for AOB personnel is organised on an annual basis in order to promote extensive exchange.

To enhance the Commission members' interviewing capabilities, the NPM organises communication workshops with professional actors who are specially trained in simulating patients. The NPM has adapted this practice-oriented training, which had initially been developed by the Teaching Centre of the Medical University of Vienna, for the Commissions' specific needs and continuously uses it in its training programmes.

6 Relations with Authorities, Civil Society and Other Partners

Apart from its monitoring activities, the NPM maintains regular communication with authorities as well as with NGOs and other representatives of civil society. Every year, the AOB hosts a forum where topics of socio-political and human rights relevance are being discussed with civil society. In May 2024, e.g. the event focused on the implementation of children's rights in Austria. Around 80 NGO representatives

[22] Ibid

came to discuss possibilities on how to improve the given situation for children and juveniles (AOB, 2025b). NGO representatives are asked to make thematic suggestions for these annual forums through the so-called NGO Sounding Board. This board was established to strengthen the NPM's exchange with civil society. In order to bring all relevant stakeholders together, usually representatives of competent authorities are also invited to participate in the discussions at the annual forum.

The NPM is not the only monitoring body whose mandate is to prevent violence or mistreatment of children/juveniles, persons with disabilities, elderly people and persons with a psychiatric diagnosis. Other bodies like e.g. the residents' representatives (*Bewohnerinnen- bzw. Bewohnervertretungen*), who examine the lawfulness of acts of deprivation of liberty applied to persons with disabilities or to elderly people, the patients' advocacies (*VertretungsNetz Patientenanwaltschaft*), who have a similar mandate regarding persons with psychiatric diagnoses, the ombuds offices for children's rights (*Kinder- und Jugendanwaltschaften*) as well as the disability ombudspersons (*Behindertenanwaltschaften*) also strive for a comprehensive promotion and protection of human rights with regard to their clients or respective target groups. They all have different approaches to their work and different access to relevant information. Therefore, it proved useful for the NPM to engage and cooperate with them, ensure a proper information flow and thereby enhance the expertise of the NPM.

The NPM is also in regular contact with several international partners. In order to present its work approach (e.g. regarding its understanding of monitoring) and to benefit from external feedback, the NPM organised, for example, so-called shadow monitoring activities with experts from the Council of Europe, SPT, CPT and APT participating. During these events, international experts were able to accompany the Austrian visiting delegations to several places of detention and give direct feedback (AOB, 2015, p. 10). As will be discussed below, the NPM engages in a dialogue with NPMs of Germany, Switzerland, Luxembourg and Liechtenstein (DACH-LU-LI). Furthermore, the NPM is also a member of the 'South East European NPM Network' (SEE NPM Network).

7 The NPMs Main Challenges

Challenges Faced Initially After Implementation of the New Mandate

New Staff, New Procedures, New Workload

The AOB itself had to hire new staff in order to be able to process the new workload and to incorporate additional expertise in its work force. This was necessary, because—although the AOB did examine some complaints through a human rights lens before—the new mandate demanded specialised human rights knowledge and in-house expertise. The work as NPM demanded a different approach than classic ombuds complaint examinations and the challenge was, besides incorporating a larger number of new staff into the AOB, to introduce new work processes.

In addition, the independent experts working for the Commissions or the HRAC had, to a large part, worked for the (former) monitoring commissions or the human rights advisory council, which had been established by Federal Ministry of the Interior prior to the NPM mandate. The members had developed their individual approach to work. Under the OPCAT mandate, the AOB, the new Commissions and the new HRAC had to align their work in order to enable a unified and standardised approach. Naturally, this was met with some resistance from the (former) commissions' members, which were used to work without the AOB. It was challenging to agree on monitoring procedures, documentation or reporting formats and a clear strategy as well as trust-building measures were needed.

To ensure this, experts from the SPT and the European NPM Network had given guidance and advice to carry out the new mandate. In addition, they provided trainings on how to apply international standards. From the first kick-off event up to this day, the AOB and the HRAC hold monthly meetings and the AOB organises sessions with the heads of Commissions every three months. As discussed above, the AOB and the independent Commissions meet once a year for a two-day workshop in order to exchange experiences.

Besides the fact that AOB and the Commissions had to find a practical way to collaborate, the sheer number of institutions falling under the scope of the NPM's mandate (at present about 5,300) posed a challenge. In order to fulfil its mandate in the best possible way, the NPM had to establish a feasible plan on the monitoring procedures, on how to get a comprehensive overview of all the institutional data and to set visiting goals accordingly.

Resistance from Authorities

Initially, some *Bundesländer* and municipalities voiced their reservation against the NPM and argued that they were not bound by OPCAT. However, the legal obligations were clear, and after sound argumentation, those stakeholders waived their objections. The *Bundesland* of *Vorarlberg* first chose to establish its own NPM, because it had its own ombuds institution carrying out public administration examinations already in place. After several years it became clear that a separate NPM led to inadvertent duplicity. Thus, *Vorarlberg* transferred its preventive mandate finally to the NPM acting on the federal level.

Another issue concerned the applicability of the OPCAT mandate for children's homes. In one *Bundesland*, the Child and Youth Welfare Authority challenged the NPM's view that such institutions would be covered by the NPM's mandate. However, after expounding the national legal framework as well as the international standards of the NPM mandate, the AOB could finally convince the responsible authorities that homes for the young and foster homes did also fall under the scope of Art. 4 OPCAT.

Challenges in the Course of the NPM's Work

Over time, both public- and private-sector organisations have generally been rather cooperative with the Austrian NPM. However, certain (private-sector) stakeholders raised concerns with regard to the limits and boundaries of the NPM's mandate, not only during the first years after the implementation of OPCAT, but also later on. In 2018, the

Austrian Economic Chambers (AEC), for example, challenged the AOB's way on how to execute the mandate. They argued that the examination of certain areas was not covered by the NPM's monitoring competencies. This included, e.g. questions on whether clinical supervision was offered to the staff of homes for elderly persons. Moreover, the AEC argued that the NPM should not speak of 'shortcomings' or 'deficiencies' in situations where all *national* provisions and regulations had been met by the facilities in question. Similar concerns were raised by a private organisation operating several nursing homes in one of the *Bundesländer* in 2020. The organisation's legal representatives claimed that health-care facilities fell within the NPM's monitoring competencies under Art. 16 para. 3 CRPD only with regard to residents with permanent and serious impairments of physical, mental, psychological or sensory functions. Accordingly, the NPM's activities should exclusively focus on persons who are or had been deprived of their liberty as well as on the rights of persons with disabilities. In response to these concerns, the AOB referred to its constitutional competencies emerging from Art. 4 OPCAT and Art. 16 para. 3 CRPD and once again elaborated on its broad understanding of mandate.

8 Major Improvements and Impact on Policies (in Austria and Across Europe)

Over the years, the NPM's efforts had a strong impact on the human rights situation of persons deprived of their liberty as well as on the human rights standards for persons with disabilities. The NPM's work led to changes in legislation and the implementation of certain standards as well as to structural reforms.

For example, the law protecting persons with disabilities from unlawful acts of deprivation of liberty initially was not applicable for child welfare institutions. After having observed mistreatments of minors with disability in such facilities, the NPM lobbied alongside the residents' representative's organisation for the change of the applicable law.

This has been done through request for statements by public authorities, reporting, media work, liaising with judges and through academic research papers. Finally, the law had been changed and applies to child welfare facilities as well.

Another amendment the NPM accounted for concerned the use of so-called net beds in psychiatric hospitals. Since 1999, the CPT had reiterated its recommendation that 'net beds [should] be withdrawn from service as a tool for managing agitated persons in all psychiatric/social welfare institutions and facilities in Austria'.[23] Certain *Bundesländer*, however, had not yet followed the CPT's advice. In accordance with the NPM's recommendation, the Federal Ministry of Health finally prohibited the use of psychiatric intensive beds (net beds) as well as other 'cage-like beds' by way of decree[24] in July 2014.

In other cases, the legislation has not been changed yet, but a process to change the law has been established. From the outset of its work, the NPM, for example, observed the risk of exploitation of persons with disabilities in sheltered workshops. This risk was caused by the applicable law that did not categorise this kind of occupation as labour in the legal sense. As a consequence, the clients only receive a small amount of pocket money for their work, thereby being completely dependent on social welfare and the institution they live in. Furthermore, they do not have the possibility to retire and get a pension. The NPM visited workshops where clients during an eight-hour working day produced goods for high-end fashion brands and other top consumer companies and did not receive adequate salaries. To lobby for a systemic change, the AOB presented a special, public report on this topic to the national and regional parliaments. As a result, the Ministry for Social Affairs had established a high-profile working group with all major stakeholders in order to change the legal framework. Although this topic is not resolved yet, all stakeholders agreed that a change was important and several pilot projects had been set up since.

---

[23] E.g. CPT, Report to the Austrian Government on the visit to Austria carried out by the CPT from 15 to 25 February 2009, CPT/Inf (2010) 5, 11 March 2010, para. 134.

[24] Federal Ministry of Health, *Decree on the use of psychiatric intensive beds in institutions based on the Hospitalisation of Mentally Ill Persons Act and the Nursing and Residential Homes Residence Act,* 22 July 2014.

Occasionally, the Commissions had to visit institutions and facilities where people had to live under unacceptable conditions. Presented with the observations of gravest mistreatments, the relevant public authorities (or sometimes even the service providers themselves) closed the respective facilities.

In early 2022, serious findings in a nursing home in one of the *Bundesländer* prompted the NPM to closely monitor the duties and obligations of supervisory authorities to guarantee adequate fostering and care as well as the compliance with legal (and ethical) standards. In the course of its visit, the competent regional Commission identified a clear shortage of staff, a very high number of employees on (long-term) sick leave and overworked staff. Moreover, it observed serious care deficits in the areas of care planning, care reports and the execution of risk assessments (in particular regarding pain, malnourishment and bedsores). Based on these observations, the Commission's experts assumed that the (mental and physical) integrity of the residents was at risk. Apart from the unbearable conditions in the visited nursing home, the NPM observed insufficient quality management on the part of the respective supervisory authority. The deficits outlined by the NPM led to nationwide media coverage and criminal investigations (AOB, 2022, p. 32 et seq.).

On a more general level, service providers, public authorities and lawmakers, after 13 years of NPM's work, accept the necessity of deinstitutionalisation for persons with disabilities. Although there is no concerted process throughout Austria yet, there are efforts to close or downsize existing institutions and not to approve large facilities anymore.

In the field of prisons, the NPM could convince the Ministry of Justice and prison managements to establish accessible visitor rooms, to improve safety in special secured detention cells or to digitise documentation and make it traceable thereby.

As far as standard setting is concerned, certain standards are now widely accepted as indispensable in Austria due to the NPM's continuous efforts. While in the initial phase of the NPM's monitoring, many facilities did not have a proper complaint mechanism, violence prevention and protection concepts, elected self-representative bodies, supervision possibilities or sex education concepts for sexual self-determination and protection in place, these necessities are widely undisputed today. Furthermore, the NPM is informing service providers as well as public authorities on the indispensability of having individual augmented and alternative communication in place. The NPM demands for institutions to provide such communication tools and collects relevant data during its visits.

The ultimate goal of the NPM's work is the prevention of torture as well as of inhuman or degrading treatment or punishment. To reach this goal, the NPM regarded it of great importance to convince service providers that such risks are unacceptable and to give feedback on what might pose a threat to persons deprived of their liberty. Certain small risks can easily be eliminated and it might be useful just to ask the facility to do so (and check the results during a follow-up visit). Other observations should be raised with the service provider companies, while some findings need to be brought to the supervision authorities' attention. As mentioned above, the NPM strives to establish respectful relationships with service providers and motivate them to improve their services. The different ways on how to raise risk assessment topics contribute to this goal.

Since 2013, the NPM has participated in various activities of mutual exchange throughout Europe. In order to share experiences with other preventive mechanisms in the German-speaking world, the NPM, e.g. regularly participates in meetings with the NPMs of Germany, Switzerland, Luxembourg and Liechtenstein (DACH-LU-LI), where ideas about effective preventive work, successful working methodologies and tried-and-tested strategies are shared. Moreover, the NPM has been a member of the so-called South East European NPM Network since its establishment in 2013. This association of NPM institutions from Albania, Bosnia and Herzegovina, Bulgaria, Croatia, Greece, Hungary, Montenegro, North Macedonia, Romania, Serbia, Slovenia and Austria (as well as Kosovo as an observer) provides a forum where knowledge and experiences are shared and mutual support is provided. During such meetings, the NPM together with its European partners, for example, visited homes and hospitals partly with the support of (consented) video broadcasting or conducted role-play trainings with actors. The goal of such exercises was and is to enhance the Commission members' interviewing techniques.

9 Conclusion

After 13 years of implementing the OPCAT mandate, it is useful to reflect more comprehensively on the NPM's performance and developments. In our opinion, the AOB, alongside the visiting Commissions and the HRAC as advisory body, was an appropriate choice to carry out the new preventive monitoring tasks. It enjoys a good reputation as an impartial actor and can rely on a high level of recognition among the general public. Due to its decades long work experience, the AOB has a tradition of dealing with the highest public administration authorities, voicing criticism against them in a constructive way, making recommendations and act as an impartial actor. Those features proved to be useful when starting to carry out the mandate and touching on difficult, sensitive topics in course of the monitoring activities and enabled the AOB and the visiting Commissions to contribute extensively to human rights-related improvements for persons deprived of their liberty. The good reputation of the NPM as a whole is also evident from the fact that the NPM is regularly invited to teach police cadets on human rights obligations during police trainings.

We are convinced that having the classic ombudsman mandate and the OPCAT mandate in-house influenced the respective work positively. Although there is a clear procedural and focal difference between individual complaints procedures and a preventive human rights mandate, there are nevertheless potential issues of thematic overlapping. Points that are raised in individual complaints can give insights into institutional shortcomings. Those could in turn be very relevant for the preventive work and the related risk assessment. When the AOB, for example, holds consultation days for prison inmates as part of its ombudsman work, it can learn about potential systematic problems from individual examples. This might influence its ability to carry out risk assessments in course of its preventive work.

Furthermore, the additional mandate as the independent authority according to Art. 16 para 3 CRPD widened the focus of the NPM in a special way. Through the CRPD mandate, the NPM included CRPD obligations in a comprehensive way in its preventive risk assessment. This approach did not only influence the work relating to facilities for persons with disabilities, but also spilled over to other institutions. Certain standards that were developed for the risk minimising in places for persons with disabilities were later also aligned for other institutions. Therefore, the special focus on disability rights in combination with the prevention of violence widened the NPM's view and contributed to a more comprehensive risk assessments in other institutions.

Since the NPM has been interpreting Art. 4 OPCAT in a broad way from the very beginning and thereby has been focusing also on less traditional places of detention, it was able to do some pioneering work with a view to homes for the elderly or facilities for persons with disabilities. It is fair to say that the NPM did shed light on the human rights situation in those institutions and contributed to improvements with a view to reduce risks for torture and other cruel, inhuman or degrading treatment or punishment.

Finally, an important factor for the success of the NPM's work is also the independence of the AOB as a NHRI in full compliance with the Paris Principles (GANHRI, 2022) and the visiting Commissions as well as the HRAC as a consulting body. Those actors have, potentially, three different approaches to assessments and can freely issue their opinions and reports. This plurality of expertise gives weight and informal authority to the NPM.

Bibliography

Association for the Prevention of Torture. (2026). *APT OPCAT database.* https://www.apt.ch/knowledge-hub/opcat

Austria Presse Agentur/OGM research & communication, APA/OGM. (2025). *Confidence index 2025.* https://www.ogm.at/2025/10/17/vertrauensindex-institutionen-oesterreich-2025/

Association for the Prevention of Torture. (2026). *OPCAT database*. https://www.apt.ch/knowledge-hub/opcat

Austrian Ombudsman Board. (2013). *Report of the Austrian Ombudsman Board on the activities of the National Preventive Mechanism 2012*. https://volksanwaltschaft.gv.at/fileadmin/user_upload/Downloads/Berichte/IntBe/Report_of_the_AOB_on_the_activities_of_the_NPM_2012.pdf

Austrian Ombudsman Board. (2015). *Annual Report on the activities of the Austrian National Preventive Mechanism (NPM), 2014, Protection and Promotion of Human Rights*. https://volksanwaltschaft.gv.at/fileadmin/user_upload/Downloads/Berichte/IntBe/Report_on_the_activities_of_the_NPM_-_2014.pdf

Austrian Ombudsman Board. (2016). *Annual Report on the activities of the Austrian National Preventive Mechanism (NPM), 2015, Protection and Promotion of Human Rights*. https://volksanwaltschaft.gv.at/fileadmin/user_upload/Downloads/Berichte/IntBe/Report_on_the_Activities_of_the_Austrian_NPM_2015.pdf

Austrian Ombudsman Board. (2022). *Annual Report on the activities of the Austrian National Preventive Mechanism (NPM), 2021, Protection and Promotion of Human Rights*. https://volksanwaltschaft.gv.at/fileadmin/user_upload/Downloads/Berichte/IntBe/pb-2022-vol-2-en_bf-3.pdf.

Austrian Ombudsman Board. (2024). *Annual Report on the activities of the Austrian National Preventive Mechanism (NPM), 2023, Protection and Promotion of Human Rights*. https://volksanwaltschaft.gv.at/fileadmin/user_upload/Downloads/Berichte/IntBe/47_Annual_Report_2023_-_Protection_Promotion_of_Human_Rights_bf.pdf

Austrian Ombudsman Board. (2025a). *Annual Report on the activities of the Austrian National Preventive Mechanism (NPM), 2024, Protection and Promotion of Human Rights*. https://volksanwaltschaft.gv.at/fileadmin/user_upload/Annual_Report_2024_-_Activities_of_the_NPM_bf.pdf.

Austrian Ombudsman Board. (2025b, May 26). *Austrian Ombudsman Board NGO Forum: 'Human Rights First – despite austerity measures'* [Press release]. https://volksanwaltschaft.gv.at/en/news/article/austrian-ombudsman-board-ngo-forum-human-rights-first-despite-austerity-measures/

Barth, P. (2012). Die Volksanwaltschaft als Kontrollinstanz an „Orten der Freiheitsentziehung". *Interdisziplinäre Zeitschrift Für Familienrecht (iFamZ), 3*, 116.

Berka, W. (2018). Zum Mandat und zur Stellung des Menschenrechtsbeirats im Rahmen des Menschenrechtsschutzes durch die Volksanwaltschaft, *Newsletter Menschenrechte (NLMR)*, 3.

Bertel, M. (2013). Menschenrechtsschutz und Volksanwaltschaft. *Spektrum der Rechtswissenschaft (SPRW)*, VuV A, 69.

Bundes-Verfassungsgesetz (B-VG), Federal Law Gazette (BGBl.) Nr.1/1930 as amended by BGBl. 194/1999.

Bundesgesetz, mit dem das Bundes-Verfassungsgesetz, das Volksanwaltschaftsgesetz 1982, das Sicherheitspolizeigesetz, das Strafvollzugsgesetz und das Bundesgesetzblattgesetz geändert werden (Bundesgesetz zur Durchführung des Fakultativprotokolls vom 18. Dezember 2002 zum Übereinkommen der Vereinten Nationen gegen Folter und andere grausame, unmenschliche oder erniedrigende Behandlung oder Strafe – OPCAT-Durchführungsgesetz), Federal Law Gazette (BGBl.) 1/2012 – OPCAT Implementation Act.

Czech, P. (2016). Schutzmechanismen des öffentlichen Rechts für Menschen mit Behinderungen in institutioneller Unterbringung. *Newsletter Menschenrechte (NLMR), 1*, 90.

ErlRV 1515 BlgNR XXIV. GP, pp. 1–13.

Funk, B.-C. (2008). Menschenrechtsbeirat, OPCAT und Nationaler Präventionsmechanismus in Österreich. Entwicklungen im kommissarischen Grundrechtsschutz. *FS Machacek/Mascher, 121.*

Global Alliance of National Human Rights Institutions [GANHRI]. (2022). *Sub-committee on accreditation report*—March 2022. https://ganhri.org/wp-content/uploads/2022/04/SCA-Report-March-2022_EN.pdf

Klaushofer, R. (2013). Besuche von Kommissionen der Volksanwaltschaft in Alten- und Pflegeheimen. *Österreichische Zeitschrift Für Pflegerecht (ÖZPR), 2*, 53.

Kopetzki, C. (2012). Neue Kontrollmechanismen für Krankenanstalten und Heime. *Recht der Medizin (RdM), 1*, 1.

Kucsko-Stadlmayer, G. (2013a). Die Volksanwaltschaft als „Nationaler Präventionsmechanismus". *Österreichische Juristenzeitung (ÖJZ), 20*, 913.

Kucsko-Stadlmayer, G. (2013b). Art 148a-j B-VG. *Korinek/Holoubek, Kommentar zum Österreichischen Bundesverfassungsrecht.*

Möstl, M. (2017). Die Anwendung präventiver Standards zum Schutz und zur Förderung der Menschenrechte: Die Praxis des Nationalen Präventionsmechanismus Österreichs. *Newsletter Menschenrechte (NLMR), 3*, 207.

Ombudsman Act 1982 (Bundesgesetz über die Volksanwaltschaft, Volksanwaltschaftgesetz 1982 - VAG), Federal Law Gazette (BGBl.) 433/1982 as amended by BGBl. 50/2025.

Optional Protocol to the Convention against Torture (adopted 18 December 2002, entered into force 22 June 2006) 2375 U.N.T.S. 237

Pratscher, E., & Carniel, J. (2012). OPCAT, UN-Behindertenrechtskonvention und die Rolle der Volksanwaltschaft. *Österreichische Zeitschrift Für Pflegerecht (ÖZPR), 5*, 118.

Subcommittee for the Prevention of Torture and Other Cruel, Inhuman or Degrading Treatment or Punishment (SPT). General comment No. 1 (2024) on article 4 of the Optional Protocol (places of deprivation of liberty), CAT/OP/GC/1.

Vogl, M. (2013). Der neue Menschenrechtsbeirat bei der Volksanwaltschaft. In K. Giese, G. Holzinger & C. Jabloner (Eds.), *Verwaltung im demokratischen Rechtsstaat: Festschrift für Harald Stolzlechner zum 65. Geburtstag* (pp. 679–704). Verlag Österreich.

Belgium's Long Road to OPCAT Ratification: Challenges and Prospects of the Belgian NPM

Olivia Nederlandt and Aurore Vanliefde De Keyser

1 Introduction

Belgium signed the Optional Protocol to the Convention against Torture (OPCAT) on 24 October 2005. More than twenty years later, it remains, together with Ireland, the only EU Member State that has not ratified the Optional Protocol. Nonetheless, important steps have been taken, culminating in the legal establishment in 2024 of a National Preventive Mechanism for places of deprivation of liberty under federal competence (hereafter: the federal NPM) and its operational set-up in 2025.

Belgium has opted for an 'umbrella model,' designating the Federal Institute for the Protection and Promotion of Human Rights (hereafter: FIHR), as the federal NPM. The FIHR works in close collaboration with three specialised bodies mandated to carry out visits: the Central Prison

O. Nederlandt (✉)
UCLouvain Saint-Louis, Bruxelles, Belgium
e-mail: olivia.nederlandt@uclouvain.be

A. Vanliefde De Keyser
KU Leuven, Leuven, Belgium

T. Daems et al. (eds.), *Preventing Torture and Monitoring Places of Detention*,
https://doi.org/10.1007/978-3-032-28285-9_10

Monitoring Council (CPMC), the Federal Migration Centre (Myria), and the Standing Police Monitoring Committee (Committee P). These institutions, which predate the federal NPM, have historically exercised partial monitoring of places of detention within their respective areas of competence—namely prisons, immigration and asylum detention, and places of detention under police surveillance (Derclaye et al., 2026).

Belgium is a federal state structured by one federal level, three Regions (based on territory: Flanders, Wallonia, Brussels-Capital), and three Communities (based on language: French-speaking/Federation Wallonia-Brussels, Flemish, German-speaking), each with distinct and autonomous powers and competences.[1] The federal NPM's current mandate covers all places of deprivation of liberty under federal competence, that is, among others, prisons and high-security forensic psychiatric centres for people with psychiatric disorders who have committed criminal offences, immigration detention centres, and police custody facilities. By contrast, places of deprivation of liberty such as closed juvenile institutions, closed psychiatric hospitals, and care homes for the elderly that fall under the competence of federated entities (Communities and Regions) are excluded from the federal NPM's remit. For Belgium to fully meet the requirements of the OPCAT, the federated entities must designate a NPM responsible for places of detention that fall under their authority.[2] However, Belgium's ratification of the OPCAT does not need to be postponed until such mechanisms at the level of the federated entities are created. In principle, the ratification of the OPCAT provides a period of one year to establish a NPM covering all places where people are deprived of their liberty.[3]

---

[1] The Regions mainly deal with economic and territorial aspects (employment, environment, etc.), while the Communities are responsible for matters involving personal services (culture, education, etc.).

[2] It should be noted that certain monitoring bodies already exist to conduct preventive visits in specific settings, particularly those where minors are detained. These bodies fall under the authority of the Communities and, at the time of publication of this chapter, are not part of the federal NPM.

[3] Art. 17 of the OPCAT. Yet art. 24 of the OPCAT allows postponing this for a year, and exceptional extensions may be granted by the Committee against Torture (Bernath & Šteinerte, 2026, in this volume).

This chapter traces the process of constructing the Belgian federal NPM: from the conceptual choices underpinning its design and the institutions selected for involvement, through the adoption of the 2024 law as a foundational step. Drawing on legal and documentary analysis, and interviews conducted between July and September 2025 with members of the FIHR, the three specialised bodies (CPMC, Myria, and Committee P),[4] as well as with the consulting body Unia (the Interfederal Equal Opportunities Centre), we also outline the current configuration of the federal NPM and consider the key challenges and opportunities inherent in this model.

2 NPM Blueprint: The Umbrella Model

The long-standing non-compliance with OPCAT and the delay in establishing a NPM by the Belgian authorities became a growing concern for human rights and anti-torture bodies, as well as for civil society. Two main factors may explain Belgium's slow ratification of the OPCAT. First, Belgium's complex institutional structure makes coordination between the federal level and the federated entities particularly challenging. Second, many of the bodies entrusted with oversight functions already existed prior to the creation of the federal NPM. As a result, the process required adapting and integrating these existing institutions into the NPM framework while preserving their established mandates and competences, which they were keen to maintain.

Legislative Steps and Choice of Model

After signing the OPCAT in 2005, the next legislative steps towards establishing a NPM at federal level were taken in 2018, when the federal Parliament adopted an approval act for the establishment of

[4] We would like to thank all the representatives of the federal NPM and the specialised bodies for the time they dedicated to us and the clarifications they provided us with.

the NPM.[5] At that time, an initial assessment was undertaken of the institutions already exercising a degree of monitoring in places of deprivation of liberty: the CPMC (for prisons), the Committee P and the General Inspectorate of the Federal and Local Police (AIG) (for police detention facilities), Myria (for detention relating to migration and asylum), Unia (for persons with disabilities and racial discrimination), the French-speaking *Délégué général aux droits de l'enfant* and the Flemish *Kinderrechtencommissaris* (with regard to places of deprivation of liberty of minors), as well as the various ombuds services (who, among other things, have expertise in handling complaints for all administrative services). The purpose of this mapping exercise was to explore how a NPM could be established within this landscape while complying with the OPCAT's requirements. Regarding the possible institutional model for the NPM, three options emerged: (a) the expansion of the competences of the CPMC, (b) the extension of the competences of the federal Ombudsman (*Médiateur fédéral—federale Ombudsman*), and (c) the designation of the Federal Institute for the Protection and Promotion of Human Rights (FIHR) as the NPM. This Institute was established in 2019[6] to provide Belgium with an independent national human rights institution (NHRI) in accordance with the Paris Principles.[7]

After a consultation conducted by the Federal Public Service Justice with all relevant stakeholders (the institutions mentioned above, authorities of places of deprivation of liberty and NGOs active in this field) in 2020, a set of recommendations was transmitted to the federal Parliament in spring 2021. This coincided with the UN Committee against Torture's (CAT) fourth periodic report on Belgium, where it urged Belgian authorities to ratify the OPCAT as soon as possible for it to

[5] Draft Act approving the OPCAT, *Parl. Doc.* Belgian Chamber of Representatives 2017–2018, n° 543,192/004, 19 July 2018.

[6] Act of 12 May 2019 on the establishment of the Federal Institute for the Protection and Promotion of Human Rights, *Belgian Official Gazette,* 12 June 2019.

[7] UN Principles relating to the Status of National Institutions (The Paris Principles), adopted by the UN Human Rights Commission by Resolution 1992/54, and by the UN General Assembly in its Resolution 48/134 on National Institutions for the Promotion and Protection of Human Rights *UN Doc.* A/RES/48/134, 20 December 1993.

establish or designate a NPM.[8] Jointly with this, the *OPCAT Coalition*—a coalition of eight Belgian civil society organisations which work, fully or partially, on deprivation of liberty—issued recommendations to the government, pressing to urgently take action to establish a NPM.[9] This Coalition was in favour of creating a new body exclusively dedicated to the NPM mission.

Ultimately, the FIHR was designated as the NPM in early 2023, after several rounds of consultation within the executive and legislative power in 2021 and 2022.[10]

The NPM Mandate within the Federal Institute for Human Rights (FIHR)

The federal NPM is established through a law that modifies the status of the FIHR, adding its new scope of competences for the NPM while maintaining its previous mandate.[11] The law designates the FIHR as the NPM at the federal level, that closely collaborates with existing

[8] CAT, Concluding observations on the fourth periodic report of Belgium, *UN Doc.* CAT/C/BEL/CO/4, 51 August 2021. See also *UN Doc.* CAT/C/SR.1830 and 1831.

[9] The OPCAT Coalition is comprised of the Belgian branch of Action by Christians for the Abolition of Torture (ACAT-Belgium), the International Federation of ACAT (FIACAT), the francophone umbrella organisation of numerous secularist associations Centre d'Action Laïque (CAL), the Belgian branch of Defence for Children International (DEI-Belgique), a francophone association for health services and promotion in prisons I.Care, the Belgian francophone Human Rights League (LDH), the Belgian coalition of associations working in places of deprivation of liberty for migrants and asylum seekers Move (itself including Caritas International, CIRÉ, Jesuit Refugee Service Belgium and Vluchtelingenwerk Vlaanderen), and the Belgian section of the Observatoire International des Prisons (OIP–section belge). Their recommendations can be consulted at https://www.dei-belgique.be/index.php/toutes-les-ressources/send/41-publications/540-advies-van-de-opcat-coalitie-oktober-2021-ratificatie-van-het-opcat-en-instelling-van-een-nationaal-preventief-mechanisme-tegen-foltering-in-belgie.html. Their observations pertaining to the CAT's fourth periodic report are available at https://www.laicite.be/app/uploads/2021/06/OPCAT_RapportAlternatif_2021.pdf.

[10] Explanatory memorandum of the Draft Act modifying the Act of 12 May 2019 on the establishment of the Federal Institute for the Protection and Promotion of Human Rights, *Parl. Doc.* Belgian Chamber of Representatives 2023–2024, n° 553,736/001, 21 December 2023, pp. 7–8.

[11] Act of 21 April 2024 modifying the Act of 12 May 2019 on the establishment of the Federal Institute for the Protection and Promotion of Human Rights, *Belgian Official Gazette*, 3 May 2024. Hereafter: Federal Institute for Human Rights Act.

specialised bodies, who carry out most monitoring visits (alone or jointly with the NPM).

The NPM is defined as "an independent mechanism referred to in Article 3 of the OPCAT, entrusted with carrying out regular visits to places where persons are deprived of their liberty, in order to prevent torture and other cruel, inhuman or degrading treatment or punishment."[12] The legislator intentionally defined places of deprivation of liberty very broadly so as "to guarantee maximum protection for persons deprived of their liberty."[13] Indeed, the federal NPM is mandated to visit "any place under the jurisdiction or control of Belgium where persons are or may be deprived of their liberty by order of, or at the instigation of, or with the express or tacit consent of a public authority."[14] The definition comprises official or unofficial places of detention and sites still under construction; it is sufficient that the places are intended to hold individuals who cannot leave the place freely and that there exists a link, even indirect, with a (federal) public authority for it to fall under the competence of the federal NPM.[15] Although the Act itself contains no specific provision regarding relations between the federal NPM and the monitored state authorities, the legislative preparatory works on the NPM emphasise that dialogue with the authorities constitutes the "key to its success."[16] In the event of a lack of cooperation from state authorities,

---

[12] Art. 8/2, 2° Federal Institute for Human Rights Act.

[13] Art. 8/2, 3° of Federal Institute for Human Rights Act defines deprivation of liberty as "any form of detention or imprisonment, or the placement of a person in a public or private custodial setting which they are not permitted to leave at will, ordered by a judicial, administrative or other public authority." For the rationale, see the Explanatory memorandum of the Draft Act modifying the Act of 12 May 2019 on the establishment of the Federal Institute for the Protection and Promotion of Human Rights, *Parl. Doc.* Belgian Chamber of Representatives 2023–2024, n° 553,736/001, 21 December 2023, p. 25.

[14] Art. 8/2, 4° Federal Institute for Human Rights Act.

[15] Explanatory memorandum of the Draft Act modifying the Act of 12 May 2019 on the establishment of the Federal Institute for the Protection and Promotion of Human Rights, *Parl. Doc.* Belgian Chamber of Representatives 2023–2024, n° 553,736/001, 21 December 2023, p. 25.

[16] Explanatory memorandum of the Draft Act modifying the Act of 12 May 2019 on the establishment of the Federal Institute for the Protection and Promotion of Human Rights, *Parl. Doc.* Belgian Chamber of Representatives 2023–2024, n° 553,736/001, 21 December 2023, p. 14.

several responses are available to the federal NPM, such as the publication of any failures to provide access to the NPM or recourses to the Council of State, e.g. for the denial of access to certain documents.[17]

In carrying out preventive visits, the federal NPM is granted unrestricted and unannounced access to all places of deprivation of liberty under its remit. It is free to select the places to be visited and the persons to be interviewed, may hold confidential discussions with any person deprived of liberty or with anyone likely to provide relevant information, and is entitled to receive all necessary data relating to the number and location of detention facilities, the conditions of detention, and the treatment of persons held therein.[18]

The legal framework also contains provisions relating to the expertise of those working within the federal NPM, as well as aims pertaining to gender balance and adequate representation of ethnic and minority groups.[19] Furthermore, the FIHR Act outlines the framework of the NPM pertaining to data protection and the confidentiality of information.[20] Staff members are bound by professional secrecy, and a specific provision establishes that individuals who communicate or provide information to the NPM must not suffer reprisals.[21] Although the Act does not detail how to prevent or deal with reprisals, nor provides a mechanism for it, the legislative preparatory works express the aspiration that the NPM's regular presence through frequent visits in places of deprivation of liberty should prevent reprisals by its visibility and give the opportunity for individuals deprived of their liberty to report any reprisals they may have suffered either to the NPM or other existing complaint mechanisms available to persons subjected to reprisals.[22] Finally, the Act contains provisions on the review of the adequacy of the

---

[17] Explanatory memorandum of the Draft Act modifying the Act of 12 May 2019 on the establishment of the Federal Institute for the Protection and Promotion of Human Rights, *Parl. Doc.* Belgian Chamber of Representatives 2023–2024, n° 553,736/001, 21 December 2023, p. 18.

[18] Art. 8/4, §4 Federal Institute for Human Rights Act.

[19] Art. 8/5 Federal Institute for Human Rights Act.

[20] Art. 8/6 and 8/7 Federal Institute for Human Rights Act.

[21] Art. 8/8 and 8/9 Federal Institute for Human Rights Act.

[22] Explanatory memorandum of the Draft Act modifying the Act of 12 May 2019 on the establishment of the Federal Institute for the Protection and Promotion of Human Rights,

allocated budget of the NPM and the specialised bodies two years after its entry into force, as well as a comprehensive evaluation of the functioning and budget of the NPM five years after its implementation.[23]

3 Foundations and Pillars: Coordinating NPM and Specialised Bodies

The Belgian federal NPM is established within the FIHR, working in close cooperation with specialised bodies.[24] The law does not define which institutions are designated as specialised bodies, but the current model has three: the Central Prison Monitoring Council (CPMC), the Standing Police Monitoring Committee (Committee P), and the Federal Migration Centre (Myria). The FIHR, the specialised bodies, and the ways in which they relate to each other are outlined in this section and in Table 1.

The Federal Institute for Human Rights as NPM and Coordinating Body

As the Belgian NHRI, the FIHR's mandate is to promote and safeguard human rights in Belgium, in cooperation with other organisations. The FIHR has a residual competence over specific groups of people or places of detention over which no other independent federal human rights body has authority.[25] The federal Parliament appoints the members of the FIHR's board of directors and decides on its operating budget. The

---

Parl. Doc. Belgian Chamber of Representatives 2023–2024, n° 553,736/001, 21 December 2023, p. 25.

[23] Article 8/10, §7 Federal Institute for Human Rights Act.

[24] Art. 8/4, §1 and 8/2, 5° Federal Institute for Human Rights Act.

[25] In Belgium, several institutions are designated to protect the rights of specific vulnerable groups. For instance: Unia (the Interfederal Centre for Equal Opportunities, for the protection of people with disabilities and for victims of racial discrimination); the Institute for the Equality of Women and Men (for the implementation of the Convention on the Elimination of All Forms of Discrimination Against Women); Myria (protection of the rights of migrants and the fight against human trafficking)…

Table 1 Bodies involved in the Belgian federal NPM

Federal NPM and coordinating body:
• **FIHR**: Federal Institute for the Protection and Promotion of human rights (IFDH (Institut Fédéral des droits Humains)) in French or FIRM (Federal Instituut voor de Rechten van de Mens) in Dutch): Independent national human rights institution in accordance with the Paris principles, which includes a separate unit serving as the NPM that coordinates the NPM-related work carried out within the specialised bodies. This unit is made up of three people who are exclusively appointed to the NPM mission on a full-time basis.
Specialised bodies:
• **CPMC**: The Central Prison Monitoring Council (Conseil Central de Surveillance Pénitentiaire (CCSP) in French, or Centrale Toezichtsraad voor het Gevangeniswezen (CTRG) in Dutch), within which one person is dedicated full-time to the NPM mandate.
• **Committee P**: The Standing Police Monitoring Committee, some of whose members fulfil the NPM mandate alongside other functions.
• **Myria**: Federal Migration Centre, some of whose members fulfil the NPM mission alongside other functions.

FIHR comprises twenty staff members. The FIHR was granted 'B status' (partial compliance with the Paris Principles) by the Global Alliance of National Human Rights Institutions (GANHRI) after two years of operation. To attain 'A status' (full compliance), the organisation must undergo interfederalisation—that is, the extension of its competences beyond the federal level to encompass the regions and communities (Model, 2025).

The federal NPM enjoys operational independence as a separate department within the FIHR.[26] Its mandate is distinct from the other tasks of the FIHR and is carried out by staff who are exclusively mandated to do so. The federal NPM has its own budget and accounting system, but it relies on the FIHR's staff for support functions (accounting, administration, information technology, etc.).[27] The NPM

[26] Explanatory memorandum of the Draft Act modifying the Act of 12 May 2019 on the establishment of the Federal Institute for the Protection and Promotion of Human Rights, *Parl. Doc.* Belgian Chamber of Representatives 2023–2024, n° 553,736/001, 21 December 2023, pp. 12 and 24.

[27] Explanatory memorandum of the Draft Act modifying the Act of 12 May 2019 on the establishment of the Federal Institute for the Protection and Promotion of Human Rights, *Parl. Doc.* Belgian Chamber of Representatives 2023–2024, n° 553,736/001, 21 December 2023, p. 24.

is currently composed of three members with a statutory civil servant permanent mandate: a coordinator appointed by an independent expert commission, who has previous experience in a refugee protection NGO, and two other members, designated by the FIHR, one with experience at the ICRC (International Committee of the Red Cross) and the other from within the FIHR.

The federal NPM's missions are extensive. They include the regular monitoring of the situation of persons deprived of liberty, the formulation of recommendations to the competent authorities with a view to improving their treatment and preventing torture and ill-treatment, the provision of recommendations on existing and draft legislation, the publication of an annual report, the dissemination of information to the public, and the role of contact point with specialised international bodies (such as the Subcommittee for the Prevention of Torture (SPT) and the European Committee for the Prevention of Torture and Inhuman or Degrading Treatment or Punishment (CPT)) and counterpart NPMs abroad.[28]

The NPM is responsible for coordinating the specialised bodies, who conduct preventive visits in the places of deprivation of liberty they are competent for, and may also participate in these visits to ensure the consistent application of the NPM methodology.[29] Importantly, the federal NPM is competent to exercise its functions in relation to persons deprived of liberty and places of deprivation of liberty for which no specialised body has competence.[30] At present, according to the coordinator of the NPM, this residual competence is limited to one category of facilities: high-security forensic psychiatric centres (Bonamini, 2025).[31] However, the broad legal definition of the mandate offers the possibility of extending this competence to unofficial places of deprivation of liberty, such as unlicensed housing facilities.

When a specialised body lacks the requisite mandate to undertake preventive visits within its own legal framework, the federal NPM may

---

[28] Art. 8/2, 4° Federal Institute for Human Rights Act.

[29] Art. 8/4, §3 Federal Institute for Human Rights Act.

[30] Art. 8/4, §3 Federal Institute for Human Rights Act.

[31] Only two closed high-security forensic psychiatric centres (FPCs) exist in Belgium at this time, which are located in Antwerp (182 places) and Ghent (264 places).

authorise it to conduct a preventive visit, provided that the body adheres to the established NPM standards, norms, and modalities of cooperation. In cases of non-compliance, the federal NPM reserves the right to withdraw this authorisation.[32] For instance, given that the authority of the CPMC to monitor transition houses has been contested, the NPM may now grant it authorisation to conduct preventive visits to these facilities.[33]

The Specialised Bodies

The federal NPM works in close cooperation with specialised bodies, which are defined as "existing bodies established by statute which ensures respect for human rights in specific places of deprivation of liberty or with regard to particular groups of persons deprived of liberty."[34] In the current set-up of the NPM, the following three institutions are designated as specialised bodies: the CPMC, the Committee P, and Myria. These three institutions vary greatly in terms of staff, mandates, and operations, which undoubtedly poses a challenge for coordinating their work. The CPMC and the Committee P are Parliament-funded institutions (Model, 2025) housed in the same 'Forum' building of the federal Parliament in Brussels, unlike Myria. Each specialised body was allocated the budget for one full-time staff member dedicated to the new NPM function.

[32] Art. 8/4, §2 Federal Institute for Human Rights Act.

[33] Transition houses are small-scale, community-based, and open-regime establishments managed by private companies or non-profit organisations, accommodating around fifteen sentenced men who are within eighteen months of becoming eligible to apply for conditional release. The competence of the CPMC to monitor these facilities remained indeed ambiguous, as the Minister of Justice had argued that they do not constitute 'prisons' in the strict legal sense. Hence, the federal NPM has its mandate over it and designated the CPMC as its specialised body to conduct preventive monitoring visits.

[34] Art. 8/4, §1 and 8/2, 5° Federal Institute for Human Rights Act.

Central Prison Monitoring Council (CPMC)

Prison monitoring by volunteer citizens in Belgium dates back to the country's independence in 1830 (Nederlandt & Lambert, 2019). These volunteers formed what are known as 'monitoring commissions,'[35] local bodies that regularly visited the prison to which they are assigned, with the aim of observing and reporting on detention conditions (Daems et al., 2012; De Decker, 2009; Van Loock, 2006). In 2003, the CPMC was established as a federal monitoring body responsible for coordinating and supporting these local prison commissions, which were formally established on the same legal basis. The 2003 system was criticised for the fact that the commissions are composed of volunteering civilians with little to no training and a very limited operating budget, and for their limited independence, as they fell under the authority of the Minister of Justice, who appointed their members and received their reports (Claus, 2011; Daems & Vander Beken, 2011; Daems, 2012; Nederlandt, 2017; Nederlandt & Lambert, 2019; Vander Beken, 2008; Vanhouche & Nederlandt, 2019; Vanquelberghe et al., 2017).

In 2019, a major reform in prison monitoring integrated the CPMC within an institutional framework linked to the Belgian federal Parliament, which allocates its budget and appoints its twelve members for a five-year term, renewable twice, four of whom have a full-time mandate (Daems, 2017; Nederlandt & Lambert, 2019; Vanhouche & Nederlandt, 2019). The 2019 reform marked the professionalisation of the CPMC, including the development of a visual identity, a website, and a methodology modelled after the visit protocols of the CPT.[36] Professionalisation also entailed providing the CPMC with substantial administrative staff, which it had not possessed previously: a staff of around forty civil servants, both statutory and contract-based, including a director and an administrative team, six coordinators for the local

---

[35] '*Commissions de surveillance*' in French, '*commissies van toezicht*' in Dutch.

[36] The CPMC's first and current president, Marc Nève, had previously served as Belgium's representative on the CPT.

monitoring commissions, seventeen lawyers for the complaints commissions, lawyers for the appeal commission, paralegals, a communication officer, and a knowledge hub manager.

The CPMC's mandate is defined in the Belgian Prison Act, where it is entrusted with conducting independent prison monitoring.[37] Its scope currently comprises 35 prisons, one penitentiary psychiatric facility,[38] and three detention houses (in the following contribution, we will use the term "prison" to refer collectively to these three types of institutions),[39] accommodating approximately 13,700 incarcerated people. The CPMC issues statements and recommendations—either on its own initiative or upon request—to the federal Parliament and to the competent federal Ministers of Justice and Health. It also oversees the establishment, coordination, and functioning of the 37 local prison monitoring commissions, which are present in every prison, amounting to a total of more than 500 volunteers. In addition to regular visits by local commissioners to prisons, the CPMC also conducts thematic and ad hoc cross-institution visits. For example, the CPMC's 2025 thematic report, co-authored by Unia, addressed mental health and psychiatric illness in prison.[40] The CPMC also publishes an annual public report addressed to the Parliament, including a strategic plan, issued opinions, and reports from the commissions. Prior to publication, the draft report is submitted to the relevant authorities, who have two months to provide comments before its publication.

Since 2020, the CPMC has also been entrusted with a new mission, being the handling of complaints from incarcerated people regarding certain individual decisions made by prison governors. These complaints are reviewed and dealt with by complaint commissions, which are

[37] Art. 22 Belgian Prison Act of 12 January 2005.

[38] '*Établissement de Défense Sociale*' or '*Inrichting tot de Bescherming van de Maatschappij*' in Paifve.

[39] Detention houses are small-scale facilities (between 20 and 60 places) that only hold people serving sentences of up to three years (sometimes up to five years) who have not been convicted of sex offences or crimes related to terrorism.

[40] CPMC & Unia, Thematic report 'La maladie mentale derrière les barreaux: l'urgence à sortir de l'impasse' and individual visit reports to the prisons of Ghent, Turnhout, Haren, Mons and Jamioulx, 5 June 2025, https://www.unia.be/fr/connaissances-recommandations/rapport-sant%C3%A9-mentale-en-prison-pour-sortir-de-limpasse-2025.

composed of three volunteer members within the local prison monitoring commission (who exclusively handle complaints), and appeals are handled by complaint appeal commissions within the CPMC. As such, the complaint (appeal) commissions can validate, annul, or substitute decisions made by prison governors and provide non-monetary compensation for the incarcerated individual wronged by a decision.[41] Although both prison monitoring and the handling of complaints fall under the CPMC's mandate, they are carried out by different individuals. In practice, however, the separation is not always strict—e.g. members of the prison monitoring commissions assist in collecting and forwarding complaints to the complaint commission in several prisons. The complaints mechanism within the CPMC requires considerable staff and administrative resources, with 5542 complaint cases opened just in 2024 (Nève & De Temmerman, 2025).[42]

Within the CPMC, one person has been designated to carry out the NPM function, while being supported by staff members and permanent members of the Council.

Standing Police Monitoring Committee (Committee P)

The Standing Police Monitoring Committee (or Committee P), established in 1991, is a monitoring body employing approximately 85 statutory staff members.[43] Its mandate is structured around three main functions: the external monitoring of police services, the handling of complaints pertaining to the police, and the conduct of certain judicial investigations against members of police forces (Bourdoux, 2004; Bourdoux & Berkmoes, 2004; De Pauw & Vandaele, 2020; Verhage

---

[41] Art. 158 Belgian Prison Act of 12 January 2005.

[42] CPMC, Annual Report 2024, https://ctrg.belgium.be/publicaties/. The number of complaints the CPMC deals with has grown significantly over the past years (2384 in 2022, 4164 in 2023). However, it should be emphasised that the right of complaint is still in its early stages of development, which may partly explain its expansion, alongside with the detention conditions that have been increasingly deteriorating due to rising overcrowding since the end of the 2021 pandemic crisis and legislative changes in sentence execution.

[43] Art. 1 Organic Law of 18 July 1991 on the Supervision of police and intelligence services and the Coordination Unit for Threat Analysis, *Belgian Official Gazette*, 26 July 1991.

et al., 2022). Since 2023, it has also been entrusted with the competence to manage reports submitted by whistleblowers within the police. Its mandate is defined in the Organic Law of 18 July 1991 on the Supervision of police and intelligence services and the Coordination Unit for Threat Analysis, with additional legislation delineating its competences (such as the whistleblower function and the preventive monitoring) responsibilities. The Committee P has institutional ties with the federal Parliament: its members are appointed by Parliament, its budget is allocated by Parliament, it reports its annual activities to Parliament, and it can issue opinions at Parliament's request (Bourdoux, 2001; Schuermans, 2000, 2004).

The Committee P is composed of a Standing Committee, an administrative department, and an investigative department.

First, the central decision-making body of the Committee P is the Standing Committee, composed of five members appointed by Parliament for renewable six-year terms.

Second, the administrative department of the Committee P is headed by a clerk, assisted by a team of administrative staff. The Complaints Section has been created within this department, tasked with receiving and analysing the roughly 2500 complaints and reports filed each year by citizens against police forces.[44] This office examines complaints to determine the appropriate course of action, while the final decision rests with the Standing Committee. Complaints may either (a) be referred to the internal services of the relevant police zone or federal police (in the case of individual issues with one police staff member), (b) be investigated by the investigative service of the Committee P when they may indicate structural issues or shortcomings in the functioning of the police or issues pertaining to the integrity of the police mandate, or (c) where criminal offences are suspected, be transmitted to the judicial authorities (Verhage et al., 2022). A separate integrity unit, composed of two legal experts, is responsible for handling whistleblower alerts. The Committee P does not

[44] The Committee P has dealt with 2545 complaints in 2024 and 2557 in 2023; Committee P, Annual Report 2024, https://comitep.be/document/jaarverslagen/Comit%C3%A9%20P%20Rapport%20annuel%202024.pdf.

sanction police officers, as only the internal disciplinary police services or the judicial authorities have this competence (Verhage et al., 2022).[45]

Third, the operational service of the Committee P is their investigative service (Berkmoes, 2004; Schuermans, 2000, 2004). Its officers conduct inquiries on behalf of the Committee P—approximately 180 to 200 cases per year—relating to the complaints received. It also occasionally (with approximately 75 to 100 cases per year) operates at the request of judicial authorities (for instance, the public prosecutor or an investigating judge), acting in effect as a specialised police body (Berkmoes, 2004). Investigators are also part of the integrity unit and conduct investigations related to breaches of integrity. As of 2024, this service was composed of 43 investigators, 57% of whom were seconded from other police services (with the possibility of returning after their mandate at the Committee P).[46] While this secondment is regarded as an asset in terms of professional experience, it has also generated concerns about the independence of the Committee P (Verhage et al., 2022). According to the Committee P, several safeguards for independence have been put in place: these investigating officers no longer maintain any ties with the police during their mandate (in terms of hierarchy, remuneration, etc.) and will not be assigned to cases connected to the police service where they worked previously. Regarding the question of impartiality, Committee P highlighted that it focuses on the procedural quality of the investigation in the first place, following the ECtHR's arguments[47] on the requirement of an effective investigation (Bollens & Van der Auwera, 2021). Additionally, the investigative service also visits places of deprivation of liberty under the competence of police services.

[45] Art. 10 Organic Law of 18 July 1991 on the Supervision of police and intelligence services and the Coordination Unit for Threat Analysis.

[46] Committee P, Annual Report 2024.

[47] *Golubyatnikov and Zhuchkov v. Russia*, ECtHR App. nos. 49,869/06 and 44,822/069 October 2018, §§ 94–97; *Kulyk v. Ukraine*, ECtHR App. no, 30760/06, 23 June 2016, § 100; *Razzakov v. Russia*, ECtHR App. no. 57519/09, 5 February 2015, §§ 63–64; *Baysultanov v. Russia*, ECtHR App. no. 56120/13, 4 February 2020, § 79; *Mikhail Nikolayev v. Russia*, ECtHR App. no. 40192/06, 6 December 2016, §§ 99–100.

The Standing Committee submits a confidential report on each investigation to the competent minister or authority, and to the federal Parliament. It may provide opinions on draft legislation, royal decrees, circulars, or other policy documents only at the request of the federal Parliament or the competent minister. Additionally, the Standing Committee presents an annual report to the federal Parliament (Bourdoux et al., 2004; Verhage et al., 2022).

For the preventive monitoring visits, the specificity of the structure of the Committee P entails that all its findings of preventive monitoring visits will be transmitted to the federal NPM, only after approval of its Standing Committee and submitting them to the Belgian federal Parliament. While Committee P's supervisory commission in the federal Parliament cannot refrain the Committee from communicating information to the federal NPM internally, it can choose to withhold certain information from publication (and thus from the publicly available NPM reporting) in the case it may be a threat to the security of the State. These different validation steps entail that the Committee P operates with a longer timeline for the communication of its findings.

Before the establishment of the federal NPM, inspections of places of deprivation of liberty under the competence of the police were already being carried out by the Committee P's investigative service. It is the same service that carries out monitoring visits and complaint-handling functions, under the authority of the Standing Committee (De Pauw & Vandaele, 2020). These included visits to local police stations to assess police functioning and the treatment of persons deprived of liberty in police cells and courthouse holding facilities. Numerous visits were conducted in particular between 1997 and 2008 (De Pauw & Vandaele, 2020).[48] These visits changed from generic visits to places of deprivation of liberty per police zone to more thematic visits after 2010, following developments which required specific attention (e.g. procedural protection of suspects, monitoring of new legislation).

Compared to the CPMC and Myria, the number of places of deprivation of liberty under the competence of the Committee P is substantially larger, encompassing cells in police stations, courthouses, and airports,

---

[48] Committee P, thematic *cahiers*, https://comitep.be/cahiers1.html.

among others. A particular challenge arises from the fact that individuals held in such facilities are usually detained for only brief periods, and in smaller police stations it is often uncertain whether anyone is in custody at the time of the visit.

The Committee P chose not to designate a single person to perform the NPM function; instead, it assigned the role to several investigators within the investigation service, who are gradually developing their expertise in this new mission alongside their other tasks.

Myria

In 1993, Belgium established the Centre for Equal Opportunities and the Fight against Racism. The institution was restructured in 2013 as it underwent an "interfederalisation"; for its competence to extend beyond the federal level to the Regions and Communities. Two separate entities were created out of this reform: the Interfederal Centre for Equal Opportunities and the Federal Migration Centre. In 2016, both were renamed: the first became Unia, and the second Myria. Myria is headquartered in Brussels, in the same building as Unia, which is physically more remote from the other specialised bodies at the federal Parliament.

Myria's mandate is broad and multifaceted. Its core missions are: ensuring respect for the fundamental rights of foreigners and informing public authorities about the nature and scale of migration flows within the scope of federal competences; carrying out its tasks in a spirit of dialogue and cooperation with all public and private actors involved in immigration reception and integration policies; and stimulating efforts to combat human trafficking and smuggling, again within federal competences.[49] Myria is mandated to conduct studies and research, issue opinions and recommendations to public authorities and private institutions, assist individuals seeking advice on their rights and obligations, receive and process complaints, engage in mediation where appropriate,

[49] Art. 2, Act of 15 February 1993 establishing a Federal Centre for the analysis of migration flows, the protection of the fundamental rights of foreigners, and the fight against human trafficking.

initiate legal proceedings in certain cases, and produce and disseminate information and documentation.[50] It is also required to submit an annual report to the Prime Minister, who forwards it to Parliament and ensures its publication.[51] For this, it received an access mandate to places of migration detention.[52]

Unlike the two previously mentioned specialised bodies, Myria's staff—comprising approximately twenty people—is employed on a contractual basis, and its budget is not allocated through a parliamentary endowment but is instead secured through donations and bequests, income from its activities, the award of public contracts, and similar sources.[53] Regarding the NPM-budget, it is requested by the federal NPM and reallocated by them to Myria. This is an important difference, as the statutory mandate of the other specialised bodies was introduced as a complementary safeguard for their independence and their longevity. Myria chose not to appoint a single person to carry out the NPM mandate; instead, the mission was divided among four staff members who specialise in this role alongside their other duties.

Before the establishment of the federal NPM, between 2010 and 2023, Myria had already carried out around fifty visits to places where individuals without legal residence status and some asylum seekers are deprived of their liberty (closed centres, port and airport police facilities, etc.). These visits were conducted as part of its mission to ensure respect for the fundamental rights of foreigners, and to contribute to thematic reports; they were therefore more informative than preventive in nature. In 2023 and 2024, Myria visited all six closed migration detention centres in Belgium (with a maximum capacity of 459 places at the end of 2024).[54] Myria designed these visits, which lasted from one to

---

[50] Art. 3, Act establishing a Federal Centre for the analysis of migration flows, the protection of the fundamental rights of foreigners, and the fight against human trafficking.

[51] Art. 6, Act establishing a Federal Centre for the analysis of migration flows, the protection of the fundamental rights of foreigners, and the fight against human trafficking.

[52] Art. 44 Royal Decree of 2 August 2002 on migration detention, *Belgian Official Gazette,* 22 September 2002.

[53] Ar.11 and 13 of the Royal Decree of 29 June 2014 establishing the organic status of the Federal Centre.

[54] Myria, Migratie in cijfers en in rechten—Terugkeer, detentie en verwijdering, pp. 16–17, https://www.myria.be/files/2025_MYRIA_Terugkeer_detentie_en_verwijdering.pdf.

several days, as a preparatory phase for the exercise of its future NPM mandate.

An important difference with the CPMC and the Committee P is that Myria does not at present handle complaints of those deprived of their liberty in immigration detention centres, despite its mandate legally allowing it to do so. Complaints from individuals held in immigration detention centres can be addressed to the governor of the centre or to a Complaints Commission from the Department of Immigration of the Ministry of Home Affairs. This entails that complaints are handled entirely internally by staff appointed by the Ministry of Home Affairs, which does not offer the same guarantees in terms of independence as the complaint-handling bodies within the CPMC or Committee P. The Complaints Commission only notifies Myria that a complaint has been made, but not of its content or its outcome.[55] Myria has expressed its concern regarding the low number of admissible complaints in immigration detention centres and the outcome they receive.[56] In 2024, 8 of the 16 received complaints (out of 4804 people deprived of their liberty) were deemed admissible by the commission, of which all were then declared unfounded or rejected.[57] A similar figure applies to 2023 (where out of 4915 people deprived of their liberty all 10 admissible complaints out of the 19 received by the Complaints Commission were either ruled unfounded or rejected) and 2022 (where out of 4285 people deprived of their liberty, all of the 8 admissible complaints out of the 12 received were ruled unfounded by the Commission.[58]

[55] Ministerial Order of 23 January 2009 establishing the procedure and rules of operation of the Commission and the permanent secretariat, referred to in Article 130 of the Royal Decree of 2 August 2002, which lays down the regime and operating rules applicable to places located on Belgian territory, managed by the Office for Foreigners, where a foreign national is detained, made available to the government, or held, pursuant to the provisions referred to in Article 74/8, § 1, of the Law of 15 December 1980 on the entry, residence, establishment, and removal of foreigners.

[56] Centre for Equal Opportunities and the Fight against Racism, *The Complaints Commission responsible for handling complaints from persons detained in closed centres (2004–2007): Analysis and evaluation of an inadequate mechanism*, January 2008, https://www.myria.be/files/Rapport_final_commission_des_plaintes.pdf.

[57] Belgian Immigration Office, Annual Report 2024, p. 88, https://dofi.ibz.be/fr/figures/rapports-dactivites.

[58] Belgian Immigration Office, Annual Report 2023, p. 90; Annual Report 2022, pp. 93–94, https://dofi.ibz.be/fr/figures/rapports-dactivites.

Finally, a coalition of NGOs specialising in the rights and conditions of migrants and asylum seekers, operating under the name *Coalition Move*, has been granted authorisation, by the Immigration Office to conduct visits to immigration detention centres. This coalition includes Caritas International, CIRÉ, the Jesuit Refugee Service Belgium and Vluchtelingenwerk Vlaanderen. As a result, this network of civil society volunteers regularly carry out visits to these facilities and produce reports that can serve as valuable sources of information for Myria. As an observing member of *Coalition Move*, Myria also informs coalition partners of certain findings of the visits. However, their status remains precarious, as the authorisation can be revoked at any time.

Expertise from Other Institutions

Apart from the specialised bodies, the NPM and the specialised bodies may call upon external experts.[59]

Initially, Unia—which is responsible for combating discrimination, promoting equal opportunities, and implementing, monitoring, and safeguarding the United Nations Convention on the Rights of Persons with Disabilities (CRPD)—was also considered for integration into the federal NPM. Through its CRPD mandate, Unia is tasked since 2011 with ensuring that appropriate measures are taken to enable persons with disabilities to fully exercise their rights. Broadening its competence to monitor the treatment of these individuals in places of deprivation of liberty within the federal NPM could therefore have been justified. However, it was ultimately decided not to formally associate Unia with the federal NPM. Even without this mandate, Unia followed the federal NPM's set-up on a voluntary basis. However, the federal government established in 2025 decided to cut 25% of Unia's funding,[60] rendering it unable to continue its volunteer involvement alongside the NPM.

[59] Article 8/4, §8 Federal Institute for Human Rights Act.

[60] Coalition agreement of the Belgian federal government 2025–2029 of 31 January 2025, p. 85, https://www.belgium.be/sites/default/files/resources/publication/files/Accord_gouvernemental-Bart_De_Wever_fr.pdf.

4 Building the NPM Framework: Collaboration, Protocols, and Visit Methodology

The establishment of the federal NPM, which relies on close collaboration with specialised bodies, necessitates extensive cooperation among institutions with distinct competences, divergent historical trajectories, and established operational practices. Notwithstanding these differences, the bodies comprising the federal NPM are not unfamiliar with one another. The following section outlines their prior collaborations and examines the nature of cooperation within the federal NPM framework.

Pre-NPM Collaborations

The FIHR and its specialised bodies had already worked together on several occasions prior to the creation of the federal NPM. Several of them had entered cooperation protocols, and they are all part of the Belgian human rights platform.

The Belgian Human Rights Platform

The Belgian human rights platform (*Plateforme des Droits Humains—Mensenrechtenplatform*) is a forum for dialogue between independent federal, regional, and community institutions whose mandates concern, in whole or in part, the protection of fundamental rights (Model, 2025); these seven institutions and associations signed a protocol of cooperation on 28 April 2026.[61] This network meets monthly since its establishment

[61] It brings together the Federal Ombudsman, the Ombudsman of Wallonia and of the French-speaking Community, the Ombudsman of the German-speaking Community, the High Council of Justice, the CPMC, the Committee P, the Committee R (the Standing Committee for the Oversight of Intelligence and Security Services), Myria, UNIA, the General Delegate for Children's Rights, the *Kinderrechtencommissariaat* (Flemish Children's Rights Commissioner), the National Commission on the Rights of the Child, the Institute for the Equality of Women and Men, the Data Protection Authority, and the Belgian Anti-Poverty Network (Model, 2025).

in 2014 with the aim of exchanging expertise, views, and good practices on human rights-related issues across institutions.

Although the network has not produced specific outputs on preventive monitoring, representatives of the federal NPM and specialised bodies emphasised that the inter-institutional exchange through the platform, grounded in a shared concern for the protection of fundamental rights, had made them accustomed to each other and provided an important basis for fostering dialogue and collaboration in relation to their NPM mandate.

Collaborations between Specialised Bodies

The implementation of the federal NPM is further facilitated by the fact that several specialised bodies had established protocols of collaboration well before the federal NPM mandate. For instance, Myria had concluded a cooperation protocol with the Committee P, the CPMC, as well as Unia.[62] Similarly, the FIHR had formalised a cooperation agreement with the CPMC, among others.

In addition, certain specialised bodies had undertaken joint visits, drawing on each other's expertise.[63] For example, the CPMC and Myria conducted visits in 2023 and subsequently published a special report on a prison exclusively accommodating undocumented foreign nationals.[64] In 2025, the CPMC also undertook visits in collaboration with Unia to several prisons housing individuals with mental health disorders.[65]

---

62 Collaboration protocol Myria—Unia, 20 October 2017, https://www.unia.be/fr/connaissances-recommandations/protocole-de-collaboration-entre-unia-et-myria; Collaboration protocol Myria - Committee P, 2018, https://www.myria.be/files/Myria_en_action_2020.pdf; Collaboration protocol UNIA—CPMC, 25 April 2022, https://ccsp.belgium.be/wp-content/uploads/2025/04/Protocole_Unia_CCSP.pdf; Collaboration protocol Myria—CPMC, 2 May 2023, https://ccsp.belgium.be/wp-content/uploads/2025/04/myria-protocole-FR.pdf.

63 E.g. for the NHRI Communication to the Committee of Ministers of the Council of Europe pertaining to Rule 9.2—CPMC and IFDH-FIRM (17/10/2024) concerning VASILESCU v. Belgium (ECtHR app. no 64682/12), DH-DD(2024)1278.

64 CPMC & Myria, Common report on the visit to prison of Tongeren of 29 to 31 August 2023, 28 February 2024, https://www.myria.be/files/CTRG_MYRIA_Tongeren_NL_DEF.pdf.

65 CPMC & Unia, Thematic report "La maladie mentale derrière les barreaux: l'urgence à sortir de l'impasse" and individual visit reports to the prisons of Ghent, Turnhout, Haren, Mons and Jamioulx, 5 June 2025.

A Methodology for Preventive Monitoring Visits

The federal NPM is responsible for coordinating the specialised bodies and, in consultation with them, has drafted a common strategy and visit methodology for the preventive monitoring of places of deprivation of liberty. Preventive monitoring visits can be conducted solitarily by the competent specialised body or jointly with the NPM.[66] To ensure compliance with the requirements of preventive monitoring visits,[67] while allowing each institution to adapt the methodology to the specific places of deprivation of liberty under their remit, a common visit methodology was developed in 2025. This methodology is intended to ensure uniformity of practice, transparency of procedure, and effective follow-up of findings and recommendations. The adopted common methodology includes provisions on the different types of visits (e.g. generic or thematic), the composition of visit teams, the circumstances under which visits may be unannounced, incident management procedures, sources of information to consult, guidelines on conducting confidential interviews, all while allowing flexibility to adapt to the specific realities of different places of deprivation of liberty.

For matters beyond the internal preventive monitoring visit methodology, the NPM and the specialised bodies elaborated a cooperation protocol, which was adopted on 22 April 2025, exactly a year after the creation of the federal NPM.[68] The cooperation protocol details the NPM's coordinating role, which includes developing multiyear annual plans, training, and generating recommendations, annual reports, and general, cross-cutting, or thematic reports. The protocol also addresses internal and external communication and representation

---

[66] Article 8/4, §7 Federal Institute for Human Rights Act.

[67] Article 8/4, §6 Federal Institute for Human Rights Act refers to the requirements in the OPCAT and in the guidelines of the Subcommittee on Prevention of Torture on preventive monitoring visits.

[68] Protocol between the Federal Institute for the Protection and Promotion of Human Rights, acting on behalf of the Preventive Mechanism, on the one hand, and the CPMC, the Committee P, and Myria, establishing the detailed rules of cooperation between the Preventive Mechanism and the specialised bodies in the performance of the OPCAT mandate, *Belgian Official Gazette,* 21 May 2025.

by the specialised bodies, and provides guidance to avoid duplication of monitoring activities.

Finally, the five-year multiannual strategy for the federal NPM was adopted at the end of 2025, but had not yet been published at the time of finalising this publication.

According to the interviewed representatives of the NPM and the specialised bodies, devising this common methodology absorbed much of the NPM's efforts during its first year of operation, which was necessary as these three documents constitute the foundation for the mechanism's future work. They generally considered the process as an enriching one, as it involved sharing expertise and learning from one another's visit practices and specific approaches.

5 Mise-En-Route: The First Year of the NPM and its First Visits

The federal NPM considered its first year to be an experimental one to 'test out' the visit methodology and build up the collaboration in practice, despite the scarcity of the resources currently available (Bonamini, 2025). Hence, it chose to conduct its first visits in detention houses and transition houses, jointly with the CPMC. The decision to begin with these places—recently established small-scale facilities with a largely open regime for low-risk profiles—is a notable choice, given the context of acute and chronic issues pertaining to overcrowding and human rights violations in Belgian prisons. The NPM's rationale was that selecting a low-risk environment for the first visits offered a practical opportunity to test the methodology and collaborative approach for the first time. Besides, it established the CPMC's competence to carry out preventive monitoring visits to transition houses as a specialised body of the NPM. The findings of the joint NPM and CPMC visits to detention houses published in March 2026 constitute the first visit report of the federal NPM.[69]

Initially envisaged visits to closed forensic psychiatric centres were postponed by the federal NPM given the CPT visit to these facilities in May 2025. The federal NPM preferred conducting these visits after the CPT's findings are published, rather than simultaneously, as this allows the NPM to follow up on the CPT's recommendations. Furthermore, the NPM meant to avoid overburdening the visited institutions by subjecting them to multiple inspections simultaneously, highlighting a key principle of the NPM methodology: ensuring dialogue and collaboration with the authorities being monitored.

Alongside these prison visits, the federal NPM also conducted a joint visit with Myria to one closed centre for people without residence permit, and Committee P carried out four visits under the NPM mandate. The reports of these visits conducted in 2025 are expected to be published in 2026.

6 Conclusion: Challenges and Prospects of the Belgian NPM

While an assessment of Belgium's federal NPM model would be premature, the outline of the model and the interviews with the representatives of the mechanism and the specialised bodies prompt several future-oriented questions. To conclude this chapter, we reflect on opportunities and challenges of the Belgian model and discuss the potential evolution towards a 'full' NPM extending to the places of deprivation of liberty within the federated entities, the latter being a necessary step to conclude the OPCAT ratification process.

[69] Belgian federal NPM, Visit report on the detention houses of Forest-Vorst and Kortrijk, 23 March 2026, https://www.federaalinstituutmensenrechten.be/nl/bezoekrapport-detentiehuizen-van-vorst-en-kortrijk.

Opportunities

All the representatives of the federal NPM and the specialised bodies who were interviewed for this chapter expressed that, despite the challenges inherent in creating a NPM based on cooperation between existing institutions with distinct mandates, it represents an important opportunity to strengthen fundamental rights in Belgium. Over the course of its first year, they have observed that the exchange of expertise among the federal NPM and the specialised bodies has been highly instructive and has fostered an integrated approach, helping to dismantle the silos that too often separate institutions with different competences. This is particularly significant given that individuals frequently move between places of deprivation of liberty (e.g. from prison to an immigration detention centre or a psychiatric hospital) and that competences often overlap (e.g. foreign nationals may be held in prisons or in police detention facilities). The institutions stressed that, since each of them pursues distinct missions alongside their NPM mandate, they contribute specialised expertise to the mechanism.

Beyond the sharing of expertise, another advantage identified is that the federal NPM provides a new mandate which enhances the visibility of these institutions and their work, both nationally and internationally. At present, the reports produced by the CPMC and the Committee P are published only in the national languages and not in English, while Myria's reports are in English. The international character of the NPM will likely lead to its reports being published in English, giving the specialised bodies greater international visibility. Furthermore, representatives mentioned that being part of the NPM can further reinforce the legitimacy of their institutions on the ground in carrying out the monitoring of places of deprivation of liberty.

For the civil servants carrying out the NPM mandate, the fact that the former monitoring bodies have been preserved and were assigned to the federal NPM (rather than being replaced by a new structure) ensures continuity of work, as the bodies are already familiar with one another, and allows for the retention of valuable expertise built over time. Furthermore, one of the identified added values of the federal NPM lies in its potential to consolidate recommendations in a more visible and structured manner. This is particularly relevant in the current context where authorities are confronted with recommendations issued by several distinct bodies.

In short, the interviewed representatives of the federal NPM and its specialised bodies welcome this renewed attention to fundamental rights through the establishment of the NPM, yet find it somewhat counter-current within the broader human rights context in Belgium, where the rule of law appears, in certain respects, to be eroding. A telling illustration is the Belgian State's persistent failure to comply with a number of judicial rulings condemning it for breaches of its obligations regarding the fundamental rights of migrants and the problem of prison overcrowding. The central question that remains, however, is whether this strengthening of fundamental rights will be primarily institutional, through the creation of a mechanism and mandates in other institutions endowed with legitimacy and wide-ranging monitoring competences, or whether it will translate into tangible prevention of violations of fundamental rights against persons deprived of their liberty in the places subject to its mandate.

Challenges

The first, and arguably most pressing, challenge for the federal NPM lies in the inadequacy of the resources allocated to it in proportion to its mandate. All specialised bodies had requested additional human resources to fulfil the new federal NPM mandate, yet each body was attributed only one additional full-time equivalent. This shortfall is all the more striking given that the NPM's mission is expected to intensify, as the government has announced an expansion in the number of places of deprivation of liberty, including plans to build new prisons, high-security forensic psychiatric centres, and immigration detention facilities. In doing so, the legislator has put the NPM in a position where the means granted to it from the outset appear insufficient to enable it to fulfil its mission effectively. Therefore, the NPM has to define strategies to prioritise the monitoring of certain places of deprivation of liberty over others.

A second challenge arises from the fact that the federal NPM mandate is sometimes carried out by individuals working within larger specialised bodies who shoulder numerous other responsibilities. This raises the question of how the NPM mission will be prioritised in the future, particularly amid a context of limited resources and government budget cuts.

A third challenge lies in the institutional complexity of the model itself. The division of the preventive monitoring mandate between the federal NPM established within FIHR and the three specialised bodies renders the system rather opaque and difficult to interpret. In the strict sense, the federal NPM consists solely of the three members within the NPM section of FIHR.[70]

This situation creates ambiguities regarding the status of individuals performing NPM functions within specialised bodies. First, there is the extent to which members of the specialised bodies associated with the federal NPM's mission should be considered part of the NPM when assessing the independence, expertise, and resources of the NPM. Second, when these individuals carry out visits under this mandate, they must present themselves as external to the federal NPM while acting on its behalf, which could cause confusion among the people they meet. The risk of confusion in practice may also arise from the fact that, alongside visits officially identified as part of the federal NPM, specialised bodies may conduct other visits necessary for their own missions without labelling them as NPM visits. However, the interviewed representatives of the federal NPM and the specialised bodies indicated that this risk of confusion did not arise during the first visits they carried out as a consequence of their identification policy: individuals conducting a visit under the federal NPM clearly announce, at the outset and at each new interaction, the framework within which the visit takes place, and wear a badge displaying the NPM logo.

Such institutional complexity reflects a broader structural issue in Belgium, where several *sui generis* institutions (such as the FIHR, the CPMC, and the Committee P, funded by the Belgian federal Parliament) have partially overlapping mandates. While some have proposed merging

[70] Article 8/1 Federal Institute for Human Rights Act.

or centralising these bodies, their diversity in expertise may contribute to safeguarding the rule of law, transparency, and monitoring, particularly amid challenges posed by digital technologies, big data and artificial intelligence (Model, 2025).

Moreover, a system that combines four institutions inevitably rests upon a fragile balance, reliant on effective collaboration and cooperation. Yet these institutions operate under different legal frameworks and procedures, adhere to distinct working cultures, have varying established relationships with authorities, are subject to varying responsibilities and pressures, and do not necessarily share the exact same priorities. For example, the fact that the Committee P is subject to stricter security and confidentiality rules (most notably that the appointment of its members requires security clearance, and its reports must be submitted to a parliamentary monitoring committee prior to publication) can result in a different timeline for its contributions within the collaborative work of the federal NPM mandate.

Another important challenge concerns the overlap between the federal NPM mission and the other responsibilities of the institutions involved. Whereas federal NPM members within FIHR operate in a completely distinct unit from the rest of the institute, this is not the case for the specialised bodies. For instance, the CPMC member entrusted with the NPM mandate benefits from support from other CPMC members and services. Within the Committee P and Myria, different people combine NPM duties with other responsibilities. Among the tasks performed within the Committee P and the CPMC is the handling of complaints from people deprived of their liberty under their mandate. Criticism has been voiced, most notably by the OPCAT Coalition, regarding the potential incompatibility between preventive monitoring functions and complaint-handling, as both require a high degree of independence. The interviewed representatives of the CPMC and the Committee P do not perceive the co-existence of these two missions within their institution as undermining the independence of either role, as they are carried out by different services supporting the complaints (appeal) commissions in their sovereign judicial function. The interviewed representatives from the Committee P, for example, suggested that combining both monitoring and complaint-handling within the same body has several benefits. In their view, addressing individual complaints provides insights into structural problems within police services and contributes to risk analysis: a facility receiving a high volume of complaints may signal underlying issues and inform monitoring priorities. Similarly, the interviewed CPMC representatives state that they aim to ensure the independence of the prison monitoring and the complaint-handling missions in practice, and that the combination contributes to a more comprehensive overview of issues in prisons. The dual-role issue is not unique to the Committee P and the CPMC however, as several other institutions funded by the federal Parliament combine both monitoring and complaint-handling functions (e.g. the federal Ombudsman, the High Council of Justice, and the Data Protection Authority). This is likely to remain a live issue for the federal NPM, potentially prompting adjustments: either the full externalisation of complaint-handling in response to concerns regarding the independence of carried out functions, or, conversely, its formal recognition as an added value. The latter could substantiate the argument to grant Myria with both the authority and the necessary resources to handle complaints from individuals deprived of their liberty in places falling under its monitoring mandate. Model (2025) has also raised the possibility of the FIHR extending its functions to include the handling of individual complaints. The latter illustrates that the close cooperation between different institutions might, in time, lead to a homogenisation of their pre-existing structures and mandates through their federal NPM mandate.

More broadly, the question of how these bodies can guarantee their independence is a vital one, as such independence is fundamental to the fulfilment of their mandate. In our view, this independence must be ensured at multiple levels, including in their composition and in the exercise of their functions. Ultimately, the principal challenges facing the federal NPM will be to establish and sustain a constructive dialogue with the authorities it oversees and to ensure that its recommendations are duly considered, yet maintaining its independence.

Towards a 'Full' NPM and Ratification of the OPCAT

As defined above, the mandate of the federal NPM is limited to places of deprivation of liberty falling under the federal competences. Places of deprivation of liberty falling under the competences of the federated entities (such as closed juvenile institutions, residential care homes for the elderly, or certain forensic psychiatric centres) do not fall within the remit of the federal NPM. The next step on Belgium's long path towards full implementation of the OPCAT will therefore require the federated entities to designate a NPM for the places of deprivation of liberty under their authority.

While no federated entity has yet taken concrete legislative action, the Flemish Human Rights Institute (VMRI: *Vlaams Mensenrechteninstituut*), established in 2018, would appear to be the most likely candidate to assume the role as the NPM for the places of deprivation of liberty under the competence of the Flemish community (closed institutions for minors, residential care homes, and care facilities that involve restriction of movement). There is no comparable human rights institute on French-speaking and German-speaking side. Hence, the intention could be to adopt a model integrated within the federal one. In this scenario, the federal NPM would also act as a coordinating body for existing entities (in this case, the monitoring commissions for juvenile detention centres) while exercising residual competence for places not otherwise covered. Such an arrangement, however, would create a clear institutional asymmetry between the Flemish, and French and German-speaking communities, further fragmenting and complexifying an already eclectic human rights landscape.

In conclusion, it should be emphasised that the ratification of the OPCAT does not require the prior establishment of a NPM structure encompassing places of deprivation of liberty within the remit of the federated entities. Should Belgium proceed with ratification, it would benefit from a one-year period in which to establish a NPM covering all places of deprivation of liberty, and may further avail itself of a postponement of the NPM's full implementation for up to three years.[71] These

[71] Art. 17 and 24 OPCAT.

provisions leave the Belgian State with little, if any, justification for any further delay in ratifying the OPCAT, but they do require a genuine commitment of all levels of governance to ensure preventive monitoring meeting the threshold of the OPCAT.

References

Berkmoes, H. (2004). De Dienst Enquêtes van het Vast Comité van Toezicht op de politiediensten. In G. Bourdoux, H. Berkmoes, & A. Vandoren (Eds.), *Voor een verantwoorde, transparante, democratische politiezorg* (pp. 529–536). Politeia.

Bernath, B., & Šteinerte, E. (2026). The SPT and NPMs: An evolving relation. In. T. Daems, O. Nederlandt & A. Vanliefde De Keyser (Eds.), Preventing torture and monitoring places of detention: The role of national preventive mechanisms in Europe. Palgrave Macmillan.

Bollens, S., & Van der Auwera, J. (2021). De beoordeling van het recht op een eerlijk proces in het licht van een schending van de procedurele onderzoeksverplichting vervat in artikel 3 EVRM (noot onder EHRM 22 oktober 2020). *Politie & Recht,* 3, 130–136.

Bonamini, C. (2025). De oprichting van het Nationaal Preventiemechanisme tegen foltering op federaal niveau—een blik achter de schermen. *Tijdschrift voor Mensenrechten, 23*(3), 8–13.

Bourdoux, G. (2001). Neutralité, indépendance, vigilance, loyauté et transparence: Le Comité P au service du Parlement et du citoyen en partenariat avec les autres contrôles. *Custodes, 2,* 39–78.

Bourdoux, G. (2004). Waakzaamheid, onafhankelijkheid, neutraliteit en transparantie: Het Vast Comité van Toezicht op de politiediensten ten dienste van het Parlement en van de burger, in samenwerking met de andere toezichts- en inspectieorganen. In G. Bourdoux, H. Berkmoes, & A. Vandoren (Eds.), *Voor een verantwoorde, transparante, democratische politiezorg* (pp. 537–593). Politeia.

Bourdoux, G., & Berkmoes, H. (2004). Contrôle externe et contrôle interne: What's in a name? In G. Bourdoux, H. Berkmoes, & A. Vandoren (Eds.), *Voor een verantwoorde, transparante, democratische politiezorg* (pp. 615–659). Politeia.

Bourdoux, G., Berkmoes, H., & Cuvelier, C. (2004). D'une vue particulière à une vue globale: Pour une contribution du Comité permanent P à l'amélioration permanente de l'exercice de la fonction de police. In G. Bourdoux, H. Berkmoes, & A. Vandoren (Eds.), *Voor een verantwoorde, transparante, democratische politiezorg* (pp. 303–401). Politeia.

Claus, H. (2011). Waarom loopt het toezicht op de gevangenissen mank in België? Pleidooi voor een parlementaire onderzoekscommissie voor de strafuitvoering. *De Orde van de Dag, 55*(3), 79–85.

Daems, T. (2012). De heropstanding van de Centrale Toezichtsraad voor het Gevangeniswezen? Enkele kanttekeningen bij de publicatie van een markant jaarrapport. *Panopticon, 33*(2), 140–148.

Daems, T. (2017). Rijp voor puberteit: Potpourri IV en het onafhankelijk toezicht op de gevangenissen. *Fatik—Tijdschrift voor Strafbeleid en Gevangeniswezen, 153*, 13–19.

Daems, T., & Vander Beken, T. (2011). Alleen voor amateurs: Reflecties over en vanuit het extern toezicht op gevangenissen. *De Orde van de Dag, 55*(3), 73–78.

Daems, T., Vander Beken, T., & Vermeulen, G. (2012). *Toezicht op detentie: Tekst en context*. Maklu.

De Decker, S. (2009). De bewakers bewaakt: De rol van de commissies van toezicht en de Centrale Toezichtsraad voor het Gevangeniswezen. *Fatik—Tijdschrift voor Strafbeleid en Gevangeniswezen, 123*, 13–18.

De Pauw, K., & Vandaele, L. (2020). Toezicht op vrijheidsberovingen en opsluitingen door de politie in België. *Panopticon, 41*(4), 392–407.

Derclaye, G., Nederlandt, O., & Vanliefde De Keyser, A. (2026). La creation d'un mécanisme national de prévention de la torture au niveau fédéral: Un premier pas vers une culture généralisée de prévention? *Journal des Tribunaux, 145*(12), 213–224.

Model, S. (2025). Les institutions à dotation du Parlement fédéral. *Courrier Hebdomadaire du CRISP*, 2646–2647.

Nederlandt, O. (2017). La surveillance des prisons et le droit de plainte des détenus: Jusqu'où ira le bénévolat? *Journal des Tribunaux, 28*, 541–554.

Nederlandt, O., & Lambert, M. (2019). La réforme du Conseil central de surveillance pénitentiaire et des commissions de surveillance des prisons: Entre attentes déçues et raisons d'espérer? *E-legal—Revue de droit et de criminologie de l'Université libre de Bruxelles, 2*.

Nève, M., & De Temmerman, B. (2025). *Drie jaar beklagrecht. Een terugblik en een vooruitblik/Trois ans de droit de plainte. Évaluation et perspectives*. Die Keure/La Charte.

Schuermans, F. (2000). Controle op politie en inlichtingendiensten: De krachtlijnen van de wet van 1 april 1999 houdende wijziging van de wet van 18 juli 1991 tot regeling van het toezicht op politie- en inlichtingendiensten. *Tijdschrift voor Strafrecht (dossier).*

Schuermans, F. (2004). De geschiedenis van de externe controle op de politie van 1991 tot nu: Een stuk in drie bedrijven. In G. Bourdoux, H. Berkmoes, & A. Vandoren (Eds.), *Voor een verantwoorde, transparante, democratische politiezorg* (pp. 661–700). Politeia.

Van Loock, L. (2006). Het toezicht op de gevangenissen door de Commissies van Toezicht en de Centrale Toezichtsraad voor het Gevangeniswezen. *Fatik—Tijdschrift voor Strafbeleid en Gevangeniswezen, 111*, 9–14.

Vander Beken, T. (2008). Beklagrecht en toezicht op gevangenissen in tijden van nood: Zuerst kommt das Fressen und dann die Moral. *Panopticon, 29*(4), 1–6.

Vanhouche, A.-S., & Nederlandt, O. (2019). Eindelijk een onafhankelijk en effectief toezicht op de Belgische gevangenissen? Een overzicht van de recente wetswijzigingen en discussies over het toezicht op de Belgische gevangenissen. *Fatik—Tijdschrift voor Strafbeleid en Gevangeniswezen, 162*, 25–37.

Vanquelberghe, C., Breuls, L., Casier, I., Robberechts, J., Scheirs, V., & Vanhouche, A.-S. (2017). Roepen met schorre stem? Enkele reflecties bij het jaarverslag van de Centrale Toezichtsraad voor het gevangeniswezen (2011–2014). *Panopticon, 38*(1), 1–8.

Verhage, A., Feys, Y., & Stevens, A. (2022). Versnipperd toezicht? De evolutie van toezicht op de politie in België. *Panopticon, 43*(1), 29–52.

Conclusion: 20 Years of NPMs in Europe: Highlights of a Varied Preventive Monitoring Landscape

Olivia Nederlandt and Aurore Vanliefde De Keyser

This edited volume set out to examine the establishment, functioning, and legacy of various National Preventive Mechanisms (NPMs) across European countries within the framework of the Optional Protocol to the Convention against Torture (OPCAT). Adopted in 2002, the OPCAT marked a decisive shift in international efforts to prevent torture and ill-treatment by moving beyond reactive investigation towards a system of regular, independent monitoring of places where individuals are deprived of their liberty. Two decades after its adoption, the chapters[1] in this volume on the UN Subcommittee on Prevention of Torture (SPT)

[1] The eight case studies were selected to reflect variations in the European preventive monitoring landscape and do not imply that the models or experiences of other countries are any less relevant or important to document the European dynamics of the OPCAT implementation.

O. Nederlandt (✉)
UCLouvain Saint-Louis, Bruxelles, Belgium
e-mail: olivia.nederlandt@uclouvain.be

A. Vanliefde De Keyser
KU Leuven, Leuven, Belgium

T. Daems et al. (eds.), *Preventing Torture and Monitoring Places of Detention*,
https://doi.org/10.1007/978-3-032-28285-9_11

and the NPMs of Austria, Belgium, the Czech Republic, France, Italy, the Netherlands, Switzerland, and the UK have provided an overview of how some European States implemented this preventive monitoring vision through the creation and operation of their NPMs.

1 A Varied Spectrum of NPM Models

While the OPCAT establishes a shared normative framework and clear objectives of preventive monitoring, its implementation has unfolded in markedly diverse ways across Europe. The timeline of the ratification of the OPCAT and the effective establishment of the NPMs as a result of it vary widely. Where some countries have established their NPM quickly after the ratification of the OPCAT in the 2000s (like Czech Republic in 2006, France in 2007, and Switzerland and the UK in 2009), other countries have delayed parts of the process (the Netherlands in 2011, Austria in 2012, and Italy in 2014). As an exception in the European landscape, Belgium has only created a NPM with a partial competence in 2024 and has not ratified the OPCAT so far.

NPMs have developed within specific national legal traditions, institutional landscapes, and political cultures. The establishment of a NPM almost always takes place in contexts where bodies monitoring places of deprivation of liberty already exist, raising the question of whether to integrate these bodies into the new mechanism or to create a new institution for the NPM. Often, NPMs have sought to preserve and integrate existing bodies or to work alongside them in an effort to "complement rather than replace existing systems of oversight."[2]

As a result, no single institutional NPM model has emerged. Rather, the European landscape is characterised by a diversity of NPM models. Some countries, such as France and Switzerland, have created centralised and professionalised bodies dedicated exclusively to preventive monitoring, notably the French *Contrôleur général des lieux de privation de liberté* (CGLPL) and the Swiss National Commission for the Prevention

---

[2] SPT, Guidelines on National Preventive Mechanisms, *UN Doc.* CAT/OP/12/5, 9 December 2010.

of Torture (NCPT). Others, including Austria and the Czech Republic, have entrusted the mandate to pre-existing Ombudsman institutions whose competences have been correspondingly expanded.

The UK represents the most complex multi-body model, bringing together 21 distinct organisations with their own mandates, whereas Belgium has opted for an umbrella structure in which a central NPM unit is working in close cooperation with, and coordinating, three specialised monitoring bodies which pre-date the NPM per area of expertise.

The Italian National Guarantor for the Rights of persons deprived of liberty (GNPL) may, at first glance, be placed into the category of centralised NPMs. However, the Italian model combines the centralised GNPL with a historically rooted network of territorial monitoring bodies (regional, provincial and municipal guarantors), whose evolving relationship with the GNPL raises specific coordination and independence challenges. Although the GNPL was expected to foster cooperation with territorial guarantors, the lack of clear rules has left collaboration largely at its discretion, notably through limited delegation mechanisms.

The recent evolution in the Netherlands—where a fragmented, multi-body monitoring network that had remained largely dormant for several years was replaced in 2024 by a single, centralised NPM anchored within the Dutch National Human Rights Institution (NHRI)—illustrates how institutional models may be reconfigured to more effectively fulfil the mandate.

Each institutional configuration reflects not only contextual constraints—such as federalism in Belgium, Switzerland, and Austria—but also historical monitoring traditions—such as in France, Italy, Belgium, and the UK. Overall, these examples demonstrate that the OPCAT's flexibility allows States to design mechanisms that resonate with domestic structures, but they also show the structural trade-offs inherent in each choice.

2 Institutional Design and Embeddedness Within the National Human Rights Landscape: Balancing Expertise, Organisational Benefits, and Institutional (In)dependence

Whether organised as centralised bodies or as umbrella structures in which several institutions collectively discharge the mandate, many NPMs are, in practice, situated within broader multi-mandate institutions, such as Ombuds offices or National Human Rights Institutions (NHRIs). Within these configurations, the preventive function coexists with a range of other responsibilities, such as, for example, the handling of complaints, the provision of legal opinions, independent monitoring mandates—often incident-based and reactive rather than preventive—and the broader promotion of human rights.

This institutional embeddedness offers several advantages. On the one hand, NPMs may benefit from established administrative infrastructures to facilitate access to logistical resources and limit costs, including accounting services, human resources support, and operational management. On the other hand, institutional embeddedness may also enable the NPM to draw upon substantive expertise developed within related mandates. For example, complaint-handling functions within NHRIs or Ombuds offices can signal concerning systemic issues in detention settings which may inform the strategic orientation of NPM visits and highlight areas requiring particular scrutiny.

In Austria and the Czech Republic, for example, the NPM is embedded in the Ombuds offices alongside other functions, including the handling of complaints, anti-discrimination monitoring, and disability rights oversight under the Convention on the Rights of Persons with Disabilities (CRPD). Both NPMs state that their complaint-handling mandate has occasionally served as an early-warning mechanism to identify potential risk areas and facilities and adjust their preventive monitoring visit plan accordingly. A similar dynamic appears in Italy, where the GNPL may detect systemic problems through its coordinating role over the territorial guarantors who process complaints under their jurisdiction. Within the UK's multi-body NPM, certain bodies that also handle complaints or regulatory inspection provide valuable intelligence for early detection of ill-treatment risks, but not consistently throughout the 21 distinct institutions with their own mandates.

The dual NPM-CRPD mandate of both the Austrian and the Czech Ombudsman reveals important considerations regarding the choice to centralise human rights monitoring mandates and expertise within a single body. Reflecting on this in their chapter, the Austrian Ombudsman Board contends that the dual mandate enhances its sensitivity to forms of ill-treatment that might otherwise remain undetected, such as coercive practices in (psychiatric) care institutions and situations of dependency giving rise to de facto deprivation of liberty. It further supports an intersectional understanding of deprivation of liberty, recognising that persons with disabilities may be simultaneously exposed to multiple, overlapping layers of vulnerability that a more narrowly defined OPCAT mandate may fail to capture adequately. Moreover, a combined NPM-CRPD mandate has the potential to broaden the methodological repertoire, allowing principles derived from risk assessment, monitoring tools and standards developed under the CRPD framework to inform preventive monitoring in more traditional detention settings. In most countries examined in this volume, however, the NPM is not vested in a body that also holds the CRPD mandate, a configuration that, in some cases (e.g. Belgium), reflects a deliberate institutional choice.

In Belgium, the federal NPM is structurally embedded within the Federal Institute for Human Rights, a NHRI with its own broad remit. The Belgian model relies primarily on specialised bodies for carrying out visits to the places of deprivation of liberty over which they already have a specific monitoring mandate (such as prisons, police custody facilities, and migration detention facilities). However, these bodies already existed before the establishment of the NPM and retain their respective mandates, which creates a risk that, in periods of budgetary constraint, they may have to prioritise other competences over the national preventive monitoring task, for which comparatively fewer resources are allocated.

Both the centralisation of the NPM mandate within a NHRI and the close collaboration with human rights bodies show the significance of situating the NPM within the wider human rights ecosystem—including non-discrimination bodies, CRPD monitoring mechanisms, children's rights institutions, and other oversight actors—in order to ensure comprehensive territorial and thematic coverage. The capacity of a NPM to fulfil its mandate is intertwined with the broader institutional network in which it operates, which introduces important questions regarding the independence of the NPM within these institutions, and its allocation of time and resources to preventive monitoring in a system where resources are shared and, usually, scarce.

3 Independence and Resources: Pitfalls and Conditions for Effective Prevention Monitoring

Whether as part of a NHRI or as a stand-alone body, one of the most recurrent challenges identified throughout this volume is the persistent shortage of resources available to NPMs, as well as the SPT. In many jurisdictions, limited funding and staffing constrain the ability of NPMs to conduct comprehensive monitoring as intended by the OPCAT across the full range of places where individuals may be deprived of their liberty. Consequently, NPMs are often required to make strategic choices regarding which institutions to prioritise, how frequently to conduct visits, and which thematic issues to address. However, deciding to visit a particular place of deprivation of liberty inevitably entails not monitoring another, thereby exposing both the inherent fragility of the preventive monitoring mandate and the risks of shadow-casting of such strategic decisions, whereby attention directed towards certain places of deprivation of liberty simultaneously renders others less visible.

Independence and resources are closely intertwined in practice, as formal guarantees of independence risk remaining ineffective without adequate financial and human means, while resource allocation itself may affect institutional autonomy.

Although the independence of the NPM is generally enshrined in legislation, its practical scope varies considerably across systems.

Some mechanisms benefit from strong formal safeguards. Austria's Ombudsman Board, for instance, is constitutionally protected, and the members of the commissions conducting visits are selected through a public recruitment process and appointed by the Board itself. By contrast, umbrella models reveal more fragile arrangements. In the UK, the absence of a unified legal basis continues to raise questions about the overall coherence across and independence of all the bodies within the mechanism. While Belgium's recently established federal NPM meets formal independence requirements, the diversity of its specialised bodies results in differentiated institutional profiles.

In several cases, concerns relate less to formal status than to structural or functional dependencies. Switzerland's NCPT remains financially linked to a federal department, which regularly raises questions about its operational autonomy. Similarly, the Italian NPM, although formally placed 'at' rather than 'within' the Ministry of Justice, relies extensively on seconded staff from the Ministries of Justice and the Interior, creating potential forms of hierarchical dependence. The executive's decisive role in appointing the members of its governing body further illustrates the limits of the GNPL's institutional independence, notwithstanding subsequent efforts to reinforce its financial and functional autonomy.

Financial autonomy and resourcing varies widely across the NPMs of the eight countries discussed in this volume. Some mechanisms benefit from stable and clearly identified budgets (like Austria, France, or the Netherlands). Other NPMs operate with more limited or fragmented resources, sometimes embedded within broader institutional budgets or dependent on multiple funding authorities (like the UK, Belgium, or the Czech Republic). Both Italy's GNPL—whose annual budget and core staff depend on resources provided through the relevant ministries—and Switzerland's NCPT—whose limited budget is embedded within the Federal Department of Justice and Police—illustrate NPM models where financial resources remain closely tied to the executive branch, raising concerns about independence.

Taken together, these elements underscore that independence cannot be assessed in purely formal terms or by legal status. It is shaped in practice by the availability, structure, and control of resources, making (durable) financial and operational autonomy essential components of an effective preventive monitoring system.

4 There's No One Way To Do Preventive Monitoring: Visit Methodologies

Across the eight countries, preventive visits are carried out through broadly similar methodological pillars, according to the OPCAT requirements[3]: regular access, confidential interviews, document review, and on-site observation. All eight discussed NPMs have multidisciplinary teams and maintain discretion over visit timing and scope, but differ notably in the balance between announced vs. unannounced visits, the length and depth of on-site work, and the degree to which volunteers, external experts, or specialised inspectors participate in the monitoring process.

Austria conducts both short half-day and multi-day visits, mostly unannounced, with at least two experts and strongly interdisciplinary commissions (medicine, psychology, law, social work, disability specialists). Switzerland also uses mixed announced and unannounced visits, with teams composed based on expertise and regional balance. Their visit duration and form vary: highly specialised long visits such as deportation-flight monitoring are often done by a single expert, while visits to institutions involve multi-member teams. France's CGLPL conducts exclusively unannounced visits lasting one to two weeks, carried out by a large multidisciplinary team of full-time controllers and external experts (from judicial, medical, administrative, and military backgrounds).

The Netherlands' reconfigured NPM has only conducted announced visits in 2024 to ensure quality and build institutional visibility, although unannounced visits are planned in the future. The Dutch NPM teams are small, multidisciplinary, and supported by external experts, with visit lengths varying depending on the type of institution and thematic focus.

---

[3] Art. 20 OPCAT.

The UK's multi-body NPM combines frequent unannounced volunteer-based monitoring with periodic professional inspections lasting several days. Both announced and unannounced modalities are used, except in military detention, where visits occur only by invitation. The bodies of the UK NPM range from individual volunteer monitors to large interdisciplinary inspection teams. The Czech NPM undertakes exclusively unannounced visits lasting one to three days, with teams of two to four staff plus external professionals (medical, social-care, educational), using a highly structured methodology and the possibility of night inspections. Italy's GNPL carries out regular, ad hoc, thematic, and follow-up visits, both announced and unannounced, with interdisciplinary teams drawn from its board and a 25-person technical staff. Their visit duration varies widely, from short ad hoc interventions to longer thematic missions. Belgium's newly created federal NPM conducts mainly announced visits, ranging from one day to several days, with teams that may be composed of federal NPM staff, specialised bodies (prison, police, migration), and external experts.

5 Shedding Light, yet Casting Shadows: Defining Places of Deprivation of Liberty

Beyond the visit methodology, a key issue concerns the scope of places of deprivation of liberty falling under the competence of NPMs. The OPCAT deliberately adopts a broad definition, encompassing any place (public or private) where individuals are deprived of their liberty by order of a public authority or with its consent or acquiescence.[4] Many national legislative frameworks reflect this expansive understanding in principle, confirming the broad scope of what is understood as places of deprivation of liberty. In practice, however, the range of institutions visited and the methods employed by NPMs vary significantly between countries.

Across the eight countries examined, only two categories of places of deprivation of liberty are monitored systematically by all NPMs: prisons

[4] Art. 4(2) OPCAT; SPT, General comment No. 1 (2024) on article 4 of the Optional Protocol (places of deprivation of liberty), 4 July 2024, CAT/OP/GC/1.

and police custody facilities. Beyond this common baseline, however, the range of monitored places diverges substantially. Immigration detention centres and administrative holding facilities are visited in nearly all jurisdictions, including Austria, Switzerland, France, the Netherlands, the UK, Italy, Belgium, and also the Czech Republic—but not with equal breadth or frequency across systems. Likewise, psychiatric hospitals or secure psychiatric units fall under the mandate of most NPMs, though the scope varies: Switzerland, France, Italy, Austria, and the Czech Republic conduct extensive monitoring in mental-health settings, while Belgium's federal NPM currently only covers forensic psychiatric centres and one prison psychiatric facility under the federal state competence.

Significant discrepancies appear in the monitoring of care environments and disability-related residential facilities. Some NPMs—notably those in Austria, Switzerland, Italy, and the Czech Republic—have considerably widened their remit to include residential care homes for people with disabilities and/or the elderly, crisis centres, youth residential facilities and even unregistered private care homes. Certain NPMs also extend their monitoring to non-traditional or mobile settings, including deportation flights (as in Switzerland, France, Italy, and the UK), quarantine ships and emergency shelters (Italy), and a broad range of children's institutions (France, the UK, and the Czech Republic). Of particular concern are settings in which only specific units or rooms constitute places of deprivation of liberty—for example, within healthcare facilities where certain wards are closed while others remain open. While the Dutch NPM has explicitly extended its mandate to cover such places, they fall outside the remit of the French CGLPL.

In Belgium, by contrast, the limitations of the federal NPM stem not from definitional issues but from institutional complexity: its mandate currently extends only to facilities within federal competence, leaving gaps pending the establishment of complementary mechanisms at the level of the federated entities. Other institutional limitations occur (yet are evolving) in the case of France and the Netherlands for the remit of the NPM mandate in their overseas territories.

These developments illustrate that determining which places fall under NPM jurisdiction remains dynamic and is inherently shaped by resource constraints, constitutional agreements, legal interpretation, and emerging forms of confinement. The achievements of longer-lasting NPMs and their systematic preventive monitoring of places of detention testify to significant advances in the protection of human rights, as NPM visits have contributed to identifying abusive practices and improving detention conditions and are generally aimed at fostering dialogue between authorities and NPMs. Furthermore, the cross-institutional scope of the NPM mandate affords a valuable opportunity to document the experiences of individuals as they move across different places of deprivation of liberty—for example, between police custody, juvenile institutions, prisons, migration detention centres, and psychiatric facilities. Yet the developments discussed in the chapters of this book equally caution against assuming that the existence of a NPM guarantees comprehensive scrutiny.

Particularly concerning in this regard are places of deprivation of liberty situated at the margins of traditional detention systems or places that remain largely invisible to public oversight. These may include places where persons are confined in privately operated facilities, sites where migrants or victims of human trafficking are held, deportation flights, or closed sections of otherwise open (forensic) psychiatric institutions or care homes for the elderly or persons with disabilities. Although individuals in such settings may experience restrictions on their liberty that fall within the spirit of Art. 4 of the OPCAT, they may in practice receive little or no attention from certain NPMs, depending on their remit and operational capacity.

Acknowledging that certain places of deprivation of liberty remain in the shadows is just as essential as recognising the light that NPMs have cast on other detention facilities. Without careful reflection on the limits of existing monitoring structures, however, the presence of NPMs may create an illusion of comprehensive scrutiny while significant areas remain beyond effective monitoring. The European experiences, as described and discussed in this edited volume (which are not exhaustive, as we were unfortunately not able to include other NPM experiences in this book project), illustrate both the adaptability of this framework and the importance of sustained commitment to torture prevention at the national level.

6 The Triad of NPMs, States Parties, and the SPT: A Multilevel Human Rights Dialogue

The diversity of NPM models examined in this volume should not be understood merely as a reflection of national variation but also as a learning opportunity. Mapping and critically reflecting on convergences and divergences in institutional design, monitoring practices, and the challenges encountered across jurisdictions contributes to a clearer understanding of the conditions under which NPMs are most capable of fulfilling their preventive mandate. At the same time, this comparative exercise reveals that NPMs do not evolve in isolation: their development is deeply connected to the exchange space created in fora such as the European NPM Forum,[5] and to guidelines and standards emitted by the Association for the Prevention of Torture (APT) and—most prominently—by the SPT.

Bernath and Šteinerte's chapter on the evolving relation between the SPT and NPMs within this volume has made clear that NPMs are but one type of cog wheel in the broader torture prevention mechanism laid out by the OPCAT. As highlighted in the SPT chapter, the OPCAT entrusts the Subcommittee not only with visiting places of deprivation of liberty in States Parties but also with advising, assisting, and supporting NPMs in a manner that preserves their independence. The SPT is therefore uniquely positioned to foster harmonisation without imposing uniformity, to identify good practices across regions, and to provide authoritative guidance on emerging challenges—such as defining new forms of deprivation of liberty, safeguarding independence in hybrid or multi-body systems, or ensuring effective follow-up to recommendations. Moreover, the SPT's capacity to intervene when NPMs face political pressure, institutional fragility, or attempts at interference—through confidential dialogue but also, where necessary, through public statements—makes it a central driving and safeguarding element in the intricate OPCAT preventive monitoring machinery.

---

[5] European Union & Council of Europe, *European NPM Forum,* https://www.coe.int/en/web/implementation/european-npm-forum.

With the proliferation of NPMs and in the context of limited resources, the SPT has increasingly shifted from conducting its own preventive monitoring visits towards this advisory and supporting role vis-à-vis NPMs in their diverse configurations (see Bernath & Šteinerte, *this volume*). This role mainly manifests in different forms of dialogue between the SPT, NPMs, and States Parties. The significance of this triadic relationship is reflected in a range of practices, including joint SPT-NPM visits in Switzerland, methodological exchanges with Austria, and interventions by the SPT when a NPM's functioning was under threat. While the SPT has a tradition of cooperation and (at times confidential) dialogue with States Parties, it is noteworthy that, since 2016, it also holds States Parties publicly accountable through its 'Art. 17 list' for failure to comply with the OPCAT by being significantly overdue in the obligation to designate a NPM following the ratification of the OPCAT.[6]

NPMs across the eight countries consistently draw on the standards, guidance, and jurisprudence developed at the level of the UN (SPT[7] or the Office of the High Commissioner of Human Rights[8]) or by civil society through the APT.[9] Several NPMs explicitly model their methodologies on the SPT's recommendations following country visits—for example in Switzerland, where the SPT's concerns about the NPM's independence directly shaped reforms, and in Italy, where the SPT's 2016[10] report contributed to the strengthening of the GNPL's powers and practices.

[6] SPT, *Non-compliance with Article 17*, https://www.ohchr.org/en/treaty-bodies/spt/non-compliance-article-17.

[7] SPT, Guidelines on National Preventive Mechanisms, *UN Doc.* CAT/OP/12/5, 9 December 2010; Analytical self-assessment tool for National Prevention Mechanisms, *UN Doc.* CAT/OP/1/Rev.1, 25 January 2016; General Comment No. 1 (2024) on Article 4 of the Optional Protocol (Places of Deprivation of Liberty), *UN Doc.* CAT/OP/GC/1, 4 July 2024.

[8] OHCHR, Preventing Torture: The Role of National Preventive Mechanisms—A Practical Guide, *UN Doc.* HR/P/PT/21, 2018, https://www.ohchr.org/sites/default/files/Documents/Publications/NPM_Guide_EN.pdf.

[9] APT, The Optional Protocol Implementation Manual, 2010, revised edition, https://www.apt.ch/knowledge-hub/publications/optional-protocol-implementation-manual-2010; *NPM toolkit webpage*, https://www.apt.ch/knowledge-hub/npm-toolkit.

[10] SPT, Report on the visit made by SPT to Italy, *UN Doc.* CAT/OP/ITA/1, 23 September 2016.

Within the European human rights landscape, several chapters show how NPM findings contribute to or are shaped by case law on detention, such as the Italian GNPL's role following the *Torreggiani* case and the Swiss national courts referencing findings from the NCPT's preventive monitoring reports.

The fact that most European countries have ratified both the OPCAT and the European Convention for the Prevention of Torture and Inhuman or Degrading Treatment or Punishment (ECPT) entails that European NPMs can also draw from practices and findings of the CPT and follow up on its observations and recommendations. Yet the monitoring of places of deprivation of liberty by NPMs and the CPT holds several risks, as outlined in the introduction of this volume. These include the potential for duplication of monitoring activities between different bodies, the emergence of divergent approaches and findings, and the possibility of over-scrutiny of certain institutions due to repeat visits. In the introductory chapter, we have argued that NPMs possess considerable potential to follow up on the CPT's findings and recommendations. At the same time, it is essential to acknowledge the attendant risk of a 'monitoring echo chamber.' The CPT routinely consults a country's NPM both prior to and during its visits, while NPMs may, in turn, organise their visiting programmes in the light of the CPT's schedule and findings. Although mutual follow-up may enable the optimal use of monitoring resources, NPMs must carefully balance the benefits of engaging with existing recommendations against the imperative to exercise their own independent and comprehensive mandate. Notwithstanding these risks, the coexistence of the OPCAT and ECPT monitoring systems also creates opportunities for strengthened action and dialogue with States Parties. In Scotland, for example, the closure of Cornton Vale prison for juvenile and adult women resulted from combined scrutiny by bodies of the UK NPM and the CPT. Moreover, the long-standing presence of the CPT in Europe is reflected in the extent to which NPMs or their bodies frequently align their visiting methodologies with CPT standards, as evidenced in France, Belgium, and Italy.

Ultimately, the comparative insights gathered in this volume invite both reflection and projection, demonstrating that torture prevention advances when NPMs, States, the SPT, and civil society engage in sustained, critical dialogue. The success of the OPCAT implementation in the coming decades will depend upon the capacity of all relevant bodies and authorities to acknowledge and address their institutional blind spots and operational constraints—whether relating to resources, strategic decision-making, or emerging challenges—in order to uphold the preventive ethos at the core of the OPCAT framework, in which primary attention must remain on persons deprived of their liberty rather than on institutional imperatives.

Index

T. Daems et al. (eds.), *Preventing Torture and Monitoring Places of Detention*, https://doi.org/10.1007/978-3-032-28285-9

The manufacturer's authorised representative in the EU is Springer Nature Customer Service Centre GmbH, Europaplatz 3, 69115 Heidelberg, Germany. If you have any concerns regarding our products, please contact ProductSafety@springernature.com

Printed and bound by CPI Group (UK) Ltd, Croydon, CR0 4YY

17/09/2026

02218454-0010